Real Estate

EXAM GUIDE

William H. Pivar

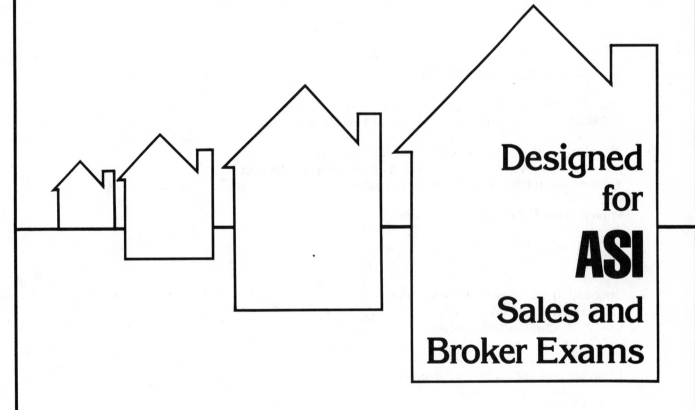

Designed
for
ASI
Sales and
Broker Exams

REAL ESTATE EDUCATION COMPANY
a division of Longman Financial Services Publishing, Inc.

While a great deal of care has been taken to provide accurate and current information, the ideas, suggestions, general principles, and conclusions presented in this book are subject to local, state, and federal laws and regulations, court cases, and any revisions of same. The reader is thus urged to consult legal counsel regarding any points of law—this publication should not be used as a substitute for competent legal advice.

© 1985 by Longman Group USA Inc.

Published by Real Estate Education Company/Chicago,
A division of Longman Financial Services Publishing, Inc.

Printed in the United States of America.

86 87 10 9 8 7 6 5 4

Sponsoring Editor: Bobbye Middendorf
Project Editor: David Walker
Cover Design: Constance Meyer

Library of Congress Cataloging in Publication Data

Pivar, William H.
    Real estate exam guide.

    1. Real estate agents—Licenses—United States—
Examinations, questions, etc. 2. Real estate business—
Licenses—United States—Examinations, questions, etc.
3. Real Property—United States—Examinations, questions,
etc. I. Title.
HD278.P58   1985   333.33'076   85-8318
ISBN 0-88462-525-7

Contents

FOREWORD

In compiling this study guide for the Real Estate Assessment for Licensure Program (REAL), we have tried to provide vital information to candidates prior to taking the examination. It is important to note, however, that Assessment Systems, Inc. (ASI) is not responsible for the contents of this book. The structure of this book follows very closely the content outline that was put together by the examination committee and accepted by jurisdictions for use in their licensure process. ASI is a testing service, and as such is responsible for the structure of testing programs, but not for the specific content of test questions. They employ job analysis, statistical and operational techniques that support the validity of examinations. A brief description of these techniques may be helpful.

The process of licensure is intended to determine which candidates have attained a level of knowledge sufficient for safe practice. In order to determine what that level is, one must first identify what the job of real estate practitioner entails and the knowledges and skills required to perform each. This is accomplished by performing analyses of the real estate profession with the guidance of a representative committee of real estate personnel. After the opinions of the committee are confirmed by analysis, test questions are written specifically to address the knowledges and skills that were identified as important and currently performed by practitioners. Committees of practitioners then review and approve all test questions. Representatives from each jurisdiction using ASI examination materials also review questions and other program-related materials. The validity of the examinations is dependent upon the judgments of many content experts, not upon the opinions of a few test editors at ASI.

We hope that you find the information in this study guide helpful. The intent of this guide is to provide helpful information to candidates preparing for the examination. It is very possible, however, that you will encounter questions on the actual examination that are not covered in this book. Please use this guide, then, accordingly with its intended purpose. We wish you success on the examination and in your career.

—The Editors

ONE
The REAL Examination

The Real Estate Assessment for Licensure (REAL) examination was developed by the staff of Assessment Systems Inc. (ASI) in conjunction with local and national examination committees. ASI, an independent testing company, administers the exam under contract with state licensing authorities.

The REAL examination is not a test of language ability, reading, or knowing how to take tests. It is designed to identify candidates who have sufficient skills and knowledge to serve the interests of the public, and to lead those who are lacking in these skills to further study.

The REAL examination is divided into two parts: Section A covers general topics and Section B covers state laws. All questions are of the four-answer multiple-choice variety. Both the salespersons' and the brokers' general sections contain 80 questions on general real estate knowledge. The state section contains 30 questions for salespersons and 30 to 40 questions for brokers.

Candidates have 3½ hours to take the test. Test scores are based upon the number of questions answered correctly. The passing score for each state is established by the state real estate board or commission based upon standards of competence which they deem appropriate for licensure.

The examination will test your ability to recall relevant material, your ability to apply what you have learned to real life situations, as well as your ability to analyze a problem. Questions are based upon topics that real estate salespeople or brokers actually deal with in the course of their work. Nonrelevant or obscure areas and archaic terms are not included.

Candidates interested in real estate as a profession are generally people who are positively motivated. They are likely to read a question written in the negative as if a positive answer were called for. Because of this, the examination includes very few negative questions. When a negative word such as *not* or *except* is used, it will be **CAPITALIZED IN BOLD FACE TYPE.**

The examination may contain case-study questions in which a block of information is given, followed by two or three related questions. However, questions stand by themselves and are not based upon previous questions. One wrong answer does not affect the score on any other question.

Questions are carefully reviewed to make certain that there are no clues to the answer which would aid a candidate who doesn't know the material. Each question is either a clear and straightforward statement which calls for one of four answers, or it is an incomplete statement (stem), with the correct answer completing the statement.

Every question has one right answer which will be clear to candidates who have prepared themselves for the examination.

Wrong answers or distractors are likely to be:

a Common misconceptions.
b Common errors (if you make a common error on a mathematical computation, it is likely that one of the distractors will agree with your answer).

c A carefully worded but incorrect statement which will appear plausible to an uninformed candidate.

The REAL examination takes a positive approach to achieve fair measurement of a candidate's knowledge and skills. You should therefore not fear your examination. You should treat it instead as an opportunity to demonstrate the knowledge and skills you have acquired to serve others as a real estate professional.

STUDY AND EXAMINATION AIDS

How to Study

Any career decision, to become a reality, requires preparation; and preparing for a career in real estate is going to take both time and dedication. While your motivation to spend the necessary time must come from within yourself, a few simple suggestions can make the hours you spend more productive.

1. Study on a Daily Basis   You will retain much more information if you study over many days than if you try to cram everything into a few marathon sessions. You should set aside particular blocks of time for your study. If at all possible, early mornings are preferred because you are more likely to be at your mental peak for the day. Try to avoid study periods after heavy meals or in too warm a study area, as you will find concentration very difficult.

2. Find a Quiet Place   Your study place should have as few distractions as possible. Studying near televisions, phones, or even outside can be extremely difficult. Many students use their neighborhood libraries as their quiet place for study.

3. Break Up Your Study Time   The second straight hour of study is much less productive than the first; the third is even worse. I recommend study periods of about 45 minutes each, separated by other activities. A short walk is an excellent way to refresh yourself and aid your concentration.

4. Use Good Study Techniques   Before you study each section, spend no more than 5 minutes scanning the material. A general understanding of what you will be studying aids your retention.

   Read and Paraphrase   As you read each paragraph, stop and close your eyes and ask yourself what you have read. By putting the material into your own words (mentally, or verbally if your study area permits it), your likelihood of retaining the information will be dramatically increased. By forcing yourself to paraphrase the material, you will avoid the likelihood of giving too light a treatment to any area.

   Reread and Paraphrase   A second reading should involve paraphrasing of more than one paragraph. It could be of whole topic areas.

   Take the Test   After the second reading, take the quiz at the end of the chapter as if it were an actual examination, allowing at least two hours. An answer sheet similar to the one you'll use on the actual exam is included after each chapter quiz and review examination. You may want to remove it from the book and use it to mark your answers. This will ensure that you are fully familiar with the use of the answer grid by the time you take the actual licensing exam.

   After taking the test, check your results. Don't limit your evaluation to just those questions you answered wrong. Understanding why a correct answer was correct is really more important than the fact that it was correct.

Group Study   Group study, when used properly, can help maintain high levels of concentration for extended periods. For it to be effective, every member of the group must have studied the material so each can contribute to the group and not hold it back. The group must also have a strong leader who can keep the session going on a straight course.

5. Study Before Class   You should complete your study of a subject before it is covered in class. Immediately before class, spend another few minutes quickly scanning the material so it is fresh in your mind.

By coming to class already understanding the topic, you get the greatest possible benefit from your instructor. Instead of trying to learn basic facts, you can use classroom time as it is meant to be used—asking questions, clarifying difficult points, and learning about changes as well as material specific to your state.

6. Mark Your Book   Highlighting key areas in the text will help you to recall and review particularly important points. Too much special emphasis, though, defeats the purpose of making a few points stand out.

Notes on your instructor's comments are best written in the margins. This way you have one integrated text to study. State-specific information should be handled the same way.

7. Know the Vocabulary   Write the words you are having trouble with on one side of a 3" × 5" card. On the other side include definitions. Whenever you have a few minutes free during the day, review your cards. When you feel you have mastered a term, you can discard that card.

8. Review   Don't limit your review to just the material you feel you are weak in, or what you think the examination will emphasize. Your review should be comprehensive. A good starting point is the review examinations at the end of the book, followed by the text material. Your review process should include several readings of the complete glossary at the end of the book. It will be of great help in tying all the material together. If time permits, retake the examination in each section. Of course the same level of study must be applied to information unique to your state.

9. Don't Become Discouraged   Because of the sheer volume of new material, many students use their confusion as an excuse to drop out. You should realize that confusion is normal for the first few weeks (and sometimes months) of study. As you progress, things will slowly come together. Students are often well into the review process before they realize that they are no longer confused. When you feel that you will never understand, think of all of the people you know in real estate. The reason they succeeded is obvious. It is not because they are smarter than you are, it is because they continued to work and refused to quit.

TAKING THE REAL EXAMINATION

Proper test-taking technique can make the difference between success and failure. Keep in mind that while passing is the goal, if you fail the examination can be retaken. This is not a one-time win-all/lose-all crisis.

It is natural to be nervous before an examination. Even though you understand that nervousness can detract from your test taking ability, remaining calm isn't easy. Even the candidate who acts very blasé is going to have a few butterflies flitting around inside. You can help yourself by avoiding pre-examination socializing with those waiting for the doors to open. Nervousness breeds nervousness, so talking with a group of agitated people is not the way to relax.

Immediately after entering the examination room, and before instructions are given, you can help yourself to relax by doing a short breathing exercise such as 10 deep breaths while counting to 5 for each of them. You will find this forced activity has a calming effect. Once you begin the examination, most of your initial apprehension will disappear. Taking a seat toward the front of the examination room, but away from the entrance, will minimize distraction.

You are allowed to bring a simple non-printing electronic calculator to the examination. It can't be programmable or make an audible tone. Make certain that your calculator has fresh batteries or you may find yourself doing long division with a pencil. Worse, you may find that you've been working with false readings. A malfunctioning calculator is not grounds for challenging exam results or for getting an extension of the time limit. Even a perfect calculator is of no use if you can't operate it correctly. If you borrow one, or buy a new one for the exam, be certain you fully understand how that particular model functions.

Listen carefully to the instructions. Failure to follow them may result in a delay in issuing your test results. Any cheating will result in your immediate dismissal from the examination and notification to the state licensing agency. Attempting to copy questions or removal of examination material constitutes cheating.

Be sure to place answers in the correct space. If you are right-handed, place the answer sheet to the right of your examination booklet. If you are left-handed, place the answer sheet to the left. In this way you won't have to risk losing your place when you pass your arm over the question. You don't want to find yourself in the panic situation of answering question 80 in space 76 on the answer sheet.

Read each question carefully to be certain you understand what is being asked. Never change the wording or assume the question means something other than it says. If a question makes an assumption, assume that to be true.

Read every answer before marking your answer sheet. If you are not certain of the answer, eliminate what you believe to be the wrong answers and take a guess from the others. An informed candidate should be able to eliminate at least one answer and possibly two. An uninformed candidate will find all four answers very plausible.

Answer every question as you come to it. Never leave a question unanswered with the intention of returning to it, or you may forget about it. A pure guess gives you a 25% chance; leaving a question unanswered gives you none. Whenever you do take a guess, indicate it with a check mark in the question booklet. After you complete the rest of the examination, you can return to the ones you guessed at.

Before you work out any mathematics question, make a mental estimate of the answer and write it down. If your computed answer differs significantly, there is a good chance that you made an error in computation. Just because your computed answer agrees exactly with an answer given does not mean it is correct. The wrong answers are answers which will result if a common mistake is made. Common errors include:

1 Reversing the dividend and divisor.
2 Failure to carry the mathematics to the final step.
3 Failure to convert inches to feet, square feet to square yards, cubic feet to cubic yards, etc.

Should you find yourself spending an inordinate amount of time on a math question, take a guess and come back to it when you are finished with the rest of the examination. In that way you will be able to work on the problem without the mental pressure of an unfinished examination.

You have 3½ hours to take the examination. Even though others around you are leaving, you must fight the urge to leave. Staying longer can mean more points for you.

First complete any math questions you guessed at, then go to those questions where you were uncertain of the answer. Then start from the beginning and go through the entire examination.

For the purpose of the examination, assume:

- there are 30 days in every month;
- there are 360 days in a year;
- there are 43,560 square feet per acre;
- the seller is responsible for charges up to and including the day of settlement;
- numbers in your final answer may be rounded off (where applicable) to the nearest whole number.

When you take the examination in this book, use these techniques. Take every examination as if you were taking a state examination, using these techniques. They could just mean the extra points which are needed.

FROM THE AUTHOR

If there is any material which you feel is not adequately covered in this book or if you have any suggestions that will make the book a better preparation tool I would appreciate hearing from you.

William H. Pivar
75-496 Desert Park Drive
Indian Wells, CA 92260

TWO
Real Estate Law

CONTRACTS

A contract is an agreement enforceable by law. Four requirements must be met to have a valid contract.

1. Competent Parties   Contracting parties must have both mental and legal capacity to enter into a contract. Persons adjudged insane cannot contract. Generally minors may contract only for necessities. The legal age is set by state law. In some states emancipated minors, such as married persons, can contract.

2. Mutual Agreement   To have a valid contract there must be a meeting of the minds (mutuality). This is normally evidenced by an offer and acceptance. A unilateral mistake (mistake on the part of one party only) will not allow that person to get out of a contract, but a mutual mistake of fact or possibility of performance makes the contract unenforceable.

3. Consideration   In order for a promise to be binding on one party to an agreement, the other party must have given or promised something of value. An unsupported promise would really be a promise to make a gift and it would generally be unenforceable because of lack of consideration. Consideration does not have to be fair, although grossly inadequate consideration could be evidence of fraud or undue influence.

4. Legal Purpose   To be enforceable a contract must be for a legal purpose. A contract made for an unlawful purpose is an illegal contract and would generally be unenforceable by either party.

Statute of Frauds

In old England, real estate was considered the basis of all wealth. Real estate transactions were considered so important that the Statute of Frauds (really a statute to prevent frauds) required every contract dealing in real estate to be in writing. Every state has a Statute of Frauds which requires the writing to show a definite agreement and to be signed by the person who is to be held to the agreement.

State statutes of fraud usually require that the following be in writing:

- all agreements for the sale of real estate;
- any lease for more than 1 year;
- contracts that by their terms cannot be fully performed within 1 year of entering into the agreement;
- promises to pay the debt of another;
- personal property contracts for $500 or more.

Valid Contracts

Contracts which meet all legal requirements are valid and enforceable by either party to the agreement.

Void Contracts

Contracts which fail to meet one or more contractual requirements are void and unenforceable by either party to the agreement.

Voidable Contracts

Voidable contracts are valid unless voided. Only one party—the innocent party to the transaction—can void the agreement or elect to be bound by it. Among the factors that may make contracts voidable are:

Duress or Menace   Contracts entered into under force or threat of force may be voided by the injured party.

Fraud   Contracts entered into because of fraud may be voided by the injured party.

Undue Influence   A party who enters into an unfair contract with another when not acting under his or her own free will because of the relationship with the other party (client/attorney, doctor/patient, father/child, etc.) can void the agreement.

Minor Status   A person generally has a reasonable period after reaching the contractual age to void contracts entered into as a minor.

The Offer and Acceptance

An offer expresses a willingness on the part of an offeror to enter into a particular agreement. An offer is not a contract until it is accepted by the offeree. Unless the offer specifies a particular period of time for acceptance, it is considered to be held open for acceptance for a reasonable period of time.

Offer Accepted

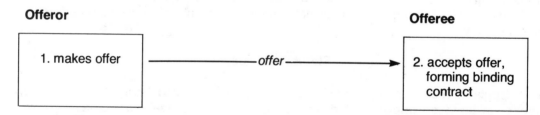

If the offer fails to specify the form for acceptance, the offer may be accepted in any reasonable manner. Under the Statute of Frauds, offers and acceptances for real estate transactions must be in writing. Acceptance does not take place until the offeror is notified of the acceptance, usually by delivery of a copy of the accepted offer to the offeror. The act of mailing an acceptance is considered an acceptance.

Revocation of Offer   An offeror can generally withdraw or revoke an offer any time prior to its acceptance. Since actual notice is required to revoke an offer, a mailed revocation does not become effective until it is received. Mailing constitutes acceptance, but receipt is necessary for revocation.

Death of Offeror   The death of the offeror or offeree *prior* to acceptance immediately voids the offer. However, the death of the offeror or offeree *after acceptance* generally has no effect on the agreement, which becomes binding on the estates of the deceased parties.

Counteroffer   An acceptance that varies from the original offer with a new or changed requirement is customarily regarded as a counteroffer. A counteroffer is really a rejection of the original offer and the original offeree now becomes an offeror with a new offer. The original offeror (now the offeree) can either accept the new offer and form a binding contract, or reject it. Once an offer is rejected it is considered dead. Any later acceptance is merely a new offer.

Counteroffer Made

Offeror   **Offeree**

1. makes offer ———offer———▶ 2. rejects offer, becomes offeror of counteroffer
3. becomes offeree— can accept or reject counteroffer ◀———counteroffer———

Option

An option is a contract that gives one party (the optionee) the right to make a contract during the period of the option if he or she wishes to do so. Ordinarily an optionor will give an optionee the right to purchase a property during a stated period of time at an agreed price.

To create a valid option, the optionee must have given the optionor something of value as consideration to keep the offer open. An option cannot be revoked by the optionor once it is given. It is an irrevocable offer.

Option

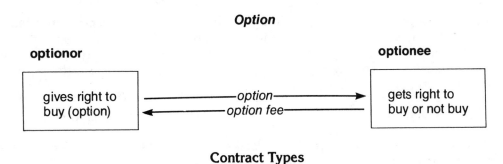

optionor   **optionee**

gives right to buy (option) ———option———▶ ———option fee——— gets right to buy or not buy

Contract Types

Bilateral Contracts   Promises made in exchange for promises are bilateral contracts. Sales agreements are generally bilateral—a promise to buy is given for a promise to sell.

Unilateral Contracts   Promises made in exchange for an act are unilateral contracts. The acceptance of the offer is not in the form of another promise, but in the form of the act. For example, assume a broker promised to pay a salesperson a bonus of $50 for listings of four-bedroom houses. If the salesperson obtained a four-bedroom house listing, the salesperson would be entitled to the bonus. While the salesperson was not obligated to perform, her performance of an act made the acceptance.

Executed Contract   An executed contract is one that has been fully performed.

Executory Contract   An executory contract has yet to be performed.

Express Contract   An express contract is one that has been specifically agreed to, either verbally or in writing. Since the Statute of Frauds requires real estate contracts to be in writing, they are express contracts.

Implied Contracts   Implied contracts are understood because of the actions of the parties, although a specific agreement is not stated. In requesting a carpenter to make repairs, you might make no agreement as to pay; it is implied, however, that you will pay a fair price for the services received.

Remedies for Breach of Contract

Specific Performance   Because every parcel of real estate is unique, money damages are not always adequate. The courts can require that a seller convey property as originally agreed to. Courts, generally, will not grant specific performance where the consideration is not considered adequate.

Compensatory Damages

Money awarded by the court to the injured party to compensate for the loss suffered is called compensatory damages.

Punitive or Exemplary Damages   Courts may award punitive or exemplary damages beyond compensatory damages to punish or make an example of a party that made a willful and/or outrageous breach of an agreement.

Nominal Damages   Token amounts awarded when the breach does not result in an actual dollar loss are called nominal damages.

Liquidated Damages   Liquidated damages are breach-of-contract compensation agreed upon by the parties at the time of their agreement. Construction contracts often have a daily liquidated damage amount when a job is not completed on time, and purchase contracts customarily provide for the forfeiture of a buyer's earnest money deposit in the event of a buyer's breach.

Restitution   Restitution is the return of consideration when a contract is rescinded.

Reformation   An action to correct a mistake in an agreement or deed is called reformation. It amends an agreement to conform to the original intention.

Rescission   A party can use a breach by the other party as the basis for rescinding the contract.

Waiver   A party to a contract can waive a contractual breach by the other party and elect to still be bound by the contract. A buyer might waive the seller's failure to correct some defect and insist upon closing. Waiver leaves the parties as they are (rescission puts them back the way they were).

Accord and Satisfaction   Accord and satisfaction occur when a party agrees to accept less than the contracted amount when the other party disputes the amount that is owing. This is common in construction contracts where a party alleges that the work was not performed as agreed upon.

Novation   A substitution of a new contract for an old one is called novation. The parties to a novation agree to cancel the old contract in favor of the new agreement, as when a buyer and a builder make a contract for a different model home than originally chosen and named in a contract. It is also considered a novation where parties agree to the substitution of a new party for one of the original parties to the contract and fully release the original party from all obligations under the agreement.

Statute of Limitations and Laches   State statutes provide for the period of time during which legal action must be brought. The statute of limitations starts on the date an obligation is due; if no payment is made or legal action taken during the prescribed period, then the right to enforce the agreement is lost.

Under the doctrine of laches, the court may refuse to grant relief to a party whose failure to bring action within a reasonable time has worked to the detriment of the other party.

The statute of limitations is based upon statute; laches is a court doctrine based on equity.

Estoppel   Parties can be prevented (estopped) from raising defenses if their words or actions have caused another party to act to its own detriment. If Bob allowed Sue to make improvements to a property based on his verbal contract to sell, Bob would likely be estopped from defending his breach of contract on the ground that it was not in writing as required by the Statute of Frauds.

Interpretation of Contracts

Ambiguities in contracts are generally resolved against the party drafting the instrument.

Typed material takes precedence over printed, and handwritten takes precedence over typed.

Written words take precedence over numerals. If a contract stated, "Four thousand dollars $400.00," then four thousand would be the contractual amount.

Parol Evidence Rule   Verbal evidence may not modify a written contract which appears to be complete. Verbal evidence can be admitted to clarify an ambiguity in a written contract or as evidence of fraud.

Assignment of Contracts   Generally, contracts that do not specifically prohibit assignment can be assigned. However, contracts that are personal in nature, such as contracts for particular personal services and contracts where consideration would be a personal note, cannot be assigned.

Assignment

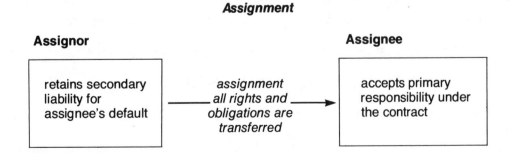

Assignor

retains secondary liability for assignee's default

assignment all rights and obligations are transferred

Assignee

accepts primary responsibility under the contract

In an assignment, the assignee becomes primarily liable under the contract and the assignor remains secondarily liable. In a novation, a new contract is written and the old party has no further obligation; in an assignment, the assignor can be held liable for damages if the assignee breaches the contract.

DEEDS

Deeds are transfer documents for an interest in real estate. A deed is only used once. When you buy, you get a deed from the seller. When you sell, you give a new deed to the buyer.

Deed Transfer

Requirements for a Valid Deed

Delivery   A valid conveyance requires that the deed be delivered to the grantee or his agent. Mailing generally constitutes delivery. In order for delivery to occur, there must be an intent to pass title immediately.

A recorded deed is presumed to have been delivered.

Conveyance   A deed must have a granting clause (words indicating that title is to pass).

Writing   All deeds must be in writing (Statute of Frauds).

Unambiguous Description   The property must be described so that boundaries can be ascertained. A legal description is not required to convey title, but it is generally required to obtain title insurance.

Habendum Clause   In most states, the deed must define the interest or estate granted (fee simple, life estate, etc.).

Competent Grantor   The grantor must be legally capable of conveying title.

Definite Grantee   The grantee must be definite. While you can convey property to a real person using a fictitious name, you cannot transfer title to a fictitious person.

Signed   The deed must be signed by the grantor. The grantee does not have to sign.

Not Required for a Valid Deed

Witnesses   A deed generally need not be witnessed (unless grantor signs with an X).

Recording   As between the parties to a deed, recording is not required. However, a deed must be recorded to give constructive notice to subsequent purchasers who first record.

Address of Parties   Some states require the address of the grantee in order to record the deed.

Seal   In most states, seals are not required for a deed. Where required, the word *"Seal"* is usually sufficient.

Acknowledgment   Acknowledgment is the admission, before a notary, by the grantor that he or she is the grantor, and that the signing is a free act. Acknowledgment is generally not required to have a valid transfer between the parties, but it is generally required in order to record the deed.

Consideration   Deeds often indicate the consideration (purchase price), but the recitation of consideration generally is not required for a valid deed.

Date   The deed need not be dated. It is considered dated as of the date of recording.

Types of Deeds

Warranty Deed   The grantor personally warrants good title and agrees to defend the title if challenged. The grantor further warrants that there are no undisclosed encumbrances, and that the grantee will be entitled to quiet enjoyment of the premises.

Grant Deed   Used in a few states, normally in conjunction with a policy of title insurance, the grant deed contains two warranties:

- The grantor has not previously conveyed the property.
- There is nothing against the property that the grantor has not disclosed.

The grant deed conveys after-acquired title. If after a sale the grantor gets a better interest, such as a quitclaim deed from an encumbrance holder, the after-acquired interest passes to the grantee.

Quitclaim Deed   This deed transfers whatever interests the grantor may have in property without making any claims as to the interest or any implied or express warranties. It is frequently used to remove clouds on title or give up an easement.

Bargain and Sale Deed   Similar to a quitclaim deed, in that the grantor is not guaranteeing title, but the grantor is asserting that he or she has an actual interest. There is no such assertion in a quitclaim deed.

Sheriff's Deed   Given at a sheriff's sale, the sheriff's deed carries no warranties or representation. It gives only the interest that was foreclosed. There could still be encumbrances.

Tax Deed   Given at a tax sale. Because taxes are a priority lien, a tax sale wipes out junior encumbrances.

Gift Deed   This is any type of deed given for love and affection. A gift deed can be voided if it can be shown that it was given to defraud creditors. As between a recorded gift deed and a prior unrecorded purchase for value, the purchase for value will generally prevail.

Clauses in Deeds

Exception   A clause which excludes a portion of the property from the grant. The word *sans* may be used in the deed; it means *without.*

Reservation   A clause which retains for the grantor some right, such as an easement.

THE REAL ESTATE PURCHASE CONTRACT

Purchase agreements in real estate are generally offers by the purchaser (offeror) to buy at a definite price and terms. Like any offer, it can be revoked prior to acceptance, but when accepted by the seller (offeree) during the period designated for acceptance, a binding contract is formed.

While various parts of the country use different forms, the form shown on the next page is included to help you understand the information normally set forth in a purchase agreement. Clauses are numbered to correspond with the explanation.

1. While a legal description is not required for a binding contract, any description included must be clear and unambiguous.

2. If the earnest money is in any form other than cash or check, the broker must notify the seller as to the form of the deposit; failure to do so can make the broker liable for the amount of the deposit in the event of a default by the buyer. If a check is to be held uncashed until the offer is accepted, the owner should be told. To protect the buyer, the deposit should be kept in a trust account or escrow.

3. Complete terms of the sale should be set forth, including assumption of existing loans; any new or seller financing; payments; interest rates; contingencies; etc.

4. Provides for the return of the deposit if offer is not accepted or seller is unable to convey marketable title.

5. By initialing, the parties agree that the forfeiture of the buyer's deposit will be the seller's only remedy should the buyer default. This election of remedies is liquidated damages. If the blocks are not initialed, the buyer could sue for actual damages or specific performance (in some states).

6. List any additional encumbrances.

7. Who pays abstract costs and title insurance varies by locality.

8. Prorating is normally based upon date of closing; however, another date could be agreed to. The seller ordinarily pays all prorations to and including the day of closing.

9. If the bonds or assessments are assumed by buyer, they may become a buyer's expense. Because bonds are generally low yielding, an assumption is often to the buyer's advantage. If the seller is to pay them, the seller receives less from the proceeds of the sale.

10. Agreeing on which items are considered fixtures and pass with the property avoids later disagreements. Any time the seller expects to keep an item which would normally go with the sale, this should be specified.

11. Different forms provide different remedies in case the property is destroyed. In this case, the buyer, at his option, can get out of the agreement. Some contracts require the seller to rebuild in case of partial or total destruction.

12. If the buyer and seller do not both agree to extensions, and the delay is caused by one party, then the other party can withdraw from the agreement if it is not closed within the time set. If no specific time for closing has been specified, then closing would have to be within a reasonable period of time.

13. In the absence of an agreement as to time of possession, possession is given at closing. If possession is to be given prior to closing, rent should be considered.

(This form is included as a sample for instructional purposes only and neither the author or publisher warrant its legality for use within any jurisdiction).

OFFER TO PURCHASE AGREEMENT

1   The undersigned buyer _____
_____
offers to purchase the property described as _____
_____
_____.

2   Buyers have deposited with broker the sum of $_____
_____ ($_____) in the form of _____
_____ as earnest money on said purchase. Said deposit to be held by broker in
a real estate trust account in _____
Bank in _____ until closing, at which time it shall apply toward the
purchase price.

3   The purchase price of the property shall be _____
($_____) and shall be paid as follows: _____
_____
_____
_____
_____.

4   In the event the offer is not accepted or seller is unable to convey marketable title, the
earnest money deposit will be returned in full to the buyer.

5   By initialing herein, Buyer (_____)
Seller (_____), the parties agree that in the event
of default by the buyer, buyer's earnest money deposit shall be forfeited to the seller as
a reasonable estimate of damages and this shall be the seller's sole remedy as to
damages.

6   Title shall be free and clear of all liens and encumbrances other than municipal zoning
ordinances, recorded utility easements, unrecorded building restrictions and _____
_____.

7   Seller shall furnish the buyer at least _____ days prior to closing at
_____ expense, either:

A. An Abstract of Title showing marketable title in the seller. The buyer shall notify the
seller within 10 days of any objection to the title and seller shall have a reasonable period
of time to cure any defect.

B. A standard policy of Title Insurance naming the buyer as insured in the amount of
_____ ($_____).
(Delivery of a preliminary title report prior to closing with the policy to be issued upon
closing shall satisfy this requirement).

8   Property taxes, insurance premiums, rents, interest and _____
_____ shall be prorated as of _____

_____ .

9 | All street, water and sewer special assessments shall be
☐ paid in full by seller.   ☐ assumed by buyer.

10 | All light fixtures, screened and/or storm windows and doors, drapery rods, draperies, fixed carpeting, shades, antennas as well as _____

_____

shall be included with the premises with the exception of _____

_____

_____ .

11 | In the event the improvements to the property are destroyed or materially damaged prior to closing, then upon buyer's request all deposits shall be returned and the parties shall be relieved of all obligations under this contract.

12 | This transaction shall be closed on _____ at ____

_____ .

13 | Possession of the premises shall be given the buyer on _____

_____ .

14 | Title shall be conveyed by Warranty Deed. Unless later designated by buyer, title shall vest as follows: _____

_____

_____

_____ .

15 | Both buyer and seller authorize the broker to advise others as to the sale price and terms.

16 | This offer must be accepted by the seller delivering a signed copy to the buyer, in person or by mail, not later than _____ .

17 | Time shall be of the essence for performing all obligations under this contract.

18 | The undersigned buyer has read and fully understands this offer to purchase and acknowledges the receipt of a copy hereof.

19 | Broker _____   Buyer _____

By _____   Buyer _____

20 | The undersigned seller accepts the buyer's offer and agrees to sell the above described property in accordance with the terms set forth above. The seller acknowledges reading and fully understanding this offer to purchase and acknowledges the receipt of a copy hereof.

21 | The undersigned seller has employed _____
as Broker and agrees to pay the sum of _____
($_____) as commission for this sale upon closing, or upon default if the closing is prevented by seller's default. In the event closing is prevented by the default of the buyer, seller agrees to pay broker as commission one half of any deposits forfeited or damages received by virtue of said buyer's default, after first deducting any costs incurred in preparation for closing and/or collection expense. In no event shall the

broker's share exceed the full commission that would have been payable had the buyer not defaulted.

22 | Broker _____ Seller _____

By _____ Seller _____

14. How the buyer is to take title should be spelled out. The manner of taking title could have tax consequences. Advising purchasers on how to take title has been held in some states to be the unauthorized practice of law.

15. Without this authorization, price and terms information could not be given to multiple listing services or others for appraisal purposes.

16. Any acceptance after the date specified would not form a binding contract. Setting forth a date for acceptance does not prevent the offeror from revoking the offer prior to the expiration of the acceptance period.

17. *Time is of the essence* means that all dates are firm and must be complied with. In the absence of this term, the courts would be likely to allow a reasonable time after the dates specified for performance.

18. By signing, the buyer acknowledges receiving a copy and claims a full understanding of the offer.

19. While one spouse can generally buy property without the other spouse, it is best to get both to sign so they are both obligated to the contract.

20. The seller by signing also acknowledges full understanding of the contract and the receipt of a copy.

21. While it is not necessary to set forth commission in the offer to purchase, it is often done to avoid any misunderstanding later. If the commission here differs from that in the listing contract, the amount in the purchase contract prevails.

22. Both spouses must sign the deed to convey jointly owned property. Therefore it is best to get both to be obligated by their signatures.

PROPERTY

Property is divided into two categories: real property and personal property.

Real Property

Real property includes land and that which goes with the land (buildings, fences, trees, water rights, mineral rights, air rights, easements, etc.). The rights, benefits, and improvements which go with the land are known as *appurtenances*.

Personal Property

Also known as chattels, personal property is any property which is not real property. Personal property is generally considered movable, while real property is generally regarded as being immovable. Naturally growing plants, perennial crops and trees are generally classified as real property, while cultivated annual crops (emblements) are considered personal property.

Chattels Real Interests in real estate less than fee ownership, such as leasehold interests, mortgages, and shares in real estate syndicates, are known as chattels real and are personal property.

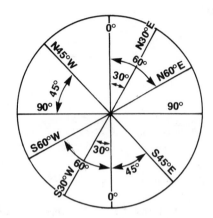

Circle Demonstrating Metes and Bounds Description
There are 360° in a circle.
There are 180° in a half-circle.
There are 90° in a quarter-circle (right angle).
Each degree is divided into 60 minutes.
Each minute is divided into 60 seconds.
The point of beginning is at the intersection of the two lines (or the center of the circle).
The "bearing" of a course is described by measuring easterly or westerly from the north and south lines.

Elements of Property Descriptions

There are three methods of legally describing real property.

Lot, Block, and Tract   This legal description uses the parcel's designation on the recorded subdivision plot. For example:

Lot 17, Block 4 of Atlantic Heights recorded on pages 814–815 in Volume 36 of the official records of the County of Oceanside.

Metes and Bounds   Also called measurements and directions, this is the oldest method of describing property. It was used extensively in our original 13 states. The method shows the boundaries of a parcel by going from point to point. The measuring points in a

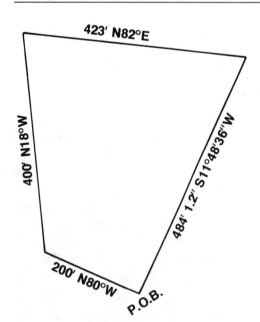

Beginning at an iron stake located 30' North of the center of County Road W and 550' West of the center of the intersection of County Road W and State Highway 17 being in Eagle Township of Clark County, thence 200' N80°W to an iron stake, thence 400' N18°W to an iron stake, thence 423' N82°E to an iron stake, thence 484' 1.2" S11°48'36"W to the point of beginning.

metes-and-bounds description are known as monuments. Natural monuments include trees, natural rocks, and rivers, while iron stakes, fences, and roads are artificial monuments. Generally metes-and-bounds descriptions are given in a clockwise manner from the point of beginning. Angles in a metes-and-bounds description are measured in degrees (°) minutes (') and seconds (") from a north-south line.

The plot shown on page 18 is the result of following the directions given in the metes-and-bounds description on the left of the diagram.

When a boundary in a metes-and-bounds description is a private road, title extends to the center of the road. If an ocean is a boundary, title is given to the average high-tide line. When a non-navigable river is used as a boundary, title is to the center of the river. For navigable rivers, the title is generally the high-water mark (set by state law).

Government Survey   Most U.S. land is laid out in a rectangular pattern by government survey. The government survey method measures land from the intersections of principal surveying lines. Those going east and west are called base lines. Those going north and south are called meridians. From the intersection of the base lines and meridians, land is measured in townships. Townships are six miles square and contain 36 square miles.

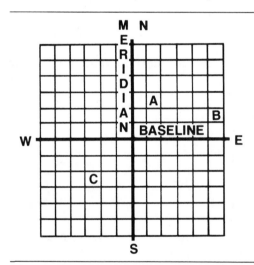

Horizontal rows of townships are known as tiers. Tiers are either North or South of the Base line.

Vertical rows of townships are known as Ranges. Ranges are either East or West of the Meridian.

The township marked "A" in the illustration is three townships north of the base line and two townships east of the meridian line. It would thus be designated Township 3 North, Range 2 East or T3N, R2E. To have a complete legal description, reference would also have to be made to the specific base line and meridian.

Township "B" is two townships above or north of the base line and four townships east of the meridian; thus it would be Township 2 North, Range 4 East or T2N, R4E (with reference to appropriate base line and meridian).

Township "C" is three townships south of the base line and three townships west of the meridian; thus it would be described as T3S, R3W (with reference to the appropriate base line and meridian).

Correction Lines   These are surveyors' lines to compensate for the curvature of the earth. These lines are run every 24 miles east and west of the principal meridian (guide meridian) and every 24 miles north or south of the base line (standard parallels). The 24-mile-square parcels resulting from the correction lines or parallels are known as "checks."

Because of the curvature of the earth, adjustments are made in sections on the north and west boundaries of a township. Eleven sections of a township could be so affected.

Each township is 6 miles square and contains 36 sections. Each section is one mile square and contains 640 acres. Sections in a township are always numbered as in the diagram shown here.

6	5	4	3	2	1
7	8	9	10	11	12
18	17	16	15	14	13
19	20	21	22	23	24
30	29	28	27	26	25
31	32	33	34	35	36

Adjoining this township are other townships, so east of Section 24 would be Section 19 of the adjoining township. In the same way, south of Section 33 would be Section 4 of another township.

You will note that numbering starts in the upper right-hand corner (NE), and continues in a zigzag pattern.

Land is normally described by its location within a specific section:

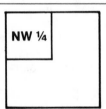

The northwest (NW) ¼ of a section. Since a section contains 640 acres, the NW ¼ contains 160 acres.

Legal descriptions are not always as simple as finding a ¼ section. Suppose the description is the S ½ of the NW ¼ of the SE ¼ of section 27, T8N,R17W,SBBL&M (San Bernardino Base Line and Meridian). We first find the township by counting 8 North from the base line and 17 West from the meridian. We find the section by the numbering as previously explained.

We can find the size of a parcel by simply going backwards using its description alone:

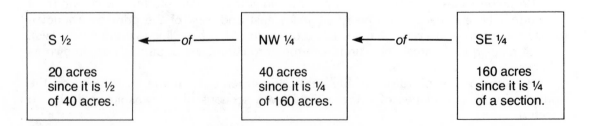

In finding S ½ of NW ¼ of SE ¼, we look at our description and *go backward.*

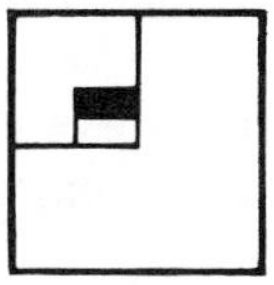

First, we find the SE ¼. Since it is ¼ of a section, it contains 160 acres (¼ of 640). Second, we find the NW ¼ of it, which gives us a 40-acre parcel (¼ of 160). Third, we find the S ½ of it, which gives us a 20-acre parcel (½ of 40).

Important land measurements are shown in the diagram, and others are defined below. They should be mastered before you take the licensing exam.

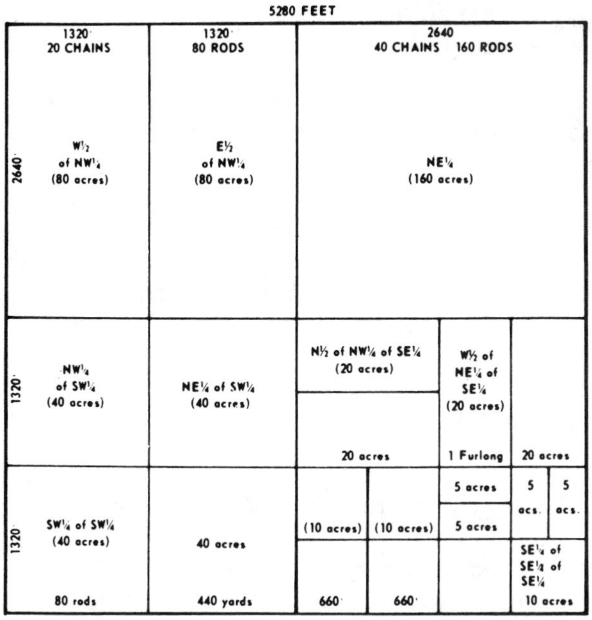

5280 FEET		
1320' 20 CHAINS	1320' 80 RODS	2640 40 CHAINS 160 RODS
W½ of NW¼ (80 acres) 2640	E½ of NW¼ (80 acres)	NE¼ (160 acres)
NW¼ of SW¼ (40 acres) 1320'	NE¼ of SW¼ (40 acres)	N½ of NW¼ of SE¼ (20 acres) / W½ of NE¼ of SE¼ (20 acres)
		20 acres 1 Furlong 20 acres
SW¼ of SW¼ (40 acres) 1320	40 acres	(10 acres) (10 acres) 5 acres / 5 acres 5 acs. 5 acs. / SE¼ of SE¼ of SE¼ 10 acres
80 rods	440 yards	660' 660'

Legal descriptions of parcels of land within a section

Know these measurements:

- one township=6 miles square containing 36 square miles
- one section=640 acres
- one mile=5,280 feet
- one acre=43,560 square feet
- one square acre=approximately 208.7 feet square
- one rod=16.5 linear feet (320 rods in a mile)
- one chain=66 linear feet

RESTRICTIVE COVENANTS

Also known as Covenants, Conditions, and Restrictions (CC&Rs), restrictive covenants are private voluntary agreements as to land use. Zoning, on the other hand, is a mandatory public control of land use.

While restrictive covenants may be placed by agreement of all of the land owners subject to the restrictions, they are normally placed on land by subdividers who record the restrictions and then sell the parcels subject to the restrictions.

Restrictive covenants are beneficial restrictions in that they seek to aid values or enjoyment by setting minimum or maximum requirements. Typically, restrictive covenants would control such things as use restrictions, setbacks, minimum lot size, minimum house size, maximum height, outbuildings, fences, keeping of animals, and even architectural styles.

Covenants are promises that can be enforced by anyone who is subject to them. They are normally enforced through an injunction—a court writ prohibiting a party from doing or continuing in some action. Courts ordinarily will not grant relief when:

- the parties have waived these rights to enforce the covenants because of failure to enforce previous breaches;
- the parties seeking to enforce the covenant are themselves in violation of the covenant (they are not entering the court with clean hands);
- there have been changes that would make the enforcement unreasonable;
- the court determines that the restrictions are against public policy.

A condition differs from a covenant in that it provides for forfeiture in the event of breach. Since courts abhor forfeiture as being too harsh, they generally treat a condition as a covenant and do not allow forfeiture.

Restrictive covenants run with the land. The rights and duties imposed are passed on to subsequent land owners. They may go on forever unless state statute sets a maximum time limit, or the restriction sets its own time limitation.

Racial restrictions are considered void and unenforceable (Shelley vs Kraemer, U.S. Sup. Ct. 1948).

EASEMENTS

An easement is an irrevocable right or interest one party has in the land of another. A typical easement might be a right of way (for ingress or egress). Easements normally run with the land (transfer with the land).

Dominant Tenement   The using land that dominates the land of another.

Servient Tenement   The land that is being used by or serves the land of another.

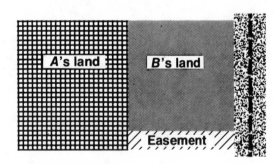

A *has an easement over the land of* B *(dominant tenement). A's easement is a benefit to his land so the easement is an* appurtenance *to A's land. The easement restricts B's use of the land (servient tenement), so the easement would be an* encumbrance *to the land of* B.

Creation of Easements

Easements may be created by any of the following means.

Grant   Either conveying the easement right or conveying the land and reserving the easement.

Agreement   Such as a common driveway or a party wall.

Implication   An easement created by law, where a single owner of two parcels of land creates a necessary use over one of the parcels, and then conveys the properties separately.

Necessity   Allowing useless landlocked property is against public policy. In many states it is possible to obtain an easement by necessity through court action, upon paying a fair value for the easement.

Prescription   This is an easement created by adverse use. Generally the use must be adverse, hostile, open, notorious, continuous, and uninterrupted for a period of time prescribed by state statute. The user can be treated as a trespasser until the easement is perfected. In many states, "tacking on" is permitted, where one user uses property for a period of time and a successor uses it for an additional period to satisfy the statutory period.

Types of Easement

Easement In Gross   This is an easement without a dominant tenement. While land of another is subject to the easement (servient tenement) there is no land being benefited, as in easements for signs or utility lines. Because an easement in gross has no dominant tenement, the easement is personal to the easement holder and does not run with the land.

Affirmative Easement   The right to use the land of another for some stated purpose.

Negative Easement   The right to prohibit an owner from some use, such as a height restriction to preserve light or view.

License   A license is a use with permission of an owner. It grants no rights to the user, as it is only a revocable privilege.

Term of an Easement

Easements created for a specific term of years end with the term. In some states, easements cannot exceed a statutory period, while in others they can go on forever.

Easements end with:

- Expiration of a stated or statutory period.
- Agreement—A quitclaim deed from the holder of the dominant tenement to the holder of the servient tenement extinguishes the easement.
- Abandonment—In some states, intentional abandonment or nonuse for a statutory period ends the easement. In other states, nonuse will only terminate an easement by prescription.
- Destruction—If the servient tenement is destroyed there can be no more easement.
- Merger—When one owner acquires ownership of both the dominant and servient tenements, the easement is lost, since an owner cannot own an easement (a lesser interest) in land that he or she holds title to.
- End of Purpose—An easement created for a particular purpose ends with that purpose.

ENCROACHMENT

Encroachment is trespass by placing improvements on or over the land of another. The property owner can take action to require the removal of the encroachment. Inaction could result in the trespasser gaining a right to continued use.

RECORDING OF DEEDS

Recording a document with a county recorder is considered to be constructive notice to the entire world as to the contents of the document. The date and time of recording determine the priority of a person's interest. Consider the following situation: A sells to B, then A sells to C. C records, then B records. As between B and C, the title goes to C. At the time C took title, the records indicated that A had title. C had no notice of B's interest. B's failure to record caused C to purchase from A. As between B and C, the one who should suffer a loss is the one whose delay caused the problem.

If, when A sold to B, B took possession (moved in), then when C purchased the property, C had constructive notice of B's interest. (Possession is considered to be constructive notice just as recording is constructive notice.) B would prevail over C, even if C had no actual notice of B's interest.

Suppose A sells to B, then to C, and then mortgages the property to D? If D records first, followed by C and B, D has the mortgage interest because it was recorded first, C gets title subject to the prior mortgage, and B gets nothing (but will be looking for A).

LIENS

A lien is a claim upon a person's property as security for a debt or obligation. The debt that gives rise to the lien may be a result of agreement between the lienor (debtor) and lienee (creditor), as in a mortgage, or may arise as a result of operation of law, as in a tax lien.

Priority

Priority of liens works similarly to priority of recordation of title, as discussed in the previous section. The first recorded lien has priority over liens placed in the public record at a later time, except for certain special cases, such as tax liens and mechanics' liens. In a foreclosure situation, liens are paid off from the sale proceeds in the order of their priority. If the foreclosing lienholder buys the property at the foreclosure sale, title is taken subject to prior liens, but liens of lesser priority are lost.

Liens for property taxes and special assessments take priority over other liens, no matter when they are incurred; however, the priority of most liens is based upon time and date of recording. To be effective, the lien must be recorded in the county where the property is located.

Judgment

A judgment is a final order by a court that an amount of money is due a plaintiff from the defendant. When recorded, a judgment becomes a general lien on all of the real property owned by the debtor within the county where the abstract of judgment was recorded. (A judgment can be recorded in more than one county.) The duration of the judgment lien and renewals vary under state law. By a writ of execution, the judgment creditor can have property sold by the sheriff to satisfy the judgment.

Attachment

An attachment is a lien on the property of a defendant before a judgment has been rendered. The purpose of the attachment is to assure the plaintiff that there will be property to levy against after a judgment is rendered.

Some states grant an attachment only when it is believed that the defendant will flee or otherwise dispose of his or her property.

Mechanics' Liens

A mechanic's lien is used to secure payment for labor, services, or materials used in construction, repair, or improvement of real property. It is specific to the property on which the work was done, and is based on statutory rights. The mechanic must file the lien within a prescribed time, and generally must verify that the facts stated are correct. Property owners can protect themselves against mechanics' liens by requiring that contractors be bonded, or by requiring lien waivers from contractors, subcontractors, and material suppliers.

In some states, the mechanic (supplier) must provide a preliminary notice to the owner that his or her work will subject the property to a lien.

Some states allow mechanics' liens to be placed against a property even though the owner did not consent to the work. Most of these states allow an owner to protect his or her interests by recording and posting a notice of nonresponsibility within a stated time after obtaining actual knowledge of the work. This type of situation most commonly arises when tenants make unauthorized improvements to rented property.

Priority of Mechanics' Liens   Mechanics' liens can be filed within a statutory period after work is completed. The priority of mechanics' liens varies greatly among the states and could be based on the:

- date that the particular contractor actually started work;
- date that the first work was performed at the property (no matter who did it);
- date of the construction contract; or
- date the lien was actually filed.

In some states, all mechanics' liens are equal as to priority; other states give different priority based on the date of the work or filing of the lien.

FAIR HOUSING

Civil Rights Act of 1866

This act gave all citizens the same rights as those enjoyed by white citizens to inherit, purchase, lease, sell, or hold real and personal property.

For many years this act was ineffective because of narrow court interpretation. *Jones* vs *Mayer* (U.S. Supreme Court 1968) held that the act was valid based upon the 13th Amendment. A victim of discrimination in the sale of housing can take the case to federal court for damages, or obtain an order that prohibits sale to another or forces the owner to sell to the plaintiff.

Federal Fair Housing Act

Title VIII of the Civil Rights Act of 1968 provides that no one can refuse to sell or rent to another because of race, color, sex, religion, or national origin, and no real estate licensee may obey his or her principal's instruction to participate in such an act. The Act is enforced by the Department of Housing and Urban Development (HUD).

Prohibitions   The act prohibits:

- broker discrimination as to clients and customers;
- refusal to show, rent, or sell by false representation that a property is not available;
- discrimination in access to multiple listing services;
- steering, i.e. directing people of different races, religions, etc., away from or toward particular areas;

- discriminatory advertising (this is prohibited even for those exempt from the act);
- retaliatory acts against those making fair housing complaints or intimidation to discourage complaints;
- discriminatory sale or loan terms;
- block busting, i.e. inducing panic selling by representing prices will drop, usually because of minority groups entering the area;
- redlining, i.e. refusal to loan or insure within an area (*Harrison* vs *Heinzeroth Mortgage Co.,* 430 F Supp 893).

Exemptions   The Act allows specific exemptions from the general provisions listed above, as follows:

- religious groups can discriminate in nonprofit housing, providing the religion is open to others regardless of race, sex, or national origin;
- private clubs can discriminate or give preference to members as to sale or lease of housing for noncommercial purposes;
- owners of a single family home can discriminate when selling or renting without an agent, providing the owner does not own more than three such homes and is not in the business of sale or leasing;
- owners of one to four residential units who occupy a unit can discriminate when renting without an agent.

Note, however, that the *Jones* vs *Mayer* decision held that the Civil Rights Act of 1866 prohibits all racial discrimination without exception. Therefore an aggrieved party may seek a remedy for racial discrimination under the 1866 Act, even though the discriminatory acts were among those covered by the exemptions in the 1968 law.

Complaints and Remedies

The statute of limitations for bringing action under the act is 180 days. The aggrieved party has a choice of:

- bringing the complaint to HUD;
- bringing an action in Federal Court;
- filing a complaint with the U.S. Attorney General.

The court can order:

- actual damages plus $1,000 punitive damages;
- a permanent or temporary injunction or restraining order.

Many states also have fair housing laws which provide remedies in state courts.

Equal Housing Opportunity Poster

An equal housing opportunity poster (supplied by HUD) should be posted in every broker's place of business. Failure to display the poster can shift the burden of proof upon the broker should a discrimination complaint be made.

CHAPTER 2 QUIZ: REAL ESTATE LAW

1. By agreement, a party to a contract was discharged and another party took her place. This is known as:

   (A) rescission
   (B) reformation
   (C) novation
   (D) revision

2. S's offer to purchase stated that it would be kept open for acceptance for three days. One day after making the offer, and before acceptance, S decides to withdraw it. The real estate agent should inform him that:

   (A) he may withdraw without penalty
   (B) revocation will mean the forfeiture of earnest money
   (C) only death can revoke the offer prior to acceptance
   (D) the offer is irrevocable

3. With the permission of W, T has used a shortcut over W's land for over twenty-five years in order to get to the highway. T has:

   (A) an appurtenant easement
   (B) an easement by implication
   (C) an easement by prescription
   (D) a license

4. An owner wishes to list an expensive home, but has requested that the home be sold to caucasians only. The agent should:

   (A) refuse the listing
   (B) explain that it would be unlikely that non-caucasians would be able to afford the house
   (C) advise owners to sell it themselves
   (D) tell seller to find another agent

5. The U.S. Supreme Court has barred racial discrimination in the rental or sale of real property based on:

   (A) the 13th Amendment
   (B) the 14th Amendment
   (C) the 18th Amendment
   (D) Jones Vs Mayer

6. A contract could best be described as:

   (A) a deliberate written agreement between competent parties to do or abstain from doing a legal act
   (B) an offer and acceptance between competent parties to do a legal act
   (C) a written offer and acceptance between legal parties to do or not do some legal act
   (D) an offer and acceptance between competent parties upon consideration to do or not do some legal act

7. After A purchased real property from S, both parties decided to rescind the recorded sale. To do so they must:

   (A) return the deed to S
   (B) record the notice of rescission
   (C) destroy the original deed
   (D) make a new deed from S to A

8. A white couple responds to a broker's ad for a property in a predominantly black neighborhood. The broker should:

   (A) try to switch them to another property in a white neighborhood
   (B) explain that the neighborhood is predominantly black
   (C) tell the prospects that they would not be comfortable in the neighborhood
   (D) show the property

9. In keeping with high professional standards of honesty and duty to both buyers and sellers, a licensee, in dealing with prospective black buyers, should:

   (A) fully explain the racial problems a neighborhood might present
   (B) suggest that they might prefer to work through a black broker
   (C) be completely color blind in all dealings
   (D) inform the owners that the prospects are black

10. Use the following illustration to answer the question below:

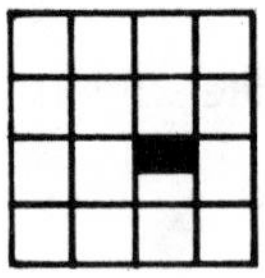

The description of the darkened parcel within this section is closest to the:

(A) N ½ of SW ¼ of SW ¼.
(B) N ½ of NW ¼ of SE ¼.
(C) N ½ of SW ¼ of SE ¼.
(D) NW ¼ of SW ¼ of N ½.

11. The S ½ of NW ¼ of SE ¼ of SW ¼ of NW ¼ of a section contains:

(A) 1¼ acres
(B) 2½ acres
(C) 5 acres
(D) 10 acres

12. A township contains:

(A) 640 acres
(B) 23,040 acres
(C) 36 acres
(D) 36 miles square

13. Section 13 in a township is located in the:

(A) NW ¼
(B) NE ¼
(C) SW ¼
(D) SE ¼

14. Title is transferred by deed at the time:

(A) of delivery
(B) the deed is executed
(C) of recording
(D) possession of the property is transferred

15. Which of the following is true of quitclaim deeds?

(A) They convey after-acquired title.
(B) They convey a warranty of merchantability.
(C) They are often used in lieu of title insurance.
(D) They can convey a partial interest.

16. Mutual assent to a real estate contract is ordinarily indicated by:

(A) attestation
(B) offer and acceptance
(C) acknowledgment
(D) seals

17. The most important element in delivery of a deed is:

(A) physical delivery
(B) intent of grantor
(C) acknowledgment
(D) grantee's signature

18. The Civil Rights Act of 1968 does **NOT** protect against discrimination as to:

(A) age
(B) sex
(C) religion
(D) national origin

19. The Federal Fair Housing Act may be enforced by bringing complaints to:

(A) Federal Housing Administration
(B) Department of Housing and Urban Development
(C) U.S. Court of Appeals
(D) U.S. Department of Commerce

20. Which of the following has the most interest in seeing that a deed is recorded?

(A) The grantor
(B) Creditors of the grantor
(C) The grantee
(D) The real estate broker

21. A verbal lease for nine months starting in six months would be:

(A) unenforceable
(B) illegal
(C) valid
(D) a unilateral contract

22. Stating that your execution of an instrument is a free act is:

    (A) an acknowledgment
    (B) an affirmation
    (C) a notarization
    (D) required for a valid deed

23. To correct a contract, the parties ask the court for:

    (A) rescission
    (B) accord and satisfaction
    (C) novation
    (D) reformation

24. The clause in a deed that defines the extent of the estate granted is known as the:

    (A) defeasance clause
    (B) habendum clause
    (C) alienation clause
    (D) subordination clause

25. Upon execution of a judgment, the deed given is a:

    (A) warranty deed
    (B) tax collector's deed
    (C) trust deed
    (D) sheriff's deed

26. A deed that conveys no promises but implies that the grantor owns the property would be a:

    (A) quitclaim deed
    (B) bargain and sale deed
    (C) gift deed
    (D) deed of trust

27. The grantor signed a deed under duress. The transaction is:

    (A) void
    (B) voidable at grantor's option
    (C) voidable at grantee's option
    (D) valid if recorded

28. Acknowledgment is required in order to:

    (A) convey legal title
    (B) execute a deed
    (C) deliver a deed
    (D) validate a deed for recording

29. The offeror dies five minutes prior to the offeree accepting the offer. The contract formed is:

    (A) illegal
    (B) voidable
    (C) unenforceable
    (D) valid

30. The offeror gave an offer on 10 December allowing ten days for acceptance. The buyer:

    (A) can withdraw the offer immediately
    (B) cannot withdraw the offer before 19 December
    (C) cannot withdraw the offer before 20 December
    (D) cannot withdraw the offer before 21 December

31. The provision in a purchase contract which provides that the buyer shall forfeit the deposit if the buyer fails to complete the purchase is known as:

    (A) liquidated damages
    (B) the defeasance clause
    (C) punitive damages
    (D) the subordination clause

32. The right of another to erect a billboard on a property is most likely:

    (A) an appurtenant easement
    (B) a prescriptive easement
    (C) an easement in gross
    (D) a license

33. Deed restrictions are created by:

    (A) the zoning commission
    (B) grantors
    (C) prescriptive use
    (D) statute

34. A contract was ambiguous in that numbers written as words differed from the numerals. The:

    (A) words take precedence over numerals
    (B) numerals take precedence over words
    (C) contract is void for uncertainty
    (D) contract is voidable at the option of either party

35. When P died, a signed and acknowledgd, but un-recorded, deed was found which gave his house to a local charity. His will provided that his entire estate was to go to his nephew. The house would therefore go to:

(A) the charity, since acknowledgment is a presumption of delivery
(B) the charity, since intent was clear
(C) the nephew, since P died owning the house
(D) the charity, since delivery is not a requirement as to charitable gifts

36. An exception in a deed:

(A) excludes part of the property
(B) reserves a right with the grantor
(C) voids the deed
(D) provides for alternate grantees

37. Which of the following voids a deed?

(A) Fraud
(B) Illegal purpose
(C) Duress
(D) Undue influence

38. The person making an acknowledgement on a deed is described as the:

(A) grantor
(B) grantee
(C) broker
(D) notary public

39. An easement is **NOT** ended by:

(A) merger
(B) a quitclaim deed from the holder of the dominant tenement to the holder of the servient tenement
(C) a sale where the deed does not reference the easement
(D) destruction of the servient tenement

40. Horizontal rows of townships are known as:

(A) tiers
(B) layers
(C) parallels
(D) ranges

41. A sold a house to B, who immediately moved in but failed to record his deed. A sold the same house to C one week later. C immediately recorded his deed, and B recorded the next day. Who has greater claim to the property?

(A) B, because his deed was delivered
(B) B, because he had possession before C purchased the property
(C) B, because he recorded his deed within a reasonable period of time
(D) C, because he recorded first

42. If you were standing in the center of a clock with the 12 facing North, you would describe 7 o'clock as:

(A) N60°W
(B) S15°W
(C) S30°W
(D) S30°E

43. The landmark case concerning the constitutionality of fair housing was:

(A) *Jones* vs *Mayer*
(B) *Shelley* vs *Kraemer*
(C) *Brown* vs *Board of Education*
(D) *Maxwell* vs *City of Chicago*

44. To create a lien after a court decision, the instrument to be recorded is:

(A) a writ of attachment
(B) an abstract of judgment
(C) an order for execution
(D) an order for possession

45. After accepting an offer, Y now refuses to sell her swamp to High Mountain Investments Corporation. Six months later she drains the swamp at great expense. High Mountain Investments Corporation then brings an action for specific performance. Which of the following principles would be of greatest interest to Y?

(A) Laches
(B) Mitigation of damages
(C) Accord and satisfaction
(D) Novation

46. Use the following illustration to answer the question below:

The blackened parcel is described as:

(A) the SE ¼ of NE ¼ of NE ¼
(B) the SW ½ of NE ¼ of NE ¼
(C) the SW ¼ of NE ¼ of NE ¼
(D) half of the NE ¼ of the NE ¼

47. Which of the following would most likely be legal under the law?

(A) A lender refusing to make loans in areas with more than twenty-five percent blacks
(B) A private country club where ownership of homes is tied to club membership, but all members are white
(C) A church, which excludes blacks from membership, renting its nonprofit housing to church members only
(D) Directing prospective buyers away from areas where they are likely to feel uncomfortable because of race

48. Which of the following would **NOT** terminate an offer?

(A) a request by offeree for more time for acceptance
(B) revocation by offeror
(C) an acceptance contingent upon a change in price
(D) the death of the offeror

49. A mechanic's lien is **NOT** available to a person who:

(A) graded the site for construction
(B) supplied the lumber but did not perform any labor
(C) provided the furnishings for a model house
(D) performed labor under a subcontract rather than a direct contract with the owner.

50. Voidable means:

(A) valid unless voided
(B) unenforceable
(C) not valid
(D) illegal

GENERAL TEST

PLEASE PRINT THE FOLLOWING:
YOUR NAME

LAST   FIRST   MI

STREET ADDRESS

CITY   STATE   ZIP

TEST CENTER LOCATION (CITY, STATE)

TEST BOOKLET NO.

1ST THREE LETTERS OF LAST NAME

I.D. NUMBER FROM ADMISSION TICKET OR SCANNABLE APPLICATION

SOCIAL SECURITY NUMBER

TEST CENTER CODE

TEST DATE

JAN	YR.
FEB	
MAR	0
APR	1
MAY	2
JUN	3
JUL	4
AUG	5
SEP	6
OCT	7
NOV	8
DEC	9

HAVE YOU EVER TAKEN THIS EXAMINATION BEFORE?   YES ○   NO ○

FOR WHICH LICENSE ARE YOU TAKING THIS EXAM?   BROKER ○   SALESPERSON ○

WHICH PART OF THE EXAMINATION ARE YOU TAKING?   GENERAL ○   STATE ○   BOTH ○

IN SIGNING BELOW I HEREBY AFFIRM THAT:
I AM THE UNDERSIGNED AND HAVE SIGNED MY CORRECT NAME ON THE SIGNATURE LINE BELOW. IN ADDITION TO PASSING THE EXAMINATION FOR LICENSURE, I MUST MEET ALL STATE REQUIREMENTS. I UNDERSTAND ALL EXAMINATION BOOKS ARE SECURE MATERIAL AND THAT NO BOOK OR PORTION THEREOF IS TO BE COPIED, TRANSMITTED TO ANY OTHER PERSON OR REMOVED FROM THE EXAMINATION ROOM. I WILL NEITHER ASSIST NOR RECEIVE ASSISTANCE FROM ANOTHER CANDIDATE OR USE ANY NOTES, MANUALS OR OTHER AIDS.

SIGNATURE   DATE

Questions 1–80 (A B C D answer bubbles)

PLEASE TURN TO REVERSE SIDE FOR STATE TEST.

ANSWERS

1. (C) A new contract or a new obligor for the old one.

2. (A) The offer can be revoked any time prior to acceptance.

3. (D) Since the use was not hostile, all T has is a revocable privilege.

4. (A) Violation of Civil Rights Acts of 1866 and 1968. To advise sellers to sell it themselves or find another agent is to advise them to violate the law.

5. (A) *Jones* vs *Mayer* is the case which upheld the constitutionality of the Civil Rights Act of 1866 based on the 13th Amendment to the Constitution.

6. (D) Four requirements are mutuality (offer and acceptance), competent parties, consideration and legal purpose. For a contract involving real estate, a fifth requirement is "in writing."

7. (D) A deed is only used once. The new deed should be recorded to clear the record.

8. (D) The other choices are steering, which violates the Civil Rights Act of 1968.

9. (C) You cannot treat buyers differently because of race.

10. (B) A 20-acre parcel.

11. (A) We always go backwards in finding acres from a legal description:

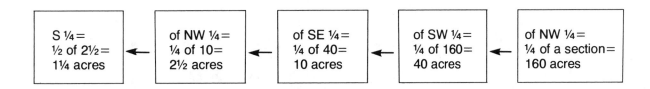

| S ¼ =
½ of 2½ =
1¼ acres | ← | of NW ¼ =
¼ of 10 =
2½ acres | ← | of SE ¼ =
¼ of 40 =
10 acres | ← | of SW ¼ =
¼ of 160 =
40 acres | ← | of NW ¼ =
¼ of a section =
160 acres |

12. (B) 36 sections of 640 acres each. There are 36 square miles not 36 miles square.

13. (B)

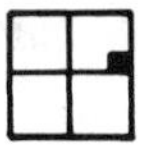

14. (A) Title does not pass until delivery. Recording is a presumption of delivery, but title can pass without recording.

15. (D) They convey whatever interest the grantor has.

16. (B) Indicates a meeting of the minds.

17. (B)

18. (A) And marital status.

19. (B) HUD, or filing a civil suit in federal district court.

20. (C) To give constructive notice of his or her interest.

21. (A) A contract that cannot be fully performed within 1 year must be in writing (Statute of Frauds).

22. (A) And it is made before a notary public.

23. (D) To reflect the real agreement of the parties.

24. (B) Usually starts with the words "to have and to hold . . . "

25. (D) Execution is the sheriff's seizure and sale to satisfy the judgment. Deed is often in the form of a quitclaim deed.

26. (B) This distinguishes it from a quitclaim deed.

27. (B) Only the wronged party can void the contract.

28. (D) A deed will generally not be accepted for recording unless acknowledged.

29. (C) There is no contract, as the offer died with the offeror.

30. (A) An offer can be withdrawn any time prior to acceptance.

31. (A) Damages agreed upon prior to the breach of contract. The courts will enforce them if they are a reasonable estimation of damages, but not if they are so excessive as to be a penalty.

32. (C) No dominant tenement being benefited. Since it is a right, it is not a license.

33. (B) Restrictive covenants are created in deeds by the grantors.

34. (A) Also, handwritten takes precedence over typed, and typed takes precedence over printed.

35. (C) The deed was never delivered. If it had been recorded, there would have been a presumption of delivery.

36. (A) And a reservation retains a right (such as an easement).

37. (B) The others make it voidable.

38. (A) The grantor acknowledges who he is and that the signature is freely given before a notary.

39. (C) Easements go with the land.

40. (A) Vertical rows are ranges.

41. (B) B's possession was constructive notice to C of B's interest.

42. (C)

43. (A) U.S. Supreme Court 1968. It upheld the Civil Rights Act of 1866 under the 13th Amendment.

44. (B) The recorded record of judgment creates a general lien on all of the debtor's property in the county where it is recorded.

45. (A) The delay in taking action has caused Y to act to her detriment. It would not now be equitable to enforce performance.

46. (B)

47. (B) The others are specifically prohibited by the Civil Rights Act of 1968. If the country club excluded blacks, then their policy could be discriminatory.

48. (A) A request for an extension is not a rejection.

49. (C) Mechanic's lien would apply to real property only—not personal property.

50. (A) Contract may only be voided by one party.

THREE
Ownership/Transfer

ESTATES (INTERESTS IN LAND)

Fee Simple (Fee Simple Absolute)   Fee simple is the highest ownership possible in real property. It is characterized by:

- no time limitation
- freely transferable
- may be inherited

Life Estate   In a life estate, the grantee holds the estate only for his or her lifetime. Therefore, it cannot be inherited or encumbered by the life tenant beyond his or her lifetime. The life tenant must make repairs and pay taxes and may not commit waste (damage or fail to make repairs).

Lenders sometimes lend on a life estate, but require that the life tenant take out a life insurance policy that will pay off the loan in the event of the tenant's death.

Upon the death of a life tenant, the property reverts either to the grantor (or heirs) if they retained a reversionary interest, or to a named third party who has a remainder interest.

Reversionary Estates

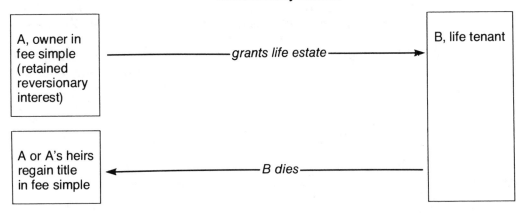

Remainder Estates

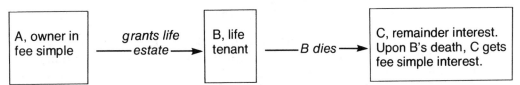

If the conveyance shown were from A to B for life and then to C, C or his heirs would be certain of receiving the estate so they would have a *vested* remainder interest. If, however, the conveyance was from A to B for life and then to C if C is still alive, C must outlive B in order to obtain the property. In this case, C would have a *contingent* remainder interest.

A life estate may be created by will or by grant where the grantor either conveys a life estate or conveys the real property, but retains a life estate.

In addition, a number of states recognize dower and curtesy as legal life estates created by law.

Dower   Right of a wife to a life estate in the husband's home upon his death.

Curtesy   Right of a husband to a life estate in the wife's home upon her death.

Freehold Estates   Fee simple and life estates are considered to be the freehold estates.

Non-Freehold Estates   Leasehold interests are the non-freehold estates. Unless specifically prohibited, leasehold interests can be freely transferred and may be inherited.

Estate for Years   A lease interest for a definite period of time. Such a lease does not automatically renew itself. Since an estate for years ends at the end of its specific term, no notice is required for termination. State laws provide for the maximum term of a leasehold interest (often 99 years).

Periodic Tenancies   These are leases from period to period such as month to month or year to year, which automatically renew themselves unless either party gives notice. Generally, notices to end the tenancy must be delivered or posted on the property a specified number of days prior to termination.

Tenancies at Will   A lease for an unspecified period which can be terminated by either party upon giving statutory notice (typically 30 days). A tenant's interests typically cease upon the death of either tenant or landlord. (Other leases are generally binding upon the estates of the parties.)

Tenancies at Sufferance   A tenant who properly came into possession of real property but who wrongfully holds over after the expiration of the tenancy is a tenant at sufferance. A tenant who fails to leave at the end of a fixed lease, for example, is a tenant at sufferance.

A tenant at sufferance may be removed without formal notice by an ejectment action. If an owner accepts rent from a tenant at sufferance, however, then the tenant becomes a periodic tenant (month to month) or a tenant at will.

OWNERSHIP

Bundle of Rights   The term bundle of rights refers to all beneficial rights of ownership, including the right to use, exclude, lease, encumber, transfer, or inherit.

Sole Ownership

Tenancy in Severalty   Ownership by one individual or corporation.

Joint Ownership

Joint Tenancy   Joint tenancy is defined as an undivided ownership by two or more people with the right of survivorship. Survivorship means that upon the death of one joint tenant, his or her interest immediately ceases. The interest passes to the surviving joint tenants. Since the interest ceases immediately upon death, it cannot be transferred by Will. Probate procedure is not necessary for joint tenancy interests. The surviving joint tenants take the interest without the personal debts of the deceased joint tenant.

A corporation cannot hold title in joint tenancy because a corporation can live forever, so survivorship is not possible.

If A, B, and C are joint tenants, the estate passes as follows under the survivorship right:

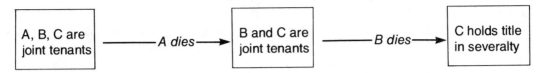

Four unities must occur in order for a joint tenancy to exist:
Time   The joint tenants must have obtained their interests at the same time.
Title   The joint tenants must have obtained their interests by the same document.
Interest   The interests of the joint tenants must be equal.
Possession   Joint tenants must have equal rights to possession.

To create a joint tenancy, it generally is necessary to clearly indicate this intent. In some states, however, a conveyance to husband and wife is presumed to be as joint tenants unless the papers state otherwise.

Tenancy in Common   Undivided interest by two or more parties without the right of survivorship is called a tenancy in common. Generally, conveyances to two or more parties that do not specify how title is to be taken give the parties title as tenants in common, except in the case of spouses.

The only one of the 4 unities required for joint tenancy that is also required for tenants in common is possession. The tenants in common have equal rights of possession. Since there is no survivorship, upon the death of a tenant in common, his or her interest would pass to the heirs rather than to surviving tenants in common.

The evolution of a tenancy in common is shown here:

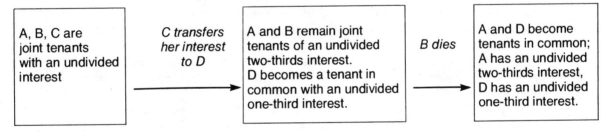

In this situation, D becomes a tenant in common because the unities of time and title do not apply to him. After C transfers her interest, the four unities continue to apply to A and B until B's death.

Community Property   While originally a Spanish concept, community property has been adopted by a number of states. Property acquired during marriage is considered to be equally owned by the husband and the wife. Property acquired before marriage is considered separate property, as is property received by either spouse as the result of a gift or inheritance. Either spouse can will his or her half of the community property to others.

Tenancy by the Entirety   In many states, when title is conveyed to a husband and wife, they each own the entire parcel as tenants by the entirety. Neither spouse can separately convey an interest during the lifetime of the other. Upon the death of one spouse, the property is owned by the survivor (similar to the survivorship of joint tenancy). Divorce would change the ownership to a tenancy in common since the survivorship was based on marriage.

Tenancy In Partnership   A partnership is an agreement of two or more co-owners to conduct a business for a profit. Generally, agreements to share in the profit create a presumption of a partnership. Title to partnership property may be held in the name of the partnership. Partnership property can be conveyed without the signatures of the spouses of the partners, although real property cannot be conveyed or encumbered without the consent of all of the partners.

Partners have equal rights to use partnership property for partnership purposes. In the absence of an agreement to the contrary, they share equally in the control of the partnership and in its profits.

Partners' Liability   General partners (active partners) have unlimited personal liability for the debts of the partnership. Limited partners (inactive partners who contribute money only) have no personal liability for the debts of the partnership beyond their investments. There must be at least one general partner in every partnership.

Death of a Partner   The heirs of a general partner have no rights to the partnership business, but are entitled to the value of the deceased partner's share in partnership assets. Limited partnership interests may be inherited.

Syndicates   A limited partnership for investment purposes, used to raise funds for large investments; subject to state regulations.

Real Estate Investment Trusts (REIT)   Under federal law a real estate investment trust must have 100 or more investors. It is taxed on retained earnings only, provided it distributes 90 percent or more of its earnings to the investors. At least 75 percent of the assets must be in real estate.

Joint Venture   A joint venture is an association for a single undertaking rather than for a continuing business. While it is treated for most purposes as a partnership, the spouses of the members must join in the conveyance of real property.

Corporations   A corporation is an artificial person created by state law. Since it is a separate entity, its shareholders have no personal liability for the debts of the corporation. Corporate profit is taxed, as are dividends received by the stockholders (double taxation).

Before a foreign corporation (incorporated in another state) can get permission to operate within another state, it generally must consent to being sued within that state by service on an agent or upon the Secretary of State.

If a corporation has a seal, then the use of the seal on a document creates the presumption that the person signing had corporate authority.

The bylaws of a corporation set forth the authority of its officers. If an officer exceeds his or her authority, the officer could be personally liable, but the corporation might not be bound by the agreement.

Chapter S Corporations   Certain small corporations can elect to become Chapter S corporations. Corporate earnings are then taxed directly to the shareholders (taxed as a partnership). The shareholders avoid the double taxation of a normal corporation, but retain the protection of not being personally liable for corporate debts.

Subdivisions   Subdivisions, land divisions for the purpose of sale or financing, are governed by state and local statutes.

Standard Subdivision   Land development with no areas owned in common.

Planned Development Project (Planned Unit Development)   A subdivision with individual lot ownership, but with common areas owned by all of the owners as tenants in common.

Cooperative   Development where each owner owns stock in a cooperative corporation with the right to occupy a unit under a proprietary lease. Taxes and mortgage payments are made by the corporation. A disadvantage is that owners don't have title, so they can't mortgage their interest. They can, however, borrow on their stock.

Condominium   Development where individual owners actually own air space of their unit but the land and common areas are owned with the other owners as tenants in common. Unlike in a cooperative, owners pay their own mortgage and taxes.

Timeshare Ownership   Also known as interval ownership, timeshare ownership is an undivided interest in a unit (usually as tenants in common), coupled with the exclusive right of occupancy for a designated period each year. Timeshare interests can also be leasehold estates where the right of occupancy ends after a stated number of years. Timeshares are customarily vacation type units where individual buyers obtain occupancy for particular weeks each year.

Interstate Land Sales Full Disclosure Act   Federal disclosure act administered by the Office of Interstate Land Sales Registration (OILSR) of HUD. Disclosure is required for subdivisions of 25 or more unimproved residential lots offered for sale in interstate commerce. The disclosure statement sets forth material facts about the development which must be provided to the purchaser prior to sale. Sales to builders are exempt from the Act. Purchasers have a 7-day right of rescission after signing the purchase agreement.

Fixtures

Fixtures are former items of personal property which have become so affixed to the real property that they have become part of the real property. Fixtures are transferred with the real estate.

Generally, a court requires that at least one of the following three tests be met in order to determine that an item is a fixture:

Intent   What the parties intended is considered the most important test of a fixture. Parties can agree as to whether or not an improvement or addition will be a fixture.

Attachment   The permanence of attachment.

Adaptability   If an item is reasonably necessary for the normal use of the property, it probably is a fixture.

Relationship of the Parties   If the other tests are inconclusive, the law would favor:

1. the buyer, as between buyer and seller;
2. the tenant, as between landlord and tenant;
3. the mortgagee (lender), as between mortgagee and mortgagor (borrower).

Trade Fixtures   Fixtures installed by a tenant for the purpose of conducting a business or trade ordinarily remain personal property and can be removed by the tenant any time prior to the expiration of the lease. The tenant is liable for any damage caused by the removal.

Emblements   Cultivated annual crops (fructus industriales) are personal property. The tenant has the right to enter the property after the expiration of the lease to harvest those crops that were the fruits of his or her labor.

INSURANCE

Insurance is a personal contract whereby an insurer agrees to indemnify an insured in the event of a specified loss. In exchange for the payment of a premium, the risk of loss is shifted from the insured to the insurer. In real estate we are concerned with title insurance and property insurance.

Abstract and Title Insurance

The sellers in real estate transactions must show the buyers that they are conveying marketable title. This is often accomplished through an abstract of title. An abstract is a copy of every recorded document dealing with a property which has been prepared by an abstractor who searched the records. The seller usually pays to update the abstract. An attorney would then give an opinion as to the marketability of the property. In preparing the abstract, the abstractor's only liability is a failure to show a recorded document. The attorney's opinion is based only on what is reported in the abstract.

Title insurance is more than an opinion—it is a guarantee of marketable title. The title insurance company checks the records and issues a preliminary title report. This is not a policy of insurance, but a statement of the condition of the title, setting forth the encumbrances and affirming that the insurance company will issue a title policy. Title policies are issued at the closing of the transaction.

Title policies with a one-time premium are available to protect the purchaser and the lender and to insure against past defects in the title up to the amount of insurance purchased.

Standard policies of title insurance generally protect against:

- forgery
- lack of capacity
- failure of delivery
- recorded but unreported liens
- tax liens

Because the standard policy does not cover matters not of public record, lenders frequently require an extended coverage American Land Title Association (ALTA) policy which includes:

- rights of parties in possession
- unrecorded liens
- unrecorded easements
- claims that a proper survey or inspection would have revealed (the property is surveyed for this coverage)
- mining claims and water rights

Similar extended coverage is also available for the purchaser.

Title insurance does not protect the purchaser against zoning restrictions or against defects the purchaser knew of but failed to tell the insurer about.

Torrens Title System   Eleven states have systems of registering title with the state. After a court determination as to title (quiet title action), a registrar keeps a record of title. When liens are placed on the property, they are entered on a master certificate of title and are removed when they are satisfied. When the grantee brings a deed to the registrar, the registrar changes the master records and issues a new certificate of title to the grantee.

Property Insurance

Basic Fire Policy   Covers loss by fire, lightning, and smoke from a hostile fire.

Extended Coverage Policy   Includes coverage for wind, hail, water damage, and other specified perils.

Co-Insurance   A requirement that an insured carry a particular percentage of the replacement value (usually 80 percent) in order to be fully reimbursed for a loss. If an insured carries less than the required coverage (a percentage of the required coverage), the insured can collect only that percentage of the loss.

Homeowners Policy   Provides a package of protection from losses beyond the extended coverage policy including vandalism, theft, personal property protection, and even liability coverage.

Tenant Policy   A package of protection for the tenants' personal property which may also include liability protection.

Condominium Owner Policy   Similar to a tenant policy; includes most of the general homeowner coverage, except for loss of the structure, which is covered by a separate policy of the condominium owners association.

Flood Insurance   The National Flood Insurance program makes flood insurance available through private insurance carriers under a government-subsidized program.

Earthquake Insurance   While earthquake coverage might be included as part of another policy, it usually requires a separate policy.

Home Warranty Plans   A buyer insurance plan which covers structural, mechanical, and electrical problems over a stated period of time.

Rent Insurance   Protects the owner against lost income while a property is being repaired or rebuilt as a result of a casualty loss.

Deductibles   Premiums can be reduced by having a deductible amount from the coverage. The higher the deductible, the lower the premium.

Riders   These are amendments to policies. They usually exclude or increase coverage.

Redlining   The refusal to provide insurance coverage (or loans) within a particular area. Redlining is a violation of the Civil Rights Act of 1968.

SETTLEMENTS

Real estate settlements are generally the responsibility of the listing broker. In some areas they are handled by escrow companies. Presettlement activities include:

1. ordering preliminary title report (for title insurance) or the update of the abstract;
2. obtaining statements from lenders as to loan balances being assumed or paid off, as well as assumption costs and/or prepayment penalties;
3. prorating taxes, insurance, rents, etc., as applicable;
4. arranging for transfer of insurance policies being assumed;
5. obtaining leases and arranging for their assignment;
6. preparing bills of sale for personal property;
7. obtaining certificate of occupancy (new structures);
8. drafting all deeds, notes, mortgages, etc.;
9. drafting settlement statements.

At the settlement, all signatures are obtained and funds disbursed. The broker generally arranges for the recording of all documents.

The broker provides separate closing statements for the buyer and the seller showing all debits and credits, and the amount to be paid or to be received.

Credits are pluses, amounts a party is entitled to. Debits are amounts to be paid or subtracted from what is coming.

Following are typical seller and buyer statements showing credits and debits of both.

SELLER'S CLOSING STATEMENT

Debit Seller	Credit Seller
Title insurance or abstract costs. Pay off on existing loan Loan being assumed Seller Financing Money received from buyer Commission to be paid broker Taxes (could be credit or debit) Documentary transfer stamps Cost to notarize deed Cost to draft deed Recording costs of new mortgage (if seller financing). NOTE: The party who gives an instrument generally pays to prepare and acknowledge it. The party receiving it pays to record it. Termite inspection fee Recording satisfaction of mortgage being paid off Prepaid rents Attorney fees Cash to be received at closing New loan points (As agreed by the parties or required by law. On VA loans the seller is required to pay the points).	Purchase price Balance in loan impound accounts Prepaid insurance (if policy is assumed) Taxes (could be credit or debit)

BUYER'S CLOSING STATEMENT

Debit Buyer	Credit Buyer
Sale price Recording deeds received Drafting new mortgages Notarizing new mortgages Balance in impound accounts of loans being assumed Insurance policies being assumed Attorney fees Interest paid in advance Advance taxes and insurance for impound account New loan costs Taxes (could be credit or debit)	Loans being assumed Money paid to seller or deposited with agent New mortgage to be given Interest on loans being assumed (if paid in arrears) Taxes (could be credit or debit) Balance paid at closing

VOLUNTARY AND INVOLUNTARY ALIENATION

Alienation is the legal term for transferring ownership or interest in real property. It is most commonly achieved by sale or lease. This section describes other means by which alienation occurs.

Dedication

A voluntary transfer of real property or property rights to a governmental unit is called dedication. Customarily either a right of way (easement) or actual title is transferred. Dedication can be for roads, school sites, parks, hospitals, etc. Dedication could be a condition for approval of a development by a city or county.

Statutory Dedication   State statutes often provide that a developer, by recording a plot map showing the streets, is in fact offering the streets to the governmental unit.

Common Law Dedication   Owner's acts that indicate it was the owner's intent to dedicate the property. A developer requesting that a city maintain a road could be construed as intending to dedicate the road to the city.

Dedication by Deed   Actual deeding of the parcel to the government unit.

Gifts

Title can pass by gift. The lack of valuable consideration will not in itself invalidate a transfer. If it can be shown that the grantor made the gift while insolvent in order to defraud creditors, the gift could be set aside and the creditors could reach the property. A deed conveying real property as a gift would normally describe the consideration as "love and affection."

Adverse Possession

Title can be acquired from another without permission by adverse possession. To obtain title there must be:

- actual continuous and uninterrupted use of the property for a period of time prescribed by statute. (In some states, the statutory period for adverse possession can be fulfilled by "Tacking On": successors in interest can add prior adverse use of their predecessors to their own use);
- the use must be exclusive;
- the use must be hostile (owner's permission would destroy the hostile nature of the use);
- the use must be open and notorious.

Some states require that the use must be under some claim of right or color of title, or provide a shorter statutory period for use when under a claim of right (example: a deed from a person who falsely claimed ownership).

A number of states add the requirement that the adverse user pay the taxes. Claims of right and paying taxes generally enhance the claims of adverse users.

By adverse possession you cannot obtain any greater rights than the former owner had. Therefore, if the former owner had only half the mineral rights, by adverse possession you would take title to the property with only half the mineral rights.

To obtain marketable title, it would be necessary to adjudicate an adverse claim through a quiet title action (ask the court to determine ownership).

Title cannot be taken from the government by adverse possession.

Sheriff's Sale

After a judgment has been rendered against a debtor, the creditor can get execution on the judgment. The sheriff can seize non-exempt property of the debtor and dispose of it by public sale to satisfy the judgment. Real property would be transferred by a sheriff's deed, which transfers no greater right than the creditor had. Purchaser takes title subject to existing liens.

Homestead Exemption   Homeowners are protected against unsecured creditors forcing the sale of their home by state homestead exemptions. If the amount of the homeowner's equity is the same or less than the statutory exemption, then the unsecured creditor cannot force the sale of the homestead. In some states, the homeowner must record the declaration of homestead to be protected.

Foreclosure

A mortgagor (borrower) who defaults on a mortgage may be foreclosed by the mortgagee (lender) through a public sale. The purchaser at a foreclosure sale takes title subject to all encumbrances senior to the foreclosing mortgage, but junior encumbrances are wiped out. (See Chapter Six for additional information.)

Condemnation

Under the police power of the state, a property may be condemned and ordered vacated or destroyed when it is unfit or unsafe for use or occupancy. When the property is so condemned the owner is not entitled to any compensation.

Another type of condemnation is the taking of private property for public use. This is known as Eminent Domain.

Eminent Domain   A government unit may take ownership of private property for public purposes without the consent of the owner. This power may be delegated to public utilities, schools, hospitals, etc.

The owner is entitled to the fair market value of the property at the time it is taken. The owner can object to the amount offered and has the right to have the court determine fair value.

Eminent domain is not authorized under the police power of the state. Under police power, the restrictions placed on property are to protect the public health, safety, morals, and general welfare; no compensation is given. Police power can never be delegated; eminent domain can.

Severance Damage   When only part of the owner's land is taken by eminent domain and it results in a reduced value for the remaining land, the owner is entitled to compensation for this additional loss.

Inverse Condemnation   An owner can take action to force the condemnation of his or her property if the government by its action has caused loss in value or inability to use a property. Such an action might occur, for example, when a government takes away a former public access so as to landlock a parcel.

INHERITANCE

Probate is the legal procedure for disposing of the estate of a deceased. If the deceased died with a will (testate), then the will would appoint an executor (man) or executrix (woman) to administer and dispose of the estate. If the deceased died intestate (without a will), then the court would appoint an administrator (man) or administratrix (woman) to administer and dispose of the estate.

An estate may be made up of three types of property:

- Devise: real property given by will
- Bequest: personal property given by will
- Legacy: money given by will

Types of Will

Formal Will   Written, signed, and witnessed, usually by at least two people.

Holographic Will   Handwritten, signed and dated (no witness required). This is not legal in all states.

Nuncupative   Oral deathbed will, usually only allowed for personal property of low value. Not legal in all states.

A will can be canceled anytime prior to the testator's death. A new will cancels a prior will. A codicil is an amendment to a will. It requires the same formalities as a will.

Intestate Succession

If a person dies intestate (without a will), property in his or her estate passes in accordance with the laws of intestate succession. Intestate succession varies among the states, with provisions for spouses and lineal descendants (children). In the event no living descendants of the deceased are found, provision is made for parents and collateral heirs (related through a common ancestor).

Generally, if a blood heir is dead but leaves children, the children share equally in the share their parent would have received (per stirpes).

Escheat   Because every property should have an owner, when a person dies without a will (intestate), and also has no known heirs, after a statutory period the title to real property goes to (escheats to) the state.

REAL PROPERTY TAXATION

Real estate taxes are *ad valorem* taxes: the tax is according to the value of the property.

The tax assessor sets the value for each property. Assessed value could be market value or a percentage of market value. Many states have state boards of equalization that ensure that valuations are at a uniform basis throughout the state. Property owners can appeal assessments (not the tax rate) within a specified period of time through appeal boards. All of the assessed valuations is known as the assessment roll.

Many states offer special homeowners' exemption for a primary residence as well as special exemptions for senior citizens.

To determine the tax rate, the taxation authority divides the budgetary needs by the assessment roll.

$$\text{Tax Rate} = \frac{\text{Budget Needs}}{\text{Assessment Roll}}$$

If a community needed $\$850,000$ and had a tax roll of $\$20,000,000$, the tax rate per dollar of assessed valuation would be $\$.0425$.

$$\frac{850{,}000}{20{,}000{,}000} = .0425$$

Since taxes are usually expressed per $100 of evaluation, the tax rate would be $4.25 per $100.

Tax rates are often expressed in mills. A mill is 1/10 of a cent, or $.001. The tax rate of $.0425 per dollar of evaluation could be expressed as 42½ mills. To determine the taxes, simply multiply the tax rate times the assessed valuation.

If the taxes are not paid, they become a specific lien on the property. After a specified period, there is a sale at public auction. Some states allow a statutory period of redemption by the property owner after the sale. The tax collector issues a tax deed or quitclaim deed to the purchaser.

Special Assessments

Special assessments are for improvements that directly benefit a property (road improvement, sidewalks, sewer, etc.). Assessments are usually made on a front-foot basis. Special assessments are also a specific lien, and nonpayment can result in a public sale of the property. Both property tax liens and special assessments are priority liens and take precedence over mortgage liens.

Capital Gains

Gains on the sale of real property held for over six months are classified as long-term capital gains. Currently 60 percent of a long-term capital gain is exempt from taxation. The taxpayer therefore adds 40 percent of the gain to his or her other income for tax purposes. Since the highest individual tax rate is currently 50 percent, the most any taxpayer would have to pay on a long-term capital gain is 20 percent of the gain—50 percent of the taxable 40 percent of the gain.

The amount of the gain is computed by deducting the seller's cost basis or book value from the net sales price. Cost basis is the original cost plus improvements, less depreciation.

Assume a property originally cost $100,000 and the buyer put $10,000 in improvements into the property, and over the years took $68,000 in depreciation. The cost basis would be $42,000:

$100,000 + $10,000 − $68,000 = $42,000
cost   improvements   depreciation   book value

If the owner then sold the property for $100,000 (the same price originally paid) there would be a long-term capital gain of $58,000, the difference between sales price and book value (cost basis). Forty percent of the $58,000 gain, or $23,200, would be added to the seller's income to determine the tax.

Dealers who regularly get a substantial portion of their income from buying and selling real property are not entitled to take long-term capital gains. Their gains are regarded as regular income.

Homeowners may defer paying capital gains on the sale of their residence if within two years of a sale they purchase a new home costing the same or more than the sale price of their former home. Assume:

Cost of Home	$14,000
Sold for	$26,000
Reinvested in home for	$29,000
Sold for	$42,000
Reinvested in home for	$44,000
Sold for	$96,000

Assume the seller did not wish to buy another home. To determine the cost basis, we start with:

	$14,000	Cost of original home.
Add	3,000	Amount added to proceeds of 1st sale to buy 2nd home.
Add	2,000	Amount added to proceeds of 2nd home to buy 3rd home.
	$19,000	Cost basis.

Sale Price	$96,000
− Cost Basis	$19,000
Capital Gain	$77,000

A capital loss may be used to offset a capital gain. However, a homeowner is not entitled to take a capital loss on the sale of his or her residence.

$125,000 Exclusion   Homeowners 55 years of age or older who have lived in a house for 3 of the 5 years preceding its sale are entitled to a one-time exclusion of $125,000 in long-term capital gains. Many states have similar exemptions for their state income taxes.

Tax-Free Exchange

By exchanging like property for like property (real property for real property), one can defer capital gains. Each party to an exchange keeps the old cost basis, increased by the amount of any boot given or decreased by the amount of boot received.

Boot is any item of personal property (usually money) given to even up a trade. Debt relief (assuming a lower indebtedness on the property received than there was on the property given) is considered boot. Boot is taxable as capital gains to the party receiving it.

Income Tax Deductions

A homeowner may take as tax deductions the interest paid on his or her home loan as well as property taxes. No other cash expenses or depreciation may be taken on a residence not used for business or income purposes.

For business and income property, all expenses are deductible, including depreciation. Keep in mind that income from such property is treated as regular income, not as capital gains.

Income Tax Liens

Income tax liens when recorded become general liens against all the property of the debtor. The property can be sold at sheriff's sale to satisfy the lien. Purchasers take title subject to all existing prior liens.

PUBLIC CONTROL

Planning

Local governments obtain their planning powers from state enabling legislation that requires city and county planning commissions to develop a master plan. This plan forces a community to consider its future goals and is implemented through zoning.

Master planning can consider not only future development, but redevelopment as well. It considers the coordination of all services, the protection of the environment, and the health, safety, morals and general welfare of the people. Master planning can provide for growth limitations as well as requirements that discourage premature development.

By allowing advantageous uses, zoning can encourage redevelopment by making it economically feasible to rip down the existing structure. Redevelopment can also be aided through special assessment districts and enterprise zones (an area where special tax or other benefits encourage redevelopment).

Some city planning commissions have powers to control land use within their sphere of influence, but outside their boundaries.

Besides providing for orderly growth and uses consistent with the needs of the people, proper planning tends to protect property values.

Environmental Impact Statement   The National Environmental Policy Act of 1969 provides for an Environmental Impact Statement (EIS) when a development is considered likely to have an effect on the environment. These statements can be required by planning commissions and serve as an aid in planning. The environmental statement considers all aspects of a development such as schools, services, transportation, utilities, pollution, noise, future growth effects, jobs, wildlife, ecology, etc.

Rural Land Planning   Soil conditions should be considered in providing the best soils for agriculture. By exclusionary zoning (excluding other uses), land can be kept in agriculture.

Zoning

While restrictive covenants are private restrictions on land use, zoning is a public restriction that is enforceable under the police power of the state. Zoning is a local control (city and county). There are no federal zoning laws.

The zoning is ordinarily set by a local planning commission. If an owner objects to the zoning, an appeal can be made to the planning commission. The owner can ask for:

Zoning Variance   An exception to the zoning.

Rezoning   An actual change to the zoning.

If turned down, the owner can generally appeal to either the city council, county board of supervisors, or a special zoning appeals board. After exhausting all administrative remedies, the owner can appeal to the courts. Generally the courts will overrule the planning commission only if it determines that the zoning was arbitrary or capricious.

Nonconforming Use   A use that was in existence prior to zoning is generally allowed to continue (under a grandfather clause) but it may not be expanded. Zoning provisions can allow a reasonable period of time in which the use must cease, allowing the owner to recoup the investment. When a nonconforming use structure is destroyed, it generally may not be rebuilt. Once a nonconforming use has been abandoned, it usually may not be reinstated.

Exclusionary Zoning   Keeping out a use (usually people of lower income) by requiring large lots or homes of particular square footage.

Bulk Zoning   Controlling density by setbacks, height restrictions, and open space requirements.

Incentive Zoning   Zoning which allows office use, providing that the first floor be for retail use.

Aesthetic Zoning   Architectural and/or color requirements so that an area conforms to a desired plan. Aesthetic zoning can also control sign usage and size.

Spot Zoning   Zoning of parcels that are inconsistent with the area. Generally the result of political influence.

Cluster Zoning   Zoning requiring structures clustered together with the rest of the lot in open space for the use of all.

Water Rights

Riparian Rights   Right of a landowner to reasonable use of flowing water through, adjacent to, or under the property.

Littoral Rights   Right of a landowner to reasonable use of water from a lake, ocean, or pond bordering the property (nonflowing water).

Right of Correlative Use   Right of a landowner to reasonable use of underground percolating water.

Accretion   Build up of land by action of water.

Reliction   Land formed when water recedes (belongs to owner of waterfront property).

Avulsion   Sudden tearing away of land by action of water, such as a change in a river's course.

Surface Water   No defined channel. Landowner can be liable for damage caused by diverting the natural flow of surface water.

Flood Water   Water overflowing a defined channel. Landowner can dike his property against flood water.

Health and Safety/Building Codes

Building codes have been enacted by state and municipal governments under their police power to protect the health, safety, and general welfare of the people. They set minimum acceptable standards. Codes cover a wide spectrum, including construction standards and methods, plumbing, electrical, heating, fire alarm, fire suppression, sewage disposal, ventilation, etc.

Local building inspectors are the primary enforcers for compliance with code standards, although the local fire department might have jurisdiction over fire-related codes and the local health department over health codes.

Before a new structure can be occupied, a Certificate of Occupancy must be obtained which certifies that the building is in compliance with the codes.

Specification Code   Codes which specify particular methods or materials. They can be very restrictive.

Performance Code   Specifies performance requirements which give greater latitude to builders as long as a standard of performance is met.

CHAPTER 3 QUIZ: OWNERSHIP/TRANSFER

1. M wishes to leave her property to her husband and niece on a two-thirds—one-third undivided basis. This can be done as:

   (A) joint tenancy
   (B) tenancy in common
   (C) community property
   (D) tenancy in severalty

2. J, age 58, sold the home he had purchased two years before. He had paid $46,500 and received $74,800. In computing his income tax, J would add the following to his other income:

   (A) $11,320
   (B) $28,300
   (C) $16,980
   (D) nothing, as he has a $125,000 exemption

3. Time, possession, interest, and title relate to:

   (A) joint tenancy
   (B) tenancy in common
   (C) a partnership
   (D) severalty ownership

4. A city would likely own the city parks:

   (A) as a tenant in common
   (B) in partnership
   (C) as a tenant by the entirety
   (D) in severalty

5. A tenant remaining in possession after the lease has expired:

   (A) is on a periodic tenancy
   (B) has a freehold interest
   (C) is a tenant at sufferance
   (D) has a servient tenement

6. A codicil is an amendment to:

   (A) an insurance policy
   (B) a title report
   (C) an abstract
   (D) a will

7. The rental of a beachfront condominium for the month of August is:

   (A) a periodic tenancy
   (B) a tenancy at will
   (C) an estate for years
   (D) a freehold interest

8. A standard policy of title insurance protects a purchaser against:

   (A) zoning prohibitions
   (B) an existing encroachment
   (C) the rights of parties who are in possession
   (D) the lack of capacity of a previous grantor

9. At least 100 investors are required to form a:

   (A) real estate investment trust
   (B) syndicate
   (C) limited partnership
   (D) corporation

10. A man moved into a deserted home and installed kitchen cabinets, among other extensive repairs. When the owner discovered the occupancy he had him ejected. What is the status of the kitchen cabinets?

    (A) The cabinets stay, as they are trade fixtures.
    (B) The man can get them back if they can be removed without damage to the real estate.
    (C) The man cannot get the cabinets back.
    (D) While the cabinets stay, the man is entitled to the value of the improvements.

11. S and M plan to buy a home together, but they wish to leave their property to their respective children from previous marriages. They would want to hold title as:

    (A) tenants by the entirety
    (B) joint tenants
    (C) tenants in common
    (D) tenants in severalty

12. The future interest retained by a grantor is:

    (A) a remainder interest
    (B) a reversionary interest
    (C) a defeasible interest
    (D) a tenancy at sufferance

13. A tenancy for years is created by:

    (A) express agreement
    (B) adverse possession
    (C) operation of the law
    (D) holding over

14. Which of the following terms do **NOT** belong together?

    (A) Joint tenancy/survivorship
    (B) Escheat/testate
    (c) Tenancy in common/undivided interest
    (D) Fee simple/perpetuity

15. A, B, and C are joint tenants. C sells his interest to D, then B dies. As a result:

    (A) B's heirs, D and A are joint tenants
    (B) B's heirs and A are joint tenants, but D is a tenant in common
    (C) A, D, and B's heirs are tenants in common
    (D) A and D are tenants in common

16. A partition action is:

    (A) a subdivision
    (B) a court proceeding to break up a co-ownership
    (C) a conversion of rental units to condominiums
    (D) a conveyance of a partial interest

17. The following is true regarding an estate in real property:

    (A) interest must presently vest
    (B) it is always forever
    (C) more than one estate can exist in a property simultaneously
    (D) it requires ownership

18. A brother and sister hold land as joint tenants. The sister conveys one-half of her interest to her husband. Ownership is now:

    (A) by brother, sister, and her husband as tenants in common
    (B) by brother and sister as joint tenants, and by her husband as a tenant in common
    (C) by brother, sister, and her husband as joint tenants
    (D) by brother and sister as joint tenants

19. The only one of the four unities of joint tenancy that is also required for tenancy in common is:

    (A) time
    (B) title
    (C) interest
    (D) possession

20. Creditors can claim the personal assets of an investor in:

    (A) a general partnership
    (B) a syndicate
    (C) a real estate investment trust
    (D) a corporation

21. The following would be a credit on a seller's closing statement:

    (A) prepaid rents
    (B) prepaid insurance
    (C) title insurance costs
    (D) existing liens being assumed

22. In a buyer's closing statement, selling price would always be:

    (A) a debit to the buyer
    (B) a credit to the buyer
    (C) assumed by the seller
    (D) less the amount to be paid for commission

23. What form of interest is conveyed by a sale made with the provision that title shall revert to the grantor should an objectionable use take place?

    (A) An estate on a condition subsequent
    (B) An estate on a condition precedent
    (C) A fee simple absolute
    (D) A life estate

24. A standard policy of title insurance would **NOT** cover:

    (A) prescriptive easements
    (B) failure of delivery
    (C) lack of capacity
    (D) forged signatures

25. The right of a landowner to take water from a river flowing through the property is:

    (A) littoral rights
    (B) right of correlative use
    (C) riparian rights
    (D) right of prior appropriation

26. A littoral rights owner's property adjoins a:

    (A) river
    (B) sea
    (C) navigable waterway
    (D) public park

27. The following would be a specific lien on real property:

    (A) unpaid federal taxes
    (B) an easement
    (C) a special assessment
    (D) exclusionary zoning

28. Rights of occupancy of owners in a cooperative are based on:

    (A) a proprietary lease
    (B) the articles of incorporation
    (C) the bylaws of the association
    (D) individual deeds to each unit

29. A life tenant may:

    (A) commit waste
    (B) encumber the reversionary interest
    (C) lease the property to another
    (D) convey the estate by will

30. In the absence of an agreement, a tenant in common who occupies and farms the property is not specifically liable to the other tenants in common for:

    (A) mortgage payments
    (B) rent she received from a third party
    (C) income she received from oil and gas leases
    (D) rent for her occupancy

31. Ownership by husband and wife only describes:

    (A) joint tenancy
    (B) tenancy in severalty
    (C) tenancy in common
    (D) tenancy by the entirety

32. A codicil transfers personal property through:

    (A) bill of sale
    (B) devise
    (C) dedication
    (D) bequest

33. A corporation could hold title to real property as:

    (A) tenants by the entirety
    (B) joint tenants
    (C) community property owners
    (D) partners

34. A joint tenancy between 2 single men would become a tenancy in common upon:

    (A) the death of one joint tenant
    (B) one selling his interest to the other
    (C) the marriage of one of them
    (D) one selling his interest to a third party

35. W sold the home he had lived in for nine years at a $12,000 loss. In the same year he sold an apartment building he had owned for seven years at a $40,000 profit. Considering both sales, he would have a combined long-term capital gain of:

    (A) $28,000
    (B) $15,200
    (C) $16,000
    (D) $40,000

36. Which of the following is **NOT** required for adverse possession?

    (A) Continuous use
    (B) Permission
    (C) Notorious use
    (D) Exclusive use

37. A conveyance from H to A for life, and then to S if S is still alive would give S a:

    (A) contingent remainder interest
    (B) vested remainder interest
    (C) life estate
    (D) reversionary interest

38. Which of the following best describes a condominium?

    (A) Undivided interest in the whole
    (B) Undivided interest in common area and separate interest in individual units
    (C) Separate interests in the whole
    (D) A divided interest in the common areas and undivided interest in each unit

39. A's house is at the end of the runway of a new city airport. The noise has made her home uninhabitable. She would ask for:

    (A) punitive damages
    (B) inverse condemnation
    (C) severance damages
    (D) tax relief

40. The state wants to condemn a strip of land through a farm for a highway. The farm will decrease in value far more than the value of the condemned land. The farmer should ask for:

    (A) severance damages
    (B) inverse condemnation
    (C) nominal damages
    (D) an injunction

41. The cost base from which capital gains are figured is NOT affected by:

    (A) depreciation
    (B) repairs
    (C) improvements
    (D) your cost

42. Closing prorations are based on:

    (A) 365 days in a year
    (B) 52 weeks in a year
    (C) the actual days in each month
    (D) 30-day months and 360-day years

43. If B's interest in land entitles her to impose conditions on its future use, her interest is probably:

    (A) a life estate
    (B) a non-freehold interest
    (C) a fee simple estate
    (D) an estate for years

44. A capital gain CANNOT be obtained from:

    (A) the sale of your residence
    (B) the sale of stocks and bonds
    (C) the sale of raw land
    (D) increased rents

45. Interval exclusive occupancy coupled with a tenancy-in-common interest best describe:

    (A) an estate for years
    (B) a periodic tenancy
    (C) a cooperative
    (D) a timeshare ownership

46. Which of the following is true of zoning?

    (A) It is a private control over land use
    (B) It takes precedence over restrictive covenants
    (C) Its controls are limited to land use
    (D) It will not be retroactive

47. The LEAST important test of a fixture is:

    (A) adaptability
    (B) cost
    (C) intent
    (D) method of attachment

48. A church has just purchased a huge apartment complex they intend to use for an orphanage. The neighbors could expect to be affected by:

    (A) lower taxes
    (B) higher taxes
    (C) an increase in city services
    (D) an increase in values

49. Who pays the taxes on the common areas within a condominium?

    (A) The property owners association
    (B) The developer
    (C) The individual unit owners
    (D) All of the unit owners as tenants by the entirety

50. Real property includes:

    (A) leasehold interests
    (B) fixtures
    (C) mortgages
    (D) fructus industriales

GENERAL TEST

PLEASE PRINT THE FOLLOWING:
YOUR NAME

| LAST | FIRST | MI |

STREET ADDRESS

| CITY | STATE | ZIP |

TEST CENTER LOCATION (CITY, STATE)

TEST BOOKLET NO.

1ST THREE LETTERS OF LAST NAME

I.D. NUMBER FROM ADMISSION TICKET OR SCANNABLE APPLICATION

SOCIAL SECURITY NUMBER

TEST CENTER CODE

TEST DATE
JAN FEB MAR APR MAY JUN JUL AUG SEP OCT NOV DEC
YR.

HAVE YOU EVER TAKEN THIS EXAMINATION BEFORE?   YES ○   NO ○

FOR WHICH LICENSE ARE YOU TAKING THIS EXAM?   BROKER ○   SALESPERSON ○

WHICH PART OF THE EXAMINATION ARE YOU TAKING?
GENERAL ○   STATE ○   BOTH ○

IN SIGNING BELOW I HEREBY AFFIRM THAT:
I AM THE UNDERSIGNED AND HAVE SIGNED MY CORRECT NAME ON THE SIGNATURE LINE BELOW. IN ADDITION TO PASSING THE EXAMINATION FOR LICENSURE, I MUST MEET ALL STATE REQUIREMENTS. I UNDERSTAND ALL EXAMINATION BOOKS ARE SECURE MATERIAL AND THAT NO BOOK OR PORTION THEREOF IS TO BE COPIED, TRANSMITTED TO ANY OTHER PERSON OR REMOVED FROM THE EXAMINATION ROOM. I WILL NEITHER ASSIST NOR RECEIVE ASSISTANCE FROM ANOTHER CANDIDATE OR USE ANY NOTES, MANUALS OR OTHER AIDS.

SIGNATURE   DATE

(Answer grid: questions 1–80, each with options A B C D)

ANSWERS

1. (B) For joint tenancy the ownership must be equal. Community property is only for a married couple and tenancy in severalty is ownership by one person.

2. (A) J's long-term capital gain is $28,300. He would add 40% of this to his other income. To be eligible for the $125,000 exemption, he would have had to have lived there three of the preceding five years.

3. (A) Joint tenancy requirements. Survivorship is a feature of joint tenancy.

4. (D) Owned by the city alone.

5. (C) A holdover tenant can be removed by ejectment; however, if the owner accepts rent, the tenant's position is changed to either a tenancy at will or a periodic tenancy.

6. (D) It requires the same formalities as the will itself.

7. (C) A lease for a definite period of time (does not automatically renew itself).

8. (D) As well as forgery, unreported but recorded liens, failure of delivery, and tax liens. B and C are covered by extended coverage policies. No policy covers zoning restrictions.

9. (A) REIT under federal law.

10. (C) They are fixtures and have been joined to the real estate by the wrongful accession.

11. (C) A and B would go to the survivor, and D is ownership by one person only.

12. (B) At the end of the life estate, the estate reverts to the grantor. A remainder interest goes to a third person.

13. (A) Since it is a lease for a specific period of time.

14. (B) Property only escheats to the state when the owner dies intestate and has no heirs.

15. (D) When C sold to D, he broke the joint tenancy as to his interest, and D took a one-third interest as a tenant in common, while A and B remained joint tenants. When B died, A took his interest. A has two-third's interest and D has one-third.

16. (B) An action to divide the lands of a tenancy in common or joint tenancy.

17. (C) Such as a life estate and a reversionary interest or a fee simple and a leasehold interest.

18. (A) There are no longer two owners possessing the four unities of joint tenancy. (Brother has undivided one-half interest and sister and her husband each have undivided one-quarter interest.)

19.   (D) Tenants in common have equal rights of possession.

20.   (A) Unlimited personal liability.

21.   (B) When the insurance policy is assumed by buyer. Others are usually debits and never credits.

22.   (A) The buyer must come up with this amount with credits and cash.

23.   (A) Estate presently vests but can be lost. (A defeasible estate.)

24.   (A) Others are covered.

25.   (C) Littoral rights deals with non-flowing water (lakes).

26.   (B) And a riparian rights owner adjoins moving water (stream).

27.   (C) B and D are not liens. Federal tax liens are general liens against all the debtor's property.

28.   (A) That sets forth the occupancy rights of each shareholder.

29.   (C) But the lease would end with the death of the life tenant. The life estate holder cannot obligate the property beyond his or her lifetime.

30.   (D) All tenants in common have equal rights as to possession.

31.   (D)

32.   (D) A codicil is an amendment to a will.

33.   (D) The corporation can be a partner with others. They could hold title as tenants in common or in severalty. A and C require marriage, and corporations can't hold title in joint tenancy because they do not die (no survivorship).

34.   (D) Neither of the two owners would have the four unities of joint tenancy. A and B result in severalty ownership.

35.   (D) A capital loss cannot be taken on the sale of his residence.

36.   (B) The use is hostile to the owner's interests. Permission defeats a claim of adverse possession.

37.   (A) Since he must outlive A for the interest to vest. A reversionary interest goes back to the original grantor.

38.   (B) Owners own their own units but own common areas as tenants in common.

39.   (B) To force the city to take her property by eminent domain and pay its fair value.

40.   (A) To be compensated for the loss of value in the land that is left when part is taken by eminent domain.

41. (B) Repairs are expenses and do not affect the cost base. Cost basis is cost plus improvements less depreciation.

42. (D)

43. (C) She can place restrictive covenants which will affect future owners.

44. (D) Rents are always regular income.

45. (D) A timeshare could also be a leasehold interest.

46. (D) When zoning and restrictive covenants differ, the more restrictive takes precedence.

47. (B) Cost is not considered one of the three tests of a fixture.

48. (B) Because the tax assessment roll would be reduced. This use would generally be exempt from property taxes.

49. (C) Value of common areas is assessed to individual units.

50. (B) Fixtures by definition have become part of the real property.

FOUR
Brokerage/Agency

AGENCY

An agency is a personal relationship freely entered into whereby the agent acts for another, the principal. In order to appoint an agent, the principal must have contractual capacity.

A power of attorney is a particular written agency whereby the principal authorizes another person, the agent, to act in the place of the principal as an attorney-in-fact. A power of attorney might apply to only a particular act, such as signing a deed in place of the principal; a general power of attorney allows the attorney-in-fact to obligate a principal in any way that the principal could have obligated him- or herself. Powers of attorney are often used in real estate where the principal is unavailable. If the power of attorney involves conveying real property, it must be recorded in order for the attorney-in-fact to convey a marketable title.

The real estate broker normally is the agent of the owners. The salesperson is the employee (or independent contractor) of the broker and a subagent of the principal (owner). Much less commonly, a broker may act as agent for the buyer.

Duties of the Agent

Fiduciary Duty   The agent has a duty of financial trust and must protect the principal's interests. The agent must account for any and all funds received or disbursed on behalf of the principal. Making any secret profit would be a violation of the agent's fiduciary duty. The agent must place deposits received in a trust account. Placing money received in trust into the agent's personal account is "commingling," a grounds for disciplinary action. Wrongful personal use of trust monies by the agent is conversion, which is criminal theft.

Full Disclosure   The agent must inform the principal of any facts likely to influence the principal in decision-making. All offers received must be promptly transmitted to the principal.

Due Care   The agent must exercise reasonable care in carrying out the duties of the agency.

Loyalty   The agent cannot disclose to third parties any facts about the principal or the agency that would not be in the best interests of the principal. An agent may not act for more than one party in a transaction without the knowledge and approval of all the parties.

Obedience   The agent has a duty to obey the instructions of his or her principal. An agent who fails to obey instructions, or who exceeds the authority given by the principal, could be liable for resulting damages.

Agents' Duties to Buyers   Even though a broker's primary duties, under a listing, are to his or her principal, the agent has a duty of good-faith dealing to buyers. The agent must disclose any known facts of a detrimental nature to the buyer. If an agent knows that an intended use by a prospective buyer is not feasible or possible, the agent has the affirmative duty to disclose that fact.

Even though the agent only repeated representations made by an owner, the agent could be held liable for the misrepresentations providing the agent knew, or should have known, them to be false.

The broker must, of course, protect buyers' deposits and promptly return them when an offer is not accepted.

Termination of the Agency

If the agency is for a specified period of time, such as an exclusive listing, the expiration of that period would end the agency.

Since an agency requires consent of both the principal and the agent, either party can end the agreement. The courts will not force the agency to continue; however, the party who wrongfully breached the agency agreement could be held liable for damages.

An exception to the principal's right to terminate an agency is an agency coupled with an interest. An agent advancing the owner funds to stop a foreclosure in order to obtain the listing, for example, couples a financial interest to the agency, so the principal cannot terminate the agency.

An agency is a personal relationship; therefore the death of either the principal or the agent terminates the agency. Because a corporation is a separate legal entity, the death of a corporate officer does not affect the agency.

The agency terminates when the agent has fully performed his or her duties (usually to procure a buyer at the price and terms stated in the listing, or any other price and terms the principal agrees to accept).

Impossibility of performance, such as destruction of the property, would generally terminate the agency.

LISTINGS

A listing is a contract where a principal (an owner) employs an agent (a real estate broker) to procure a buyer for his or her property. Because of the Statute of Frauds, most states require that all real estate listings be in writing. Verbal listings are therefore generally unenforceable.

Exclusive Right to Sell Listing   Under the exclusive right to sell listing, the agent is entitled to a commission if, during the term of the listing or any extension thereto, the agent or anyone else procures a buyer who is ready, able, and willing to purchase the listed property under the terms of the listing or any other terms which the principal agrees to.

Because the broker is assured a commission if the property is sold by anyone, this is the type of listing most commonly advertised.

Listings do not give brokers rights in property; therefore, they cannot be recorded.

When, after accepting an offer, the seller refuses to sell, the broker cannot force the sale. While the broker may be entitled to sue for a commission, specific performance is a legal remedy of the buyer.

Exclusive Agency Listing   The exclusive agency listing appoints the broker as the owner's exclusive agent to sell the property. It differs from the exclusive right to sell listing in that the owners retain the right to sell the property themselves without being obligated to pay a commission.

Exclusive listings generally are required to have a definite termination date and the broker must give the owner a copy at the time it is signed. Exclusive listings are considered to be bilateral contracts, in that the broker promises to use diligence to obtain a buyer in return for the owner's promise to pay a fee should the broker succeed.

Open Listing   Unless a listing agreement specifically states that it is an exclusive one, the listing is considered to be an open listing. Open, or nonexclusive right to sell, listings may be given concurrently to more than one agent. If the owner or another agent sells the property, the broker is not entitled to any compensation.

To earn a commission under an open listing, the broker must be the procuring cause, which means that the broker's efforts must have started an uninterrupted chain of events which resulted in the sale. Because open listings are often nothing more than a letter from an owner, it is generally not necessary to give a copy to the owner or that the listing contain a definite termination date. Letter listings from the owner are unilateral contracts in that the owner offers to pay a fee if a buyer is procured. The broker is not obligated to use any effort to locate a buyer, but the broker's act forms the acceptance to the offer.

Net Listing   A net listing can be an exclusive or open listing. Net refers to the broker's fee. Under the net listing the broker gets everything over a net amount that the owner is to receive. Because the agent is likely to be more interested his or her own profit than the benefit of the owner, net listings are regarded as unethical. In a number of states they are also illegal.

Multiple Listing Services (MLS)

Listings which authorize brokers to employ subagents or cooperate with other brokers may be submitted to listing services that publish and distribute listings. These services are usually run by the local Board of Realtors®. In the absence of any authorization to cooperate with others, the broker has no right to give the listing to other agents.

It is considered a restraint of trade for listing organizations to set minimum fees or to exclude brokers from access to their services.

Sample Listing

A representative exclusive right to sell listing begins on the next page. The numbered clauses are explained below.

Comments on Listing Clauses

(1) The promise of the agent to use diligence, or his or her efforts in exchange for the owner's promise to pay a commission if the agent is successful, makes an exclusive listing a bilateral contract (a promise for a promise).
(2) The listing is given to the broker, not the salesperson.
(3) The words *exclusive and irrevocable,* coupled with the language in (10) "... if the property is sold or exchanged by the agent, by the owner or by any other party ... " makes this an exclusive right to sell listing. To change it to an open listing, the words *exclusive and irrevocable* should be removed, as well as "by the owner or by any other party" (10).
(4) While a legal description is not required in a listing, the description must be "clear and unambiguous."

(This form is included as a sample for instructional purposes only and neither the author nor publisher warrant its legality for use within any jurisdiction.)

EXCLUSIVE RIGHT TO SELL LISTING (RESIDENTIAL)

1   In consideration of the terms of this listing and the promises of the undersigned agent to use diligence to affect a sale or exchange of this property, the undersigned owner(s) hereby appoint _____

2   _____
_____.

3   as agent and grant said agent the exclusive and irrevocable right to sell or exchange real property situated in the _____ of _____
_____ County of _____
more particularly described as:_____

4   _____
_____
_____.

5   The term of this agreement shall commence on _____, 19____
and expire on midnight on _____, 19____.

6   The price of the property shall be _____
$_____ and shall be paid as follows: _____
_____
_____
_____
_____.

7   Personal property that shall be incuded with the real property includes: drapes, shades, fixed carpeting, storm and screen windows and doors, _____
_____
_____.

8   The owner(s) represent having ownership of the described property and shall evidence a marketable title by means of _____
_____.

9   The owner(s) authorize the agent to place FOR SALE sign(s) on the property and to advertise its availability.

10 The owner(s) agree to pay the agent, as compensation for services, ____% of the selling price if the property is sold or exchanged by the agent, by the owner, or by any other party during the term of this listing or any extensions hereto.

11 If within 90 days of the termination of this listing a sale or exchange is made to any party the agent negotiated with while this listing was in effect and whose name the agent furnished to the owner(s) in writing prior to the expiration of the listing; then the agent shall be entitled to the commission as if the sale or exchange was consummated during the listing period. This provision shall not be in effect if the owner(s) is obligated to another agent for a commission because of a subsequent listing.

12 In the event the property is withdrawn from the market, leased without the agent's consent or otherwise made unmarketable by any voluntary act of the owner(s) during the term of this listing, the agent shall be entitled to ____% of the listed price.

13 | In the event of a buyer's default, the agent shall receive ½ of any damages received and/or deposits retained after deducting actual costs incurred by the owner as to the sale and/or collection. In no event shall this amount exceed the commission that would have been paid to the agent had the sale been completed.

14 | It is understood that the commission set forth was not set by any trade group but was negotiated between the parties.

15 | If an action is instituted to collect compensation under this listing agreement, the prevailing party shall be entitled to court costs and reasonable attorney's fees as set by the court.

16 | The owner(s) authorize the agent to cooperate with subagents and to disburse property information through a multiple listing service. Commission splits between the agent and subagent(s) shall be the sole concern of the agent.

17 | The owner(s) authorize the agent to accept, on the owner's behalf, a deposit of not less than $_____.

18 | The owner(s) agree to hold the agent harmless for any loss or liability incurred by reason of inaccurate information furnished by the owner(s) or the failure of the owner(s) to inform the agent as to any matter.

19 | It is understood by the owner(s) that this property shall be offered without regard as to race, creed, color, sex or national origin of any purchaser.

20 | The owner(s) acknowledge by their signature(s) that they have read and fully understand the terms of this listing and acknowledge that they have received a copy of it.

21 |

_____   _____
Owner   Date   Owner   Date

_____   _____
Address   Address

Accepted for _____
                                Broker

By _____   _____
                                                          Date

(5) Failure to include a termination date on an exclusive listing is grounds for disciplinary action against the licensee in many states.

(6) Set forth any assumable loans or seller financing. Unless you specify other terms, the owner would only be obligated to pay a commission if you obtained a full-price cash offer.

(7) Poor draftsmanship can lead to misunderstandings and lawsuits. You should determine now what items shall be included with the real property. If the seller intends to remove any item that would ordinarily be regarded as a fixture, it should be specifically excluded.

(8) The persons signing are warranting that they are the owners and indicate how they will evidence marketable title. The listing will specify either title insurance or abstract to show marketable title. Who pays for the title insurance and abstract costs varies according to local custom.

(9) Without this authorization the agent would not have the right to place a sign on the property. In many areas, placing of a sign without the owner's permission is a misdemeanor.

(10) This sets forth the agent's compensation if anyone makes a sale during the term of the listing. Commissions are negotiable between the parties.

(11) This is known as the safety clause. It protects against the owner and a buyer getting together after the listing expires to avoid paying a commission. This particular safety clause becomes inoperative if another listing is entered into.

(12) The agent is entitled to a commission if the owner withdraws the listing or makes the property unmarketable by a voluntary act.

(13) Provides for splitting buyer's liquidated damages or compensatory damages if the buyer defaults.

(14) It is an unfair trade practice to set minimum commissions.

(15) This warns the owner that failure to honor the agreement could lead to greater damages.

(16) Without this authorization an agent has no right to deal with subagents.

(17) Without authorization to accept a deposit, any deposit taken would be as the agent of the buyer. The minimum amount protects you against wasting time with purely frivolous offers and gives the broker a reason for insisting on a substantial deposit.

(18) This hold-harmless clause gives the agent the right to be reimbursed by the owner for agent's liability resulting from repeating false or incomplete information furnished by the owner.

(19) This makes the owner aware of the legal requirements under federal (and state) fair housing laws.

(20) By signing, the owners acknowledge that they understand the agreement and that they have received a copy. Failure to give a copy of exclusive listings or offers to purchase to the parties signing, at the time they sign, is generally grounds for disciplinary action.

(21) While one joint owner can be obligated to a commission by signing a listing, all joint owners must sign to convey property. Therefore the signatures of all owners should be obtained.

LEASES

Generally, a lease for a fixed period is more desirable than a month-to-month lease. A gross lease or flat lease is a fixed-rate rental in which the owner pays the taxes and insurance as well as agreed-upon maintenance and repairs. While a long-term gross lease ensures having a tenant, there is a danger of being tied to a low rental during an inflationary period. This risk can be offset by leases which provide for rent increases based upon some index such as the Consumer Price Index.

Long-term commercial leases are very often net leases or percentage leases.

Net Lease   The net lease, a long-term commercial lease, also known as NNN or triple net lease, provides that the owner shall receive a net amount as rent. The tenant pays the taxes and insurance and makes all repairs. To protect the purchasing power of the rent received, the net rent could be adjusted with the Consumer Price Index.

A double net or NN lease differs from the triple net lease in that the owner pays the insurance and taxes, but the tenant pays all other expenses.

Percentage Lease   The percentage lease, commonly used in shopping centers, gives the owner a percentage of the tenant's gross receipts. Generally businesses with a higher markup pay a higher percentage. The lessor usually requires that the tenant use a cash register which cannot be turned back. Percentage leases are usually coupled with a minimum rent, a covenant to remain in business, advertising requirements, and hours of operation. As an incentive for greater volume, percentage leases often provide for reductions in the percentage paid as rent as the volume increases.

Percentage leases often include a recapture clause which allows the lessor to regain possession if the lessee fails to obtain or maintain a minimum sales volume.

Lease Provisions

Description of Premises   The lease must contain an unambiguous description of the premises leased.

Term   Unless a longer term is clearly stated, the lease is generally considered to be a periodic tenancy for the length of the rent paying period.

Quiet Enjoyment   The tenant is entitled to quiet enjoyment of the premises without interference from the lessor.

Use of Premises   Leases often contain clauses which specify the specific use that the tenant may have for the premises.

Amount of Rent   The rent, or a formula to determine rent, must be set forth in the lease.

Repairs   Leases generally provide who shall be responsible for what repairs. In residential property, the lessor is generally responsible for the roof, walls and windows, heating and cooling system, as well as any appliances that are included.

Renewal Options   Leases for fixed periods often provide for renewal options at specific rents for additional periods of time.

Option to Purchase   When the lessor is more interested in selling than renting, an option to purchase may be included in the lease. As an incentive to the lessee to purchase, the lease could provide that a percentage of the rental payments can apply toward the purchase price.

First Right of Refusal   While an option gives the tenant a right to buy, the first right of refusal gives the tenant the right to buy only if the lessor wants to accept an offer from a third party. The lessee then has the option of meeting the offer as to price and terms.

Subordination Clause   Allows a later mortgage to take precedence over the lease. Should a later mortgagee foreclose without this clause, the mortgagee would take the property subject to the tenant's rights.

Security Deposit   This is a deposit by the lessee held by the lessor to ensure that the property is returned to the lessor in good repair at the end of the lease (with the exception of normal wear and tear). If necessary, the lessor could use the money to make repairs and return the balance. A security deposit is only taxed to the lessor as income if it is forfeited. The last month's rent paid in advance is taxed when it is received.

Signature   The signature of the lessor is required for the lessor to be bound. However, the lessee may be liable without signing the lease if the lessee moves in after receiving a copy of the lease—the action shows the intent to be bound by it.

Acknowledgment   To be recorded, leases must be acknowledged. In some states, leases beyond a statutory period must be recorded to give the lessee rights against a subsequent purchaser.

Merger

A lease is extinguished when the lessor and the lessee become the same person. If a tenant under a long-term lease purchased the property and later sold it, the tenant would be without a lease. It would have been lost by merger since he or she couldn't own the property in fee simple and also have a lesser interest, i.e. a leasehold interest.

Assignment and Sublease

Unless a lease specifically prohibits assignments or subleases, the lessee can assign or sublease.

Assignment   In an assignment, the lessee transfers all of his or her interests to another.

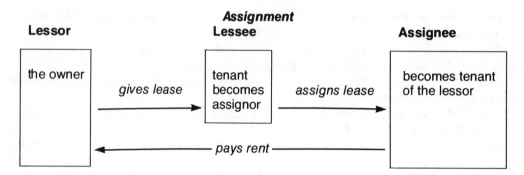

The assignee becomes the tenant of the lessor and pays the rent to the lessor in accordance with the original lease. While the original lessee remains secondarily liable under the lease the assignee is primarily liable.

Sublease   Also known as a sandwich lease, the sublease makes the lessee (under the master lease) a lessor who takes on his or her own tenant.

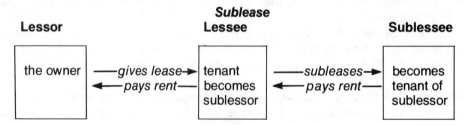

The sublessee pays the rent under the sublease to the sublessor, and the sublessor (the original lessee) pays to the lessor. The original lessee remains primarily liable for fulfillment of the lease terms. An advantage to a lessee of a sublease rather than an assumption is that the sublease could require greater rent than the original lease.

INVESTMENTS

Real estate is considered to be one of the finest investments possible because of appreciation, depreciation, taxes, leverage, income, and arbitrage. It also carries disadvantages, including low liquidity, need for management, and risk.

Appreciation

Real property has generally appreciated at a greater rate than inflation. Therefore real estate investments provide the investor with a hedge against inflation as well as appreciation possibilities.

Depreciation

Improvements on property held for income or trade can be depreciated for tax purposes. This depreciation offsets or shelters other income of the investor from regular income taxation. Depreciation can turn a negative-cash-flow investment into an economically advantageous investment. Chapter Five provides in-depth coverage of depreciation.

Taxes

Interest payments are always a deduction for tax purposes. Since the largest part of mortgage payments are interest, most of the payment is a deduction for tax purposes.

Long-term capital gains for income and investment property held over six months allow the investor a lower tax rate on profits. Our current tax laws provide a 60 percent exemption from taxation of a long-term capital gain. This means that only 40 percent of the gain is added to the investor's other income for tax purposes. Since the present maximum tax rate for individuals is 50 percent, the highest tax that an investor currently has to pay on a capital gain is 20 percent (50 percent tax on 40 percent of the gain).

Leverage

Unlike many other investments, real estate allows an investor to use other people's money for his or her investments by using available financing.

It is possible for a real estate investor to start out with very little cash and control property valued at many times his or her investment.

If an investor in stocks paid cash for the stocks and they appreciated ten percent in value, then the investor would have made a ten percent profit on the investment. If the same investor had purchased real estate with ten percent down and the real estate went up ten percent in value, then the investor would have made a 100 percent profit on the investment.

A real estate investor can trade on his or her equities by borrowing on assets to buy a property which results in a greater net return (income plus depreciation tax advantages) than he or she has to pay to borrow the money.

Because of inflation, real estate investors are often able to pay back borrowed dollars with cheaper dollars.

Income

Many real estate investments not only pay for themselves, but provide a positive cash flow for the investor. Because rents increase with inflation, the income tends to increase dramatically in relation to the investor's expenses.

Arbitrage

Real estate provides an opportunity for an investor to make money on interest differentials. By buying property at one interest rate and selling it at a higher rate (seller financing) a substantial income is possible.

Illiquidity

Real estate is considered an illiquid investment because it can often take many months to convert real estate equities to cash. Unlike the stock market, real estate does not allow an investor to quickly get out of one investment and into another that offers greater possibilities.

The illiquid nature of real estate investment may be partially overcome by the investor's ability to borrow on his or her equities.

Management

Real estate is not generally a management-free investment. Management decisions can affect income and value. Generally, real property investments which offer greater rates of return on investment also require more management effort. The management problems of real property can be met by professional real property management.

Risk

Some degree of risk is present in all real property investments. While high-leveraged investments offer greater profit potential on the investment, they also have a much greater risk. Social and economic changes can reduce values dramatically. Increases in property taxation and other expenses can result in a lower net income, which will mean a loss in value. Taxes, insurance, and principal and interest payments are generally regarded as fixed expenses. Operational expenses include maintenance, utilities, management costs, etc.

CHAPTER 4 QUIZ: BROKERAGE/AGENCY

1. A broker should **NOT** tell a prospective buyer:

   (A) about structural defects
   (B) that zoning makes the present usage noncon-forming
   (C) that she has seen evidence of termites
   (D) that the owner will accept less than the listing price

2. A salesperson may be compensated for real estate services by:

   (A) the owner
   (B) another broker
   (C) another salesperson
   (D) his or her own broker

3. After an offer is accepted, the seller finds out that the broker was the undisclosed agent for the buyer, as well as the agent for the seller. The seller:

   (A) can withdraw without obligation to broker or buyer
   (B) can withdraw but would be subject to liqui-dated damages
   (C) can withdraw only with concurrence of the buyer
   (D) would be subject to specific performance if he refused to sell

4. "Procuring cause" is most important with regard to:

   (A) options
   (B) open listings
   (C) exclusive right to sell listings
   (D) purchase agreements

5. When a lease is assigned:

   (A) the entire lease interest is transferred
   (B) the original lessor remains primarily liable on the lease
   (C) the original lessor has no liability under the lease
   (D) the assignee would pay the rent to the assig-nor

6. Prior to settlement, the broker discovers dry rot in the floor joists. The broker should:

   (A) inform the seller only
   (B) inform both the buyer and seller
   (C) refund the purchaser's deposit
   (D) inform no one, as the discovery was made after a binding contract was entered into

7. The landlord under a lease:

   (A) subordinates his interest
   (B) subrogates his interest
   (C) assigns his interest
   (D) alienates the property

8. A real estate salesperson, in selling listings of another broker, is directly responsible to:

   (A) his or her broker
   (B) the owner
   (C) the listing broker
   (D) the multiple listing service

9. Language requiring a broker to use his or her efforts is found in:

   (A) a bilateral contract
   (B) an offer to purchase
   (C) an option
   (D) an open listing

10. The holder of a general power of attorney, in dealing with real property of his or her principal, could **NOT**:

    (A) buy it
    (B) sell it
    (C) lease it
    (D) give an exclusive right to sell listing

11. A clause in a lease provides that the rent will dramatically increase when the lease expires. This is meant to discourage:

    (A) a renewal of the lease
    (B) an estate for years
    (C) a tenancy at sufferance
    (D) an extension of the lease

12. A salesperson's position to an owner-client of the broker is most nearly that of:

    (A) subagent
    (B) employee
    (C) independent contractor
    (D) principal

13. An owner gave an exclusive right to sell listing to broker A, an exclusive agency listing to broker B and an open listing to broker C. Broker C sold the house and collected a commission while the other listings were still in effect. Which of the following statements is correct?

    (A) A and B both are entitled to a split of the commission from C
    (B) A and B are entitled to a second commission to be split between them
    (C) A and B are each entitled to a full commission
    (D) Only A is entitled to a full commission

14. An unlicensed secretary in a real estate office can:

    (A) solicit listings by phone
    (B) collect rent for owner's clients
    (C) type offers to purchase
    (D) quote prices on the phone

15. The amount of commission is determined by:

    (A) local custom
    (B) the multiple listing service
    (C) the Department of Real Estate
    (D) negotiation

16. A broker sold an apartment building to a syndicate of which the broker was a member without informing the seller of this interest. Before closing, the owner discovered the broker's interest and refused to sell. The results of a suit to collect a commission would probably be:

    (A) revocation of broker's license
    (B) payment to the broker of the commission
    (C) release of the owner's obligation to pay a commission
    (D) an order that the buyer obtain specific performance

17. Which of the following false statements by a broker would most likely result in legal action by the buyer?

    (A) "It's a great investment"
    (B) "You won't make a mistake at this price"
    (C) "It's the best deal we have had in our office in over a year"
    (D) "The rents will more than make the payments"

18. A sublessee is best described as:

    (A) an assignee
    (B) an owner
    (C) a tenant
    (D) a lessor on a sublease

19. The relationship of the assignee to the original lessor is one of:

    (A) tenancy
    (B) subtenancy
    (C) agency
    (D) secondary liability

20. In order to collect a commission under an exclusive right to sell listing, it is **NOT** necessary for the broker to prove that the:

    (A) listing had been signed by the owner
    (B) listing was in effect at the time of sale
    (C) broker was the procuring cause of the sale
    (D) broker was licensed at the time the commission was earned

21. A lease prohibited assignment or subletting without the owner's prior approval. The lessee assigned without asking the lessor. The assignment is:

    (A) void
    (B) voidable
    (C) unenforceable
    (D) illegal

22. Which of the following is **NOT** essential to the creation of an agency relationship?

    (A) Agreement to pay consideration
    (B) Agreement of the parties to the agency
    (C) Competency of the principal
    (D) Right to represent

23. A listing specifically states that the broker is not to take a deposit of less than $5000, and in no form other than cash or certified check. A buyer wishes to give a personal check for $100 with his offer. The broker may:

    (A) accept the deposit but not submit the offer
    (B) refuse to accept the deposit
    (C) accept deposit as the agent of the buyer
    (D) accept deposit and present it and the offer to owner

24. Upon the death of a broker, his daughter, also a broker, wishes to take over his clients. She must:

    (A) inform all of the owners that she is the successor in interest to her father
    (B) obtain approval of the probate court
    (C) inform the state that she has taken over the responsibility for the listings
    (D) renegotiate all of the listings

25. An exclusive right to sell listing in a broker's inventory is:

    (A) an executed bilateral contract
    (B) an executory unilateral contract
    (C) an executory bilateral contract
    (D) an executory implied contract

26. An owner refuses an offer exactly in accordance with a valid exclusive right to sell listing. The owner:

    (A) does not have to sell
    (B) is liable to the buyer for money damages
    (C) would likely be sued by the broker for specific performance
    (D) is liable to the buyer for specific performance

27. The lessee pays for fire insurance under a:

    (A) gross lease
    (B) percentage lease
    (C) triple net lease
    (D) commercial lease

28. Who receives the greatest benefit from inflation?

    (A) Real estate brokers
    (B) Real estate lenders
    (C) Real estate borrowers
    (D) Renters

29. The owner sold his home without the services of the broker prior to the expiration of an exclusive agency listing. The broker is entitled to:

    (A) the full commission
    (B) ½ of the commission
    (C) costs
    (D) nothing

30. A broker would be unlikely to advertise:

    (A) an exclusive agency listing
    (B) an exclusive right to sell listing
    (C) an open listing
    (D) a listing for a rental with a purchase option

31. A commission is earned by a broker when:

    (A) the escrow is opened
    (B) funds are disbursed at settlement
    (C) the broker finds a buyer ready, willing, and able to buy
    (D) the seller is paid

32. Ethics is best described as:

    (A) what is required
    (B) obeying the law
    (C) agency duty
    (D) doing what is right

33. The business that would pay the highest percentage of the gross as rent would be:

    (A) a beauty parlor
    (B) a supermarket
    (C) a parking lot
    (D) a drugstore

34. A broker who manages property approaches a tenant for back rent a day after the owner died. The tenant refuses to pay. The broker should:

    (A) give the tenant statutory notice to quit or pay rent
    (B) start an unlawful detainer action
    (C) turn the matter over to a collection attorney
    (D) take no further action

35. Illegal blind ads do not:

   (A) provide the name of the owner
   (B) provide the property address
   (C) give the price of the property
   (D) indicate that the advertiser is an agent

36. Before settlement, the owner and the buyer have a disagreement, and both ask the broker for the earnest money she is holding. Her best course of action would be to:

   (A) obey the principal's directions
   (B) take out the commission and give the balance to her principal
   (C) do nothing until ordered by the court
   (D) file an interpleader action

37. A tenant paid the first month's rent in advance, but refuses to pay the rent at the beginning of the second month. In the absence of any specific agreement when rent is to be paid, the manager should:

   (A) start foreclosure
   (B) issue an unlawful detainer
   (C) give the tenant notice to vacate
   (D) do nothing

38. A broker, in dealing with the public, may **NOT**:

   (A) keep silent a material fact in the transaction
   (B) take an option
   (C) accept a commission from both buyer and seller
   (D) negotiate different commissions with different owners

39. It is discovered after a sale that the parcel is 20 percent smaller than the owner represented it to be. The broker, who passed on the information to the buyer:

   (A) is not liable as long as he only repeated seller's data
   (B) is not liable if the misrepresentation was unintentional
   (C) is not liable if the buyer actually saw what she was getting
   (D) is liable if he knew or should have known of the difference

40. Upon the expiration of an estate for years, the tenant and landlord agreed that the lease terms would continue on a year-to-year basis, but either party could cancel by giving a month's notice prior to the end of each rental year. The tenant has:

   (A) an estate for years
   (B) a month-to-month tenancy
   (C) a periodic tenancy
   (D) an estate at sufferance

41. Broker T took no action after discovering that salesman R acted in an unethical manner in successfully completing a large sale. The legal principle involved here is:

   (A) caveat emptor
   (B) ratification
   (C) estoppel
   (D) novation

42. A real estate salesperson may **NOT**:

   (A) buy or sell real estate as a principal
   (B) accept a commission from another broker
   (C) show property on which her office has no listing
   (D) represent both buyer and seller in a transaction

43. Commingling, one of the major reasons for revocation of real estate licenses, would occur when a licensee:

   (A) puts earnest money deposits in his personal account
   (B) engages in blockbusting
   (C) fails to indicate an agency relationship
   (D) uses unlicensed people to solicit business

44. A property manager may **NOT** be compensated by receiving:

   (A) a percentage of the gross
   (B) a fee for leasing
   (C) a fee for supervising repairs
   (D) rebates from suppliers

45. What is the advantage to the lessee in a commercial sale/leaseback?

    (A) depreciation
    (B) appreciation
    (C) easier financing of improvements
    (D) deductibility of rent

46. A lessor refused to sign the lease, but allowed the lessee to move in and accepts rent. The lessee:

    (A) has a valid lease
    (B) is on a periodic tenancy
    (C) is a tenant at sufferance
    (D) can be evicted without notice

47. A right to buy a property at a yet-undetermined price, where the seller has an option not to sell, is:

    (A) a lease option
    (B) right of first refusal
    (C) purchase contract
    (D) sale/leaseback

48. A broker exercised an option to purchase a home, but failed to indicate that the option was for her father. Her action:

    (A) is entirely proper
    (B) makes her liable for compensating damages only
    (C) makes her liable for punitive damages
    (D) allows the seller to void the conveyance

49. What type of lease is best for a commercial tenant during an inflationary period?

    (A) A flat lease
    (B) A percentage lease
    (C) An index lease
    (D) A net lease

50. A termination date is not required for an:

    (A) option
    (B) exclusive right to sell listing
    (C) exclusive agency listing
    (D) open listing

PLEASE PRINT THE FOLLOWING:
YOUR NAME

LAST	FIRST	MI

STREET ADDRESS

CITY	STATE	ZIP

TEST CENTER LOCATION (CITY, STATE)

TEST BOOKLET NO.

1ST THREE LETTERS OF LAST NAME	I.D. NUMBER FROM ADMISSION TICKET OR SCANNABLE APPLICATION	SOCIAL SECURITY NUMBER	TEST CENTER CODE	TEST DATE	YR.
○ ○ ○	0 0 0 0 0 0	0 0 0 0 0 0 0 0 0	0 0 0 0	JAN ○	
A A A	1 1 1 1 1 1	1 1 1 1 1 1 1 1 1	1 1 1 1	FEB ○	
B B B	2 2 2 2 2 2	2 2 2 2 2 2 2 2 2	2 2 2 2	MAR ○	0 0
C C C	3 3 3 3 3 3	3 3 3 3 3 3 3 3 3	3 3 3 3	APR ○	1 1
D D D	4 4 4 4 4 4	4 4 4 4 4 4 4 4 4	4 4 4 4	MAY ○	2 2
E E E	5 5 5 5 5 5	5 5 5 5 5 5 5 5 5	5 5 5 5	JUN ○	3 3
F F F	6 6 6 6 6 6	6 6 6 6 6 6 6 6 6	6 6 6 6	JUL ○	4 4
G G G	7 7 7 7 7 7	7 7 7 7 7 7 7 7 7	7 7 7 7	AUG ○	5 5
H H H	8 8 8 8 8 8	8 8 8 8 8 8 8 8 8	8 8 8 8	SEP ○	6 6
I I I	9 9 9 9 9 9	9 9 9 9 9 9 9 9 9	9 9 9 9	OCT ○	7 7
J J J				NOV ○	8 8
K K K				DEC ○	9 9
L L L					
M M M					
N N N					
O O O					
P P P					
Q Q Q					
R R R					
S S S					
T T T					
U U U					
V V V					
W W W					
X X X					
Y Y Y					
Z Z Z					

HAVE YOU EVER TAKEN THIS EXAMINATION BEFORE? YES ○ NO ○

FOR WHICH LICENSE ARE YOU TAKING THIS EXAM? BROKER ○ SALESPERSON ○

WHICH PART OF THE EXAMINATION ARE YOU TAKING?
GENERAL ○ STATE ○ BOTH ○

IN SIGNING BELOW I HEREBY AFFIRM THAT:
I AM THE UNDERSIGNED AND HAVE SIGNED MY CORRECT NAME ON THE SIGNATURE LINE BELOW.
IN ADDITION TO PASSING THE EXAMINATION FOR LICENSURE, I MUST MEET ALL STATE REQUIREMENTS.
I UNDERSTAND ALL EXAMINATION BOOKS ARE SECURE MATERIAL AND THAT NO BOOK OR PORTION THEREOF IS TO BE COPIED, TRANSMITTED TO ANY OTHER PERSON OR REMOVED FROM THE EXAMINATION ROOM.
I WILL NEITHER ASSIST NOR RECEIVE ASSISTANCE FROM ANOTHER CANDIDATE OR USE ANY NOTES, MANUALS OR OTHER AIDS.

SIGNATURE	DATE

GENERAL TEST

	A B C D		A B C D		A B C D		A B C D
1	○ ○ ○ ○	21	○ ○ ○ ○	41	○ ○ ○ ○	61	○ ○ ○ ○
2	○ ○ ○ ○	22	○ ○ ○ ○	42	○ ○ ○ ○	62	○ ○ ○ ○
3	○ ○ ○ ○	23	○ ○ ○ ○	43	○ ○ ○ ○	63	○ ○ ○ ○
4	○ ○ ○ ○	24	○ ○ ○ ○	44	○ ○ ○ ○	64	○ ○ ○ ○
5	○ ○ ○ ○	25	○ ○ ○ ○	45	○ ○ ○ ○	65	○ ○ ○ ○
6	○ ○ ○ ○	26	○ ○ ○ ○	46	○ ○ ○ ○	66	○ ○ ○ ○
7	○ ○ ○ ○	27	○ ○ ○ ○	47	○ ○ ○ ○	67	○ ○ ○ ○
8	○ ○ ○ ○	28	○ ○ ○ ○	48	○ ○ ○ ○	68	○ ○ ○ ○
9	○ ○ ○ ○	29	○ ○ ○ ○	49	○ ○ ○ ○	69	○ ○ ○ ○
10	○ ○ ○ ○	30	○ ○ ○ ○	50	○ ○ ○ ○	70	○ ○ ○ ○
11	○ ○ ○ ○	31	○ ○ ○ ○	51	○ ○ ○ ○	71	○ ○ ○ ○
12	○ ○ ○ ○	32	○ ○ ○ ○	52	○ ○ ○ ○	72	○ ○ ○ ○
13	○ ○ ○ ○	33	○ ○ ○ ○	53	○ ○ ○ ○	73	○ ○ ○ ○
14	○ ○ ○ ○	34	○ ○ ○ ○	54	○ ○ ○ ○	74	○ ○ ○ ○
15	○ ○ ○ ○	35	○ ○ ○ ○	55	○ ○ ○ ○	75	○ ○ ○ ○
16	○ ○ ○ ○	36	○ ○ ○ ○	56	○ ○ ○ ○	76	○ ○ ○ ○
17	○ ○ ○ ○	37	○ ○ ○ ○	57	○ ○ ○ ○	77	○ ○ ○ ○
18	○ ○ ○ ○	38	○ ○ ○ ○	58	○ ○ ○ ○	78	○ ○ ○ ○
19	○ ○ ○ ○	39	○ ○ ○ ○	59	○ ○ ○ ○	79	○ ○ ○ ○
20	○ ○ ○ ○	40	○ ○ ○ ○	60	○ ○ ○ ○	80	○ ○ ○ ○

PLEASE TURN TO REVERSE SIDE FOR STATE TEST.

ANSWERS

1. (D) This would be a violation of the broker's fiduciary duty to the owner to get the best price possible. A broker *must* tell prospective buyers of any negative feature.

2. (D) The only person who can pay a salesperson for an act requiring a real estate license is his or her broker.

3. (A) Because of the undisclosed agency, the seller can withdraw and the broker would be subject to disciplinary action.

4. (B) Who was the procuring cause determines who earned the commission.

5. (A) The assignee becomes the person primarily liable under the lease as the tenant of the lessor. The original lessee remains secondarily liable on the lease.

6. (B) The broker has a duty to inform the seller of any important fact concerning the property. The broker also has a duty to inform the buyer about any detrimental fact, and this duty does not cease with an offer.

7. (A) To the tenant's right to occupy.

8. (A) Although the broker and salesperson have subagent duties to the listing broker and the owner.

9. (A) An exclusive listing, which is a bilateral contract.

10. (A) An agent cannot have an interest inconsistent with his or her fiduciary duties to the principal. The agent cannot be the buyer (as he or she would be dealing for his or her own interests, not those of the principal), nor can the agent take a mortgage against the property.

11. (C) A holdover clause. The clause provides for a high rent should a tenant hold over at the end of lease in order to force the tenant to sign a new lease or vacate.

12. (A) The salesperson is either an independent contractor or the employee of the broker, not of the owner.

13. (C) By signing the two exclusive listings, the owner became obligated to both for the full commission if a sale was consummated in accordance with the listing.

14. (C) A license is not required for clerical acts. The others generally require a real estate license.

15. (D) It is illegal to set minimum fees between brokers.

16. (C) Because of agent's breach of fiduciary responsibility. Broker could be disciplined by the state department of real estate.

17. (D) A false statement of fact to induce a purchase is fraud. The other statements are really only opinions (known as puffing), and are generally not actionable.

18.   (C) Sublessee is a tenant of the sublessor (original lessee).

19.   (A) The assignee becomes primarily liable under the lease and becomes a direct tenant of the lessor.

20.   (C) On an exclusive right to sell listing, the broker is entitled to a commission if anyone sells the property.

21.   (B) Since the prohibition was for the benefit of the lessor only, the lessor could waive the breach and hold the assignee liable on the lease or void the assignment. Lessors generally are only allowed to reject assignments for valid reasons.

22.   (A) There can be a gratuitous agency.

23.   (B) The agent has a duty to obey specific instructions of the owner.

24.   (D) The listing (agency) ends with the death of either the principal or the agent.

25.   (C) Exclusive listings are bilateral contracts (mutual promises) and it would be executory until the property is sold (performance is complete).

26.   (A) There is as of yet no agreement between buyer and owner so owner has no duties toward the buyer—these begin after acceptance of an offer. While the owner does not have to accept the offer, the broker has performed, so is entitled to a commission (not specific performance).

27.   (C) Lessee pays all expenses. Not all commercial leases are net leases.

28.   (C) They are able to pay back loans with cheaper dollars.

29.   (D) Since owner can sell himself without obligation under an *exclusive agency* listing.

30.   (C) Since there is no commission if anyone else sells the property.

31.   (C) At the terms of the listing or any other terms the owner accepts. Commissions are *paid* at the settlement.

32.   (D) Ethics goes beyond the legal duties. The basic test to determine if an action is ethical is to apply the Golden Rule.

33.   (C) Businesses with higher markup pay higher percentages. A parking lot might pay 70 percent of the gross as rent.

34.   (D) Agency agreements are personal in nature and end with the death of either the principal (owner) or the agent (broker).

35.   (D) And not a principal.

36.   (D) Asking the court to determine the rights of the parties.

37.   (D) In the absence of an agreement, rent is generally due at the end of the rent-paying period. Parties usually agree that rent will be paid in advance.

38.   (A) Must disclose material facts to the parties. The broker can deal as a principal so long as the fact that he is a licensee dealing as a principal has been disclosed. The broker can accept commissions from more than one party as long as there is full disclosure and both parties agree.

39.   (D) Even when the broker only repeats information the broker could still be liable for damages.

40.   (C) From year to year.

41.   (B) Broker T, in accepting the benefits, has also accepted the responsibility for salesman R's action.

42.   (B) The only person who can compensate a salesperson for an act in real estate is his or her broker.

43.   (A) Mixing trust and personal funds.

44.   (D) This would be a secret profit.

45.   (D) A more important advantage is that capital is freed.

46.   (B) The periodic tenancy is for the length of the rent-paying period. While the lessee does not have to sign to be obligated (moving in or paying rent), the lessor must sign the lease for the tenant to have rights under it.

47.   (B) The right to buy occurs only if the owner wishes to sell. Then the right of first refusal gives the holder a right to buy at the price another party is willing to pay.

48.   (A) She was dealing as a principal, not an agent.

49.   (A) As there would be no increase. A net lease would increase taxes and expenses.

50.   (D) It can be just a letter or memorandum.

FIVE
Concepts of Appraising

Appraisal is the supported estimation of value, applicable only to the value at the time of the appraisal.

TYPES OF VALUE

Market Value   The price a willing, informed buyer will pay to a willing, informed seller. In appraisal we are primarily interested in market value.

Objective and Subjective Value   Objective value is the actual market value, while subjective value is the personal use value of the amenities of ownership. The appraiser estimates the objective value that the ultimate buyer will be willing to pay for the benefits offered.

Book Value   A property is carried at this value on the owner's books. It is the original cost plus the cost of any improvements minus the depreciation that has been taken. Book value bears no relationship to market value.

Exchange Value   The value of property that can be purchased with the sale proceeds (the relationship of the value to other goods).

Assessed Value   This is the value placed by a tax assessor. It may differ from the market value. Assessed value is often influenced by the price paid.

ELEMENTS OF VALUE

The least important factor in determining value is cost or price paid. What an owner paid in the past does not determine the present value. Cost represents what was spent in the past, not the present worth. There are four main elements of value.

Utility   To have value, there must be a useful purpose. Even an ornament serves a purpose.

Scarcity   If there are a great many similar properties on the market, the value of each will be less than if there were only a few such properties available.

Demand   Without demand there is no value. To be meaningful, demand must be coupled with purchasing power.

Transferability   To have value, the title or possession must be capable of being transferred. If an interest cannot be transferred, then it has no value. Utility and demand are considered the most important elements of market value.

Special Factors Influencing Value

Physical

Fertility   Important for agricultural land; of lesser or of no importance for other uses.

Topography   Important, as steep grades mean greater development costs. Subdividers like gentle rolling land that breaks the monotony, but does not result in excessive costs.

Location   Often said to be the single most important factor in determining value.

Economic   Economic forces affecting value include national, regional, and local economies; availability of credit; employment rates; projected growth rates; anticipated growth patterns; the economic profile of residents and businesses in the area; turnover and vacancy rates; as well as any changes in these areas.

Government   Regulations, zoning, building codes, health codes, public housing, rent control, etc., affect value.

Highest and Best Use   That use which gives the greatest net value to a property. For example, building a $300,000 apartment building on a lot will give that property a total value of $450,000. The value of the site then is $150,000. This would not be its highest and best use if $50,000 in improvements would make a parking lot worth $250,000. The value of the land would then be $200,000, making the parking lot a higher and better use.

Assemblage and Plottage   Assemblage is the process of joining several contiguous parcels of property together under common ownership to form a larger parcel. The larger parcel is likely to have a resulting value greater than the sum of the values of the smaller parcels because of the difficulty in assembling larger parcels in developed areas. The increase in value by assemblage is known as plottage or plottage increment.

Amenities   Amenities are features of a property that provide greater satisfaction in living or pride of ownership: a beautiful garden, mature trees, a magnificent view, a fountain, an extra bath, etc.

METHODS OF APPRAISAL

1. market comparison approach (comparable sales method)
2. cost approach (replacement cost method)
3. income approach (capitalization of income method)

Market Comparison

The market comparison approach is the oldest and easiest-to-learn appraisal method. The value of a property is arrived at by the recent sale prices of comparable properties. The appraiser considers terms of sale, special features, and their quality, location, etc., in the selection of the comparables. The appraiser must make adjustments when properties or features are not equally desirable.

The comparison method is the best appraisal method for single-family dwellings. It can also be used for land and other improved properties where there are sales that exhibit a high degree of similarity. The disadvantage is the difficulty of locating similar recent sales and in adjusting amenities (tangible and intangible features which enhance enjoyment and use) and sales terms.

Cost Approach

The cost approach is the best method for appraising new or service-type structures (library, county stadium, etc.). The cost approach tends to set upper limits on value.

The cost approach is a three-step appraisal process as follows:

1. Determine the present cost to replace improvements.
2. Deduct accrued depreciation. (Accrued depreciation is depreciation that has already occurred—remainder depreciation is depreciation that will occur in the future.)
3. Add the value of the land.

Cost to replace, less depreciation, plus the land equals value.

Replacement Cost   The replacement cost can be arrived at by several different methods.
  Quantity Survey Method   This is a detailed method to determine replacement costs where all material and labor is priced separately, such as in a construction estimate.
  Unit in Place Method   This method uses costs per unit, such as per square foot, per bath, per room, per electrical outlet, etc. Some appraisers consider price per square foot to be a separate method.
  Index Method   The present cost to build is arrived at by applying increases or decreases in the construction cost index since the structure was built to its original cost to build.

Accrued Depreciation   We only depreciate improvements, never land. To arrive at the depreciation of a structure, the economic life of the structure must be determined. Age-life tables provide the economic life for various types of structures and construction, often 40 to 50 years. To determine the amount of accrued depreciation, the effective age of the structure must be found. Effective age is based on the condition of the structure and can differ from chronological age.
  The appraiser analyzes the condition of the property to determine the accrued depreciation (observed condition method). If the economic life is determined to be 40 years, then each year's depreciation amounts to 2½ percent of the replacement cost:

$$100\% \div 40 = 2\frac{1}{2}\%$$

If the property had an effective age of 10 years, then it would have depreciated 25 percent:

$$2\frac{1}{2}\% \times 10 = 25\%$$

  Sample Problem   A 15,000 sq. ft. building would cost $40/square foot to build today. Its economic life is 50 years and its effective age is eight years. The land is valued at $170,000 (arrived at by market comparison method). The property is valued as follows:

$$15,000 \times \$40 = \$600,000 \text{ cost to replace}$$

$$50 \text{ year life} = 2\% \text{ depreciation/yr.}$$

$$8 \text{ yrs} \times 2\% = 16\% \text{ depreciation}$$

$$.16 \times \$600,000 = \$96,000 \text{ accrued depreciation}$$

$600,000 Cost to build today
−96,000 Accrued depreciation
$504,000 Present value of structure
+170,000 Land value
$674,000 Total value of land and improvements

A property might have a salvage value which reduces the value for depreciation.

Income Approach

The income approach is based on the net income of the property being appraised. To determine value, an appraiser determines the appropriate rate of return (capitalization rate) and divides it into the net income:

$$\frac{\text{net}}{\text{capitalization rate}} = \text{value}$$

Annual Net Income   From the gross annual income, we deduct the total annual expenses, including an allowance for vacancies and collection losses, as well as management expenses. The only two costs not deducted are payments on the loan principal and interest expenses. In determining the gross income, the appraiser is more interested in anticipated future income than in past income.

Capitalization Rate   The capitalization rate is the rate of return an investor wants on a particular property. If the investment were one of high risk, then an investor might want a 20 percent return, while a nine percent return for a secure investment might be acceptable. When interest rates are high, investors use a higher capitalization rate to reflect a higher desired return on investment.

We can determine capitalization rates for comparable sales by dividing the sale price into the net income of the comparable properties:

$$\frac{\text{net}}{\text{sale price}} = \text{rate}$$

There are a number of complex methods to determine the capitalization rate. These would be covered in separate appraisal courses.

Sample Problem   To determine the value after the net and capitalization rates have been determined you simply divide the rate into the net.

An eight-unit apartment with monthly rentals of $400 per unit has a ten percent vacancy and collection loss factor, plus total expenses of $600 per month. Find its value using a capitalization rate of 12 percent:

8 × $400 =	$3200	per month gross
$3200 × 12 =	$38,400	annual gross
Minus 10% vacancy and collection loss	3,840	
	$34,560	Effective gross income
Less expenses ($600 × 12)	7,200	
	$27,360	Net

$$\text{value} = \frac{\text{net income}}{\text{rate}} = \frac{27,360}{.12} = 228,000$$

The value, using the income approach, is therefore $228,000.

If the capitalization rate were ten percent, then:

$$27,360 \div .10 = \$273,600$$

If the rate used were 14 percent, then:

$$27,360 \div .14 = \$195,428.57$$

Value moves inversely to capitalization rate: value goes up if the rate goes down; value goes down if the rate goes up. Similarly, if expenses go up, value goes down (net decreased); if expenses go down, value goes up (net increased).

Separate capitalization rates can be used for land and improvements.

Gross Multiplier   A variation of the income approach multiplies the gross income by a figure known as the gross multiplier to arrive at value. If a property has a gross annual income of $10,000 and the property could be purchased at $70,000, then the seller believes that a gross multiplier of seven is appropriate. By knowing the average gross multipliers of similar property that has sold, a prospective purchaser will have a general idea as to the value of a property being offered. Because a property might have unusually high or low expenses, a gross multiplier merely gives a rough idea of vaule. The gross multiplier does not consider the actual net income.

Deferred Maintenance   Repairs are often deferred by an owner. In using the capitalization method or the gross multiplier, the appraiser would deduct the estimated costs to correct the deferred maintenance from the value arrived at.

Expressing Land Values
Agricultural Land   Priced per acre.
Commercial Land   Priced per square foot or per front foot.
Industrial Land   Up to approximately 20¢ per square foot, it is generally priced by the acre; over 20¢ per square foot, it is generally priced per square foot.
Residential Lots   Priced per lot (exception: waterfront lots are generally priced per front foot).
100% Location   An idiom meaning the very best commercial location within a community.

DEPRECIATION

Depreciation is a loss in value from any cause.

Types of Depreciation

Physical Deterioration   Wear and tear from use, negligence, age, or other causes of physical damage. Examples: dry rot, blistering paint, leaking roof, sagging floor, etc.
Functional Obsolescence   Loss in value that was built into the structure by poor design, lack of needed facilities, outdated equipment, or changes in demand. Examples: bedrooms without closets, small rooms, massive cornices, etc. An excessively expensive improvement is also functional obsolescence (overbuilding).
Economic or Social Obsolescence   Loss in value caused by forces outside the property itself. Examples: neighborhood change, traffic problems, parking problems, etc.

A misplaced improvement (an expensive property in an area of less expensive property) is also considered economic obsolescence.

The statement "More buildings are torn down than wear out" reflects economic obsolescence—they are not worn out, but because of outside factors, they are not economical for their designed use.

Curable Depreciation   Depreciation that can economically be corrected.

Incurable Depreciation   Depreciation that cannot be economically reversed. Because economic depreciation is caused by forces outside the property itself, it generally is incurable.

Methods of Computing Depreciation

Straight Line Method   The straight line method is used for appraisal purposes. It can also be used for income tax purposes. An equal sum is deducted each year over the life of the property.

For tax purposes, a very short 18-year life can be used to depreciate the improvements (the allowable depreciation period is subject to change by Congress). Since we can depreciate 100 percent of the value of an asset in 18 years, we can depreciate 5.555% each year:

$$100\% \div 18 = 5.555\%$$

For a $100,000 structure, you could therefore depreciate $5,555 every year for 18 years and totally depreciate the asset.

Depreciation is a paper expense, not a cash expense, so it can offset other income and protect it from taxation (tax shelter). For example, if a person broke even on an apartment building (cash expenses equalled income) and that person also had $20,000 in depreciation, then for tax purposes there would be a $20,000 loss. This means that $20,000 of additional income could go untaxed to offset this loss.

175 Percent Declining Balance Depreciation   This is an accelerated method of depreciation that is only used for tax purposes (never for appraisal). 175 percent of the straight line depreciation is allowed. Since the IRS currently allows 5.555 by the straight line method, the rate allowed would be 9.72 percent (5.555% × 175%).

If we depreciate a $100,000 asset, the first year's depreciation using the 175 percent declining balance method is:

$$\$100,000 \times 9.72\% = \$9720$$

The second year depreciation is based on a declining balance of $90,280:

$$\$100,000 - 9,720 = \$90,280$$

The second year's depreciation is:

$$9.72\% \times 90,280 = \$8,775.22$$

We then continue taking the same percentage of depreciation each year from a declining balance. The IRS has prepared a simplified table for computing 175 percent declining balance depreciation.

If we use this method on residential income property and sell before we have fully depreciated the asset, then the IRS will claim as regular income all the depreciation we took in excess of the straight-line method.

If we use this method for non-residential property and we sell the asset before it is fully depreciated, all depreciation we have taken will be taxed as regular income. A homeowner may not depreciate that portion of his or her home used as a residence—only income or business property can be depreciated for tax purposes.

Sinking Fund   This is the setting aside and investing of a sum of money each year, so that by the time an asset needs replacement, the amount set aside plus the compound interest it earns will be enough for that purpose.

Reserve for Replacement   An accounting expense for tax purposes that sets up a reserve fund to replace short-life chattels such as furniture in a furnished unit.

Appraisal Principles

Principle of Anticipation   Value is based more on anticipated future benefits than present benefits derived.

Principle of Change   Real estate values do not remain constant. An appraiser must consider how changing economic and social conditions affect the value of property.

Principle of Competition   When extraordinary profits are derived from an investment, competition will be created which will increase the supply, thus lowering profits.

Principle of Conformity   A property will achieve and maintain its maximum value when it is in a homogeneous area of similar use property.

Principle of Contribution   Maximum values are achieved when improvements return the highest net in relationship to the investment. Increasing improvements will eventually result in a decrease in their contribution to the value (principle of diminishing marginal returns).

Principle of Integration and Disintegration   Property goes through phases of development (integration), stable use (equilibrium), and decline (disintegration).

Principle of Progression   The value of a home will be increased by more expensive homes in the area (economically it is desirable to have the least expensive home in an area).

Principle of Regression   The value of a home will be reduced by the presence of homes having lesser value in the area.

Principle of Substitution   A person will not pay more for a property than for a comparable property of equal desirability (applicable to market comparison approach).

Principle of Supply and Demand   As supply increases, values drop; as demand increases, values rise.

Principle of Surplus or Surplus Productivity   After deducting the costs associated with labor, management, and capital investment, the balance of the value should be attributable to the land itself.

Appraisal Reports

Narrative Report   A narrative report is comprehensive and complete, containing the background data leading to the conclusions. These reports often include photos, maps, plot plans, floor plans, and community economic information.

Short-Form Report   A report that is completed by filling in a form or check sheet is called a short-form report.

Letter Report   A business letter report may also set forth the basis for the value arrived at.

Content

The following should be included in every appraisal report:

- Date of report (the value estimate is given as of a particular date).
- Unambiguous identification of the property appraised.
- Whether or not the appraiser has any interest in the property. An appraiser can have an interest in appraised property, but that interest must be fully disclosed.
- That the fee is in no way contingent on the appraisal results. A fee based on a percentage of the appraisal is considered unethical.
- Any limiting conditions or assumptions.
- Signature of appraiser.

CHAPTER 5 QUIZ: CONCEPTS OF APPRAISING

1. The appraisal on a quality single-family residence would be **LEAST** influenced by:

   (A) projected rental income
   (B) its location
   (C) recent comparable sales
   (D) its floor plan

2. An appraisal of a home for a lender who wishes to make a purchase loan would be concerned with:

   (A) the amount of the loan requested
   (B) unpaid special assessments
   (C) the price to be paid by the purchaser
   (D) economic changes in the area

3. An example of economic obsolescence is:

   (A) numerous pillars supporting the ceiling in a store
   (B) roof leaks making the premises unrentable
   (C) an older building with massive cornices
   (D) vacant and abandoned structures in the area

4. The best method for appraising an older home is:

   (A) income approach
   (B) cost approach
   (C) market comparison approach
   (D) the gross multiplier method

5. Accrued depreciation is most important in relation to:

   (A) economic obsolescence
   (B) the reproduction cost approach
   (C) capitalization of income
   (D) determining economic life

6. To determine effective gross income, one would deduct which of the following from gross income?

   (A) Property taxes
   (B) Income taxes on the profit
   (C) Payments on principal and interest
   (D) A vacancy and collection loss factor

7. It would be unethical for an appraiser to:

   (A) refuse to make an appraisal that he feels is beyond his expertise
   (B) appraise a property he has a disclosed interest in
   (C) accept an appraisal where the fee will be a percentage of the value arrived at
   (D) request to be paid in advance

8. The cost approach method of appraisal is most appropriate for:

   (A) older homes
   (B) new single-family homes
   (C) multifamily structure
   (D) commercial property

9. To be depreciated, real property must be:

   (A) owned in fee simple
   (B) improved
   (C) paid for
   (D) your residence

10. The advisability of including a tennis court with a planned apartment building may be determined by the principle of:

    (A) contribution
    (B) competition
    (C) substitution
    (D) change

11. Building an expensive home in an area of less expensive homes would be considered:

    (A) economic obsolescence
    (B) functional obsolescence
    (C) progression
    (D) plottage

12. The principle of substitution is related to the:

    (A) capitalization method
    (B) reproduction cost approach
    (C) market comparison method
    (D) gross multiplier

13. "It is most likely to be incurable depreciation" describes:

(A) economic obsolescence
(B) physical deterioration
(C) functional obsolescence
(D) the plottage increment

14. *Subjective Value* is:

(A) market value
(B) assessed value
(C) use value
(D) exchange value

15. Which of the following is **NOT** true regarding the capitalization rate?

(A) The rate increases when risk increases.
(B) An increase in the rate means a decrease in value.
(C) The rate is divided into net income to determine value.
(D) A decrease in rate results in a decrease in value.

16. The reason that the gross multiplier is **NOT** an accurate measurement of value is that it fails to consider:

(A) depreciation
(B) unusual expenses
(C) location
(D) amenity values

17. The highest value would most likely be maintained by having a residence:

(A) adjoining a shopping area
(B) next to a church
(C) across from a school
(D) in the center of a residential development

18. The final determination as to market value is made by:

(A) appraisers
(B) sellers
(C) buyers
(D) lenders

19. The approach that considers amenity values is the:

(A) cost approach
(B) market comparison method
(C) income approach
(D) gross multiplier

20. The time period in which a structure shows income which can be attributed to the structure itself is known as its:

(A) economic life
(B) effective age
(C) period for depreciation
(D) period of profitability

21. The last lot in a subdivision sold for over three times the price paid for the first lot sold. This is most likely to be an example of the principle of:

(A) regression
(B) diminishing returns
(C) supply and demand
(D) conformity

22. Buyers would most likely rate as the most important factor in the value of a home its:

(A) location
(B) floor plan
(C) age
(D) square footage

23. Value is best described as:

(A) price paid by owner
(B) present worth of future benefits
(C) assessed valuation
(D) price offered by a prospective buyer

24. In one building, the tenant intends to start a health food shop using her life savings; in an identical adjacent building is a catalog store leased to Sears. Both have long-term leases at identical rents. Which of the following statements is correct?

    (A) If the values of the buildings were the same before the leases, the values will be the same after they are leased.
    (B) An appraiser would likely use a higher capitalization rate for the Sears store.
    (C) The best appraisal would likely be the market comparison method.
    (D) The building with the health food shop will be worth less than the other building.

25. The highest and best use provides the:

    (A) greatest benefit to the community
    (B) greatest gross
    (C) greatest net
    (D) highest capitalization rate

26. Demand is not effective in determining value unless it is combined with:

    (A) scarcity
    (B) a use
    (C) purchasing power
    (D) access

27. An investor making extraordinary profits from a mini-warehouse would be most concerned with the principle of:

    (A) change
    (B) competition
    (C) regression
    (D) conformity

28. The principle of supply and demand predicts:

    (A) a price increase when supply increases
    (B) demand decreasing when supply increases
    (C) demand increasing when price decreases
    (D) price decreasing when demand increases

29. An apartment building appraisal focuses on:

    (A) present income
    (B) anticipated income
    (C) cost to reproduce the structure
    (D) comparable sales

30. In analyzing economic obsolescence, one wants to know:

    (A) if the builder has deferred maintenance
    (B) the income of the tenants
    (C) about changes in the neighborhood
    (D) the vacancy factor of the structure

31. The annual gross multiplier is calculated by:

    (A) capitalizing the annual gross
    (B) dividing the annual gross by the price paid
    (C) dividing the price paid by the annual gross income
    (D) multiplying the monthly gross by twelve.

32. The conditions of sale can be expected to affect the:

    (A) price of the property
    (B) value of the property
    (C) utility of the property
    (D) cost basis of the property

33. A property owner would have the greatest difficulty in correcting depreciation caused by:

    (A) age
    (B) the built-in nature of the structure
    (C) forces extraneous to the structure
    (D) wear and tear due to use

34. Deducting salvage value from the cost base for depreciation:

    (A) reduces the gross
    (B) increases the profit
    (C) decreases the net
    (D) accelerates depreciation

35. How would a substantial increase in interest rates as the only economic change affect the value of a rental property?

    (A) The value would increase.
    (B) The depreciation would change.
    (C) The value would stabilize.
    (D) The value would decline.

36. Each unit in a fourplex rents for $225 per month. With a price of $81,000, the annual gross multiplier is:

    (A) 360
    (B) 90
    (C) 30
    (D) 7.5

37. An appraiser would **NOT** depreciate:

    (A) a structure that is vacant
    (B) unimproved land leased for open storage
    (C) a single-family house used for rental purposes
    (D) a residence used for owner occupancy

38. The oldest and easiest-to-learn method of appraisal is the:

    (A) cost approach
    (B) market comparison method
    (C) capitalization of income approach
    (D) abstractive method

39. A separate value for the land is needed for the:

    (A) income approach
    (B) gross multiplier
    (C) cost approach
    (D) market comparison method

40. With fixed rents and a capitalization rate of 8%, an increase in taxes of $4,000 would result in the value of a property:

    (A) decreasing by $5,000
    (B) decreasing by $50,000
    (C) remaining unchanged
    (D) increasing

41. An appraiser counting the number of electrical outlets in a structure is probably using the:

    (A) market comparison method
    (B) income approach
    (C) cost approach
    (D) gross multiplier

42. The reproduction cost approach is **NOT** an effective method for appraising:

    (A) a new residence
    (B) an old public library
    (C) an old residence
    (D) a new commercial structure

43. Economic obsolescence is usually considered:

    (A) built-in depreciation
    (B) obsolescence resulting from "old fashioned" design
    (C) incurable depreciation
    (D) wear and tear caused by use that would be uneconomical to correct

44. Which of the following would be the most difficult appraisal task?

    (A) Determining net income
    (B) Determining the capitalization rate
    (C) Determining the chronological age
    (D) Determining the economic life

45. In the market comparison method, amenities are balanced out:

    (A) to allow for appreciation
    (B) because of the principle of competition
    (C) because the market is not static
    (D) because no two properties are identical

46. Which of the following is an example of economic obsolescence?

    (A) Leaking roof
    (B) Numerous partitions
    (C) No parking for tenants
    (D) A one way street

47. "The whole is worth more than the sum of its parts" refers to:

    (A) progression
    (B) assemblage
    (C) land residual
    (D) depreciation

48. Two adjacent residences had the same value when they were built 30 years ago. They are both in similar condition, but one is now worth a great deal more than the other. What would be a likely reason for this difference?

    (A) Physical deterioration
    (B) Economic obsolescence
    (C) Functional obsolescence
    (D) Principle of integration/disintegration

49. Which method would be used to determine the present value of future income?

    (A) Income approach
    (B) Cost approach
    (C) Quantity survey method
    (D) Market comparison approach

50. Land and improvements must be appraised separately using the:

    (A) cost approach
    (B) market comparison approach
    (C) gross multiplier
    (D) income approach

GENERAL TEST

**PLEASE PRINT THE FOLLOWING:
YOUR NAME**

LAST   FIRST   MI

STREET ADDRESS

CITY   STATE   ZIP

TEST CENTER LOCATION (CITY, STATE)

TEST BOOKLET NO.

1ST THREE LETTERS OF LAST NAME

I.D. NUMBER FROM ADMISSION TICKET OR SCANNABLE APPLICATION

SOCIAL SECURITY NUMBER

TEST CENTER CODE

TEST DATE

JAN ○	○ ○
FEB ○	○ ○
MAR ○	① ①
APR ○	② ②
MAY ○	③ ③
JUN ○	④ ④
JUL ○	⑤ ⑤
AUG ○	⑥ ⑥
SEP ○	⑦ ⑦
OCT ○	⑧ ⑧
NOV ○	⑨ ⑨
DEC ○	

YR.

HAVE YOU EVER TAKEN THIS EXAMINATION BEFORE?   YES ○   NO ○

FOR WHICH LICENSE ARE YOU TAKING THIS EXAM?   BROKER ○   SALESPERSON ○

WHICH PART OF THE EXAMINATION ARE YOU TAKING?   GENERAL ○   STATE ○   BOTH ○

IN SIGNING BELOW I HEREBY AFFIRM THAT:
I AM THE UNDERSIGNED AND HAVE SIGNED MY CORRECT NAME ON THE SIGNATURE LINE BELOW.
IN ADDITION TO PASSING THE EXAMINATION FOR LICENSURE, I MUST MEET ALL STATE REQUIREMENTS.
I UNDERSTAND ALL EXAMINATION BOOKS ARE SECURE MATERIAL AND THAT NO BOOK OR PORTION THEREOF IS TO BE
COPIED, TRANSMITTED TO ANY OTHER PERSON OR REMOVED FROM THE EXAMINATION ROOM.
I WILL NEITHER ASSIST NOR RECEIVE ASSISTANCE FROM ANOTHER CANDIDATE OR USE ANY NOTES, MANUALS OR
OTHER AIDS.

SIGNATURE   DATE

1–80 answer grid, each item with options A B C D:

1 A B C D
2 A B C D
3 A B C D
4 A B C D
5 A B C D
6 A B C D
7 A B C D
8 A B C D
9 A B C D
10 A B C D
11 A B C D
12 A B C D
13 A B C D
14 A B C D
15 A B C D
16 A B C D
17 A B C D
18 A B C D
19 A B C D
20 A B C D
21 A B C D
22 A B C D
23 A B C D
24 A B C D
25 A B C D
26 A B C D
27 A B C D
28 A B C D
29 A B C D
30 A B C D
31 A B C D
32 A B C D
33 A B C D
34 A B C D
35 A B C D
36 A B C D
37 A B C D
38 A B C D
39 A B C D
40 A B C D
41 A B C D
42 A B C D
43 A B C D
44 A B C D
45 A B C D
46 A B C D
47 A B C D
48 A B C D
49 A B C D
50 A B C D
51 A B C D
52 A B C D
53 A B C D
54 A B C D
55 A B C D
56 A B C D
57 A B C D
58 A B C D
59 A B C D
60 A B C D
61 A B C D
62 A B C D
63 A B C D
64 A B C D
65 A B C D
66 A B C D
67 A B C D
68 A B C D
69 A B C D
70 A B C D
71 A B C D
72 A B C D
73 A B C D
74 A B C D
75 A B C D
76 A B C D
77 A B C D
78 A B C D
79 A B C D
80 A B C D

PLEASE TURN TO REVERSE SIDE FOR STATE TEST.

ANSWERS

1. (A) The income approach would give an unrealistically low value for a single-family home. The market comparison method is appropriate.

2. (D) The others don't affect the property's value.

3. (D) Economic obsolescence is forces outside the property itself. *A* and *C* are functional obsolescence, while *B* is physical deterioration.

4. (C) Market comparison is the best method for single-family homes, although the cost approach can be effective for new homes.

5. (B) It is cost to build today *less accrued depreciation* plus the value of the land.

6. (D)

7. (C) This could create the appearance of a conflict of interest. It is all right to have an interest in the property being appraised, so long as there is open and full disclosure.

8. (B) The cost approach can be used for new homes. It is the preferred method for service-type structures.

9. (B) Since we never depreciate raw land, only the improvements.

10. (A) What will the tennis court contribute to the anticipated net income?

11. (A) It would be regression, which is economic obsolescence.

12. (C) You would not pay more for a property than you would for one of equal utility and desirability.

13. (A) It is forces outside the property itself over which the owner has no control.

14. (C) Market value is considered to be the "objective value."

15. (D) Value moves inversely to the rate.

16. (B) Because of unusual expenses, the gross may bear little relationship to the net.

17. (D) Principle of conformity: values are maintained when a property is located in an area of similar properties.

18. (C) What a buyer will actually pay is the final determinant of value.

19. (B) It balances the amenities.

20. (A) When the property no longer returns an income attributable to the structure itself, it has exceeded its economic life.

21. (C) Sellers market, with limited supply and greater demand.

22. (A) It is often said that location, location, and location are the three most important determinants of value.

23. (B) While an appraiser estimates the value, B is its definition. What a buyer paid does not determine its value.

24. (D) An appraiser would use a lower capitalization rate in appraising the Sears building because of the quality of the income (lower risk).

25. (C)

26. (C) Otherwise it is only a wish.

27. (B) Whenever extraordinary profits are being made, competition will produce additional units which reduce the profits.

28. (C) When supply exceeds demand, prices drop. When demand exceeds supply, prices rise. As prices drop, there are more buyers (demand); as prices rise, there are fewer buyers.

29. (B) What a property should bring in is more important to an appraiser than what the rents actually are. The best appraisal method for income property is the income approach.

30. (C) Since economic obsolescence is caused by forces outside the property itself.

31. (C) And you can get the monthly gross multiplier by dividing the monthly gross income into the sales price.

32. (A) Advantageous sales terms will result in a higher price; however, the value of the property is intrinsic in the property and remains the same.

33. (C) Economic obsolescence. Because it is caused by forces outside the property, it is extremely difficult for a property owner alone to correct. A and D refer to physical deterioration and B to functional obsolescence.

34. (B) Less depreciation results in a greater profit and increases tax liability.

35. (D) Value moves inversely to the capitalization rate.

36. (D) $225 × 4 = $900 per month
                  $900 × 12 = $10,800 per year
                  81,000 ÷ 10,800 = 7.5

37. (B) We only depreciate improvements, not land. Appraisers would depreciate A, C, and D, but would not depreciate D for income tax purposes.

38. (B)

39. (C) Cost to reproduce less depreciation *plus* the value of the land.

40. (B) The increase in expenses of $4,000 with fixed rents will mean a $4,000 reduction in net. The value of $4,000 income by capitalizing 4000 ÷ .08 = $50,000.

41. (C) Unit cost in place method to determine the reproduction cost.

42. (C) Most effective for new or service-type buildings.

43. (C) Because it is caused by forces outside the property itself.

44. (B) The net income is simply an accounting task; chronological age can be determined from the building or tax records, and economic life can be determined from age/life tables. Determining the capitalization rate can be a complex process.

45. (D) Because of condition and features. We balance out these features (amenities) to evaluate comparables.

46. (D) This is a force outside the property itself. *B* and *C* are functional obsolescence, while *A* is physical deterioration.

47. (B) Added value due to assemblage.

48. (C) Built-in obsolescence by design.

49. (A) When we capitalize the net, we determine the present value of future income.

50. (A) Cost to build today less depreciation (present value of structure) plus the value of the land.

SIX
Finance

For financing purposes, real estate is typically hypothecated—that is, the borrower retains possession, while the lender holds a security interest.

The three basic instruments to finance real estate are the *mortgage,* the *trust deed,* and the *land contract or contract of sale.*

MORTGAGE

The mortgage is a two-party instrument whereby the mortgagor (the borrower) gives an interest and a note to a mortgagee (the lender) in exchange for a loan. The promissory note is the primary evidence of the debt, and the real estate interest is given as security for that debt.

Mortgage

mortgagor (borrower)	*gives promissory note, plus mortgage interest as security*	mortgagee (lender)
	loans money	

Lien Theory   In most states the mortgagor retains title and gives the mortgagee a lien on the property. The lien is perfected when the mortgage is recorded in the county where the real estate is located. When the mortgagor has paid off the loan the mortgagee gives the mortgagor a satisfaction of mortgage which, when recorded, removes the lien.

Title Theory   In title theory states, mortgages transfer title to the mortgagee on a condition subsequent. This means that when the condition is met (the payment of the mortgage note), the title reverts back to the mortgagor. Title theory states are Alabama, Arkansas, Connecticut, Maine, Maryland, Massachusetts, New Hampshire, Pennsylvania, Rhode Island, Tennessee, Vermont, and West Virginia.

Intermediate Theory   Under the intermediate theory, the title remains with the mortgagor (as in the lien theory) but it automatically transfers to the mortgagee in the event the mortgagor defaults. Intermediate theory states are Arkansas, Illinois, Mississippi, New Jersey, North Carolina, and Ohio.

Foreclosure by Sale

If the mortgagor defaults on the promissory note, then foreclosure normally involves a public sale. The mortgagee could bid the amount owing on the mortgage. Other bidders would have to bid cash. Should the sale bring more than the amount owed on the foreclosing mortgage, the balance would go to pay off junior encumbrances in the order of their priority. Should there be an excess, it would be paid to the mortgagor.

The priority of mortgages is determined by the time and date of recording. The first mortgage to be recorded is the priority lien. All other mortgages become junior to it. When a mortgage is foreclosed, the encumbrances junior to the foreclosing mortgage are wiped out. A purchaser at a foreclosure sale takes title subject to the encumbrances that are senior to the mortgage being foreclosed, but all junior encumbrances are eliminated.

Suppose there were 5 mortgages on a property:

- Mortgage 1 recorded 1 Sep 1969
- Mortgage 2 recorded 3 Aug 1973
- Mortgage 3 recorded 15 May 1978
- Mortgage 4 recorded 9 Jul 1983
- Mortgage 5 recorded 24 Dec 1984

If the mortgagee on mortgage 3 foreclosed, then the purchaser would take title subject to mortgages 1 and 2; mortgages 4 and 5 would be wiped out.

The mortgagee on a junior lien that contains a default clause could protect his or her interest prior to foreclosure by making the payments on the senior mortgage in default and then foreclosing on the junior mortgage. This would leave the junior mortgagee as the owner, subject to the senior encumbrances.

Period of Redemption   Mortgagors have a statutory period to redeem the property after a foreclosure sale by paying the sale price. In many states the mortgagor is allowed possession during the redemption period, which in a number of states is one year.

Deficiency Judgments   When the amount realized at a foreclosure sale is not sufficient to satisfy the debt owed to the foreclosing mortgagee, it is possible for a deficiency judgment to be granted for the difference between the sale price and the amount owing. The foreclosed mortgagor not only loses the property which secured the mortgage, but is still liable for the deficiency. Several states prohibit deficiency judgments. Many others place strong limitations on their use.

Deficiency judgments are not generally allowed where the foreclosing mortgagee purchases the property for less than its fair market value, or where the foreclosing mortgagee is the seller who is simply taking the property back by bidding at the foreclosure sale.

In several states strict foreclosure is allowed, whereby the court orders the mortgagor's interest to be terminated without a sale. Some New England states allow foreclosure by entry. If the mortgagee can peaceably take possession, then after a required period of time, the mortgagor's interests are terminated. Deficiency judgments are not allowed in cases of strict foreclosure or foreclosure by entry.

Deed in Lieu of Foreclosure   To avoid the credit stigma of a foreclosure sale, owners sometimes deed their interest to the lender. While a foreclosure sale wipes out junior liens, accepting a deed in lieu of foreclosure can give title to the mortgagee with subsequent liens intact.

TRUST DEEDS

A trust deed or trust indenture is a three-party instrument where the borrower (trustor) gives a note to the lender (beneficiary) and, as security for the note, conveys title to a third person (trustee).

Trust Deed

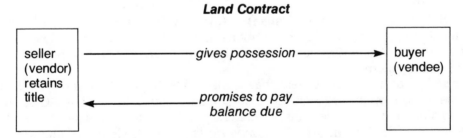

When the trustor has paid the note in full, the beneficiary directs the trustee to return the title to the trustor with a deed of reconveyance. Should the trustor default on the note, the beneficiary orders the trustee to conduct a trustee's sale. The trustee is said to hold only a naked legal title because the trustee's rights are so limited.

Trust deeds have an advantage over mortgages for lenders because they provide for a quick foreclosure sale and avoid lengthy mortgage redemption periods. However, a disadvantage is that deficiency judgments are generally not allowed when foreclosure is by trustee sale.

Trust deeds are commonly used in Alabama, Alaska, California, Colorado, Delaware, District of Columbia, Illinois, Mississippi, Missouri, Nevada, New Mexico, Oregon, Tennessee, Texas, Utah, Virginia, and West Virginia.

LAND CONTRACTS

Also known as real property sales contracts, land sales contracts, or contracts for deed, land contracts are financing agreements whereby the seller retains the legal title as security for the buyer's promise to pay.

Land Contract

Because land contracts provide for relatively quick forfeiture of the buyer's interests in event of default, they are often used in sales with low down payments.

A deed is not given until the property is paid for. This can create a danger to the buyer in that the seller might be unable to provide good title.

Courts in many states have placed restrictions on the quick and easy forfeiture provisions of land contracts, and in some cases judicial foreclosure is required.

While land contracts should be recorded to protect the buyer's interests, they often are not.

SPECIAL PROVISIONS OF FINANCING AGREEMENTS

Loan Assumptions   A buyer who assumes a loan agrees to be primarily liable for payment of the loan. The seller remains secondarily liable. Because the buyer has agreed to pay, a deficiency judgment is possible against the buyer in event of default.

Subject to a Loan   When a buyer purchases "subject to" an existing loan, the buyer acknowledges the existence of a loan but does not agree to pay it. In the event of foreclosure, the buyer loses the property but is not liable for a deficiency judgment. In a "subject to" sale, the seller remains primarily liable on the loan, and could be held liable for a deficiency judgment.

Late Charges   Grace periods (number of days allowed for a late payment) and charges for late payments are generally set forth in the loan agreement, and may be regulated by state statutes. Courts will not allow excessive late charges, nor will they allow late charges to be pyramided.

Defeasance Clause   The defeasance clause provides for the release of the lien when the obligation under the note is discharged by payment.

Prepayment Penalty Clause   Without special authorization, the mortgagor has no right to repay a loan in any manner other than is set forth in the note. Prepayment clauses allow a prepayment, but specify a penalty such as, "six months interest based upon the amount prepaid." Prepayment penalties cannot be charged when an early payment is required under a due on sale clause. Many states regulate prepayment penalties.

Or More Clause   The use of words such as, "payments of $550 or more per month," allows the mortgagor to prepay a loan without penalty.

Lock-In Clause   A lock-in clause allows prepayment, but requires that all interest be paid as if the original loan schedule were followed. It is really a severe prepayment penalty. Many states strictly regulate the use of such clauses.

Due On Sale Clause (Alienation Clause)   A loan with a due on sale clause must be paid in full if the property is sold, so cannot be assumed. Because such a loan is likely to be repaid prior to its due date, loans with these clauses are valued at a premium on the secondary mortgage market.

   A number of state courts held that loans made by state-chartered lenders were assumable, even though they included a due on sale clause. In 1982, the U.S. Supreme Court held that the due on sale clauses were enforceable as to federally-chartered lenders *(Fidelity Federal Savings and Loan Assn v de la Cuesta)*. Congress then passed the Garn Act (October 15, 1982), which provides for the assumability of loans. The Garn Act sets a three-year window period which allows for the assumption of loans until October 15, 1985, if those loans were originated, assumed, or taken subject to while permitted under state law. After this window period, no loans with due on sale clauses will be assumable. Due on sale clauses on loans made by federally chartered banks and savings institutions are fully enforceable, and are not subject to the window period exemption.

Release Clause   When a mortgage covers more than one property (blanket encumbrance), release clauses allow individual properties to be freed from the lien upon payment of specified sums. Without a release clause, the entire mortgage would have to be paid off in order to sell one parcel.

Subordination Clause   This clause makes a mortgage secondary to a later recorded mortgage. It is usually used with land sales where the seller agrees to take a lien that will be subordinate to a construction loan. Subordination clauses subject the seller to great risks and there have been many cases of fraud involving their use. As partial protection for the sellers, the mortgage should include limitations on the amount and terms of the loan to which it is to be subordinated. When a specific mortgage to which a loan is subordinated is satisfied, the subordinated mortgage regains its priority. A mortgage that merely says it will be subordinate always takes last priority, increasing the seller's risk.

FINANCING SOURCES

Primary Financing refers to the first loan on a property, such as a first mortgage. *Secondary Financing* refers to second trust deeds. Characteristics of secondary financing include:

- short period: usually under 7 years
- final balloon payment
- higher interest than primary financing

Primary financing is usually the function of institutional lenders (banks, savings and loans, and insurance companies). Institutional lenders also engage in secondary financing, but much of the secondary market is handled by noninstitutional lenders (individuals, trusts, pension funds, mortgage companies, etc.). Mortgage loan brokers usually deal in secondary financing, locating borrowers and investors for a fee.

Conventional Loans

Loans made without government guarantees or insurance are conventional loans. They generally have a lower loan-to-value ratio than government-insured-or-guaranteed loans, although federally chartered savings and loan institutions can make loans up to 95 percent of value for owner-occupied dwellings if the portion of the loan exceeding 80 percent is insured by a qualified private insurer.

Commercial Banks   Prefer short-term higher interest loans. They make construction loans.

Savings & Loans   Make the largest number of housing loans. They can make loans with lower down payments than most other lenders.

Insurance Companies   Prefer large commercial and industrial loans, as well as new home loans. They seldom make individual loans on older homes. They generally do not make construction loans.

Government Loans

These loans are generally not made by the government. Most are government-insured or -guaranteed. FHA and VA loans are made by institutional lenders. FHA loans are government-insured loans, while VA loans are government-guaranteed loans.

Federal Housing Administration Loans (FHA)

1 Government Insured: A one-time premium is collected at settlement. The insurance protects the lender against default by the borrower.
2 For housing only, including mobile homes and apartments.
3 FHA appraisal is required.
4 Property must meet minimum property requirements.
5 High loan-to-value ratio loans.
6 Sets a maximum loan on single-family dwellings. (Currently $67,500 for a 1-family dwelling.)

7 Secondary financing is not allowed at time of loan.
8 Loan discount points may be paid by buyer or seller subject to their agreement.
9 Fully amortized loans. Balloon payments are not allowed.
10 Long term loans, and therefore lower monthly payments.
11 No prepayment penalty allowed.
12 Taxes and insurance are included in the payments.
13 Lower interest rate than conventional loans. (Interest rate is no longer set by FHA but floats with the market rate.)
14 Loans are assumable by anyone.
15 Loans are made by institutional lenders.

FHA will issue a six-month conditional commitment to insure a loan for a property, providing that the mortgagor (when found) qualifies for the loan. A firm commitment to insure a loan may be obtained for a property when there is a definite mortgagor.

VA Loans

1 Veteran must submit copy of discharge and obtain a Certificate of Eligibility.
2 Appraisal and Certificate of Reasonable Value (CRV) is required.
   The veteran is not obligated to complete the purchase if the sale price exceeds the CRV. (The veteran can, however, pay the difference in cash.)
3 Loans are made by institutional lenders.
4 The VA guarantees 60 percent of the loan up to a maximum of $27,500.
   Example: $50,000 loan. 60% guarantee = $30,000, but maximum guarantee = $27,500. If property is foreclosed, the sale would have to be for less than $22,500 before the lender suffered a loss: $50,000 loan −27,500 guarantee = $22,500 not covered by guarantee.
5 No limit on the amount of the loan, as long as it does not exceed the CRV.
6 Loan can be for farm, home, or business. If for a home, it must be owner occupied.
7 No down payment is required by the VA, but lenders may require a down payment.
8 Secondary financing is not allowed at the time of purchase.
9 Loans are long term (30 years for home).
10 Loans are amortized (no balloon payments).
11 Veteran may pay a one percent loan origination fee. Additional points must be paid by the seller. Should the veteran use a VA loan to refinance a home he or she owns, then the veteran would be required to pay points.
12 Veteran pays one-half of one percent of the loan as a funding fee to the VA at the time of the loan; this can be covered by the loan.
13 Loans are fully assumable by non-veterans.
14 No prepayment penalty.
15 Lower interest rate than conventional loan.
16 Payments include taxes and insurance.

Mortgage Markets

Primary market lenders make mortgages directly to borrowers. The market applies to both primary and secondary financing. The secondary mortgage market is the buying and selling of existing mortgages. Mortgage loan correspondents arrange the transfer of packages of mortgages from the original lender to investors such as insurance companies and pension funds.

Fannie Mae (Federal National Mortgage Association)   FNMA is a private corporation which sells stocks as well as participation certificates to raise money. It creates a market place for existing mortgages by buying and selling FHA, VA, and conventional mortgages in the secondary mortgage market.

Ginnie Mae (Government National Mortgage Association)   GNMA is a government corporation which guarantees government assistance loans where other financing is unavailable. It makes it easy to invest in mortgages by selling government-guaranteed certificates that are backed by mortgages.

Freddie MAC (Federal Home Loan Mortgage Corporation)   FHLMC, a subsidiary of the Federal Home Loan Bank, provides a secondary mortgage market for federal savings and loans. It buys FHA, VA, and conventional mortgages and uses the mortgages as security to sell bonds and participation certificates.

Farm Home Administration (FmHA)   FmHA guarantees as well as insures loans in rural areas and small towns. Preference is given to veterans.

LOAN TERMS AND TYPES

Hard-Money Loan   An actual advance of cash. This type of loan demands the highest market interest.

Purchase-Money Loan   A loan where the seller finances the buyer. No money changes hands. The interest rate for purchase-money loans is often less than for hard-money loans.

Amortized Loan   A loan in which the regular payments fully pay the loan during the period of the loan.

Graduated Payment Mortgage (GPM)   This loan has lower payments during its early period. It is well suited for young buyers with rising incomes.

Adjustable-Rate Mortgage (ARM) or Variable Rate Mortgage (VRM)   A mortgage where the interest rate can be adjusted up or down in relationship to some index. Normally there is a limitation on the interest swing.

Straight Mortgage   A mortgage in which interest only is paid, and the principal is all due on a specified date.

Growing Equity Mortgage (GEM)   These mortgages have increasing payments, often doubling in 15 years or less, so the mortgage is paid off in a comparatively short time.

Canadian Rollover Mortgage (also known as a renegotiable rate mortgage, RRM) A short-term mortgage (such as 5 years, with payments based upon a 25- or 30-year period). When the term expires, the lender agrees to rewrite the loan at the then-current interest rate.

Sharing Appreciation Mortgage (SAM)   The lender agrees to a below-market interest rate or to share in the down payment in exchange for a percentage of the increased value of the property.

Participation Mortgage   On large projects, lenders (usually insurance companies) insist on a share in the ownership (as a limited partner) as well as the interest on the loan.

Reverse Mortgage or Reverse Annuity Mortgage (RAM)   The owners borrow against the equity in their home by receiving a monthly payment. It provides a means for elderly people to keep their homes. The mortgage is paid off when the mortgagors die or when the property is sold.

Wrap-Around Mortgage or All-Inclusive Mortgage   This is a second mortgage which is written to cover the amounts of first and second mortgage. The buyer makes the total payment to the seller, who then makes the payment on the first mortgage. This arrangement allows the seller to make money on the interest differential between the rate on the first mortgage and the rate on the second mortgage, as well as to get the interest on his or her equity.

Open End Mortgage   A mortgage that can be increased to an agreed-upon ceiling. A dragnet clause provides for the mortgage to cover the future advances.

Open Mortgage   A mortgage that can be prepaid without penalty.

Package Mortgage   A mortgage that covers personal property as well as real property.

Construction Mortgage   The payments which are made as work progresses are known as obligatory advances. The final payment is usually not made until the lien period expires. Construction loans are at a higher interest than permanent financing.

Take Out Mortgage   This is the permanent financing which "takes out" the construction loan.

Seasoned Mortgage   This is an existing mortgage with a payment history. On the secondary mortgage market it would sell at a premium when compared to a similar new mortgage.

Mortgage Warehousing   Interim financing by a mortgage company that borrows on its inventory of loans.

Discount Mortgage   A short-term mortgage in which the interest is taken out in advance. Sometimes used for home improvement loans.

Discounting a Mortgage   Selling an existing mortgage for less than its face value.

Compound Interest   This is interest upon interest. In a mortgage, there is straight interest—the only time the interest is compounded is when payments are not made.

OTHER LOAN PAYMENT COMPONENTS

Most real estate loans require payment for items besides principal and interest, such as insurance, taxes, and lender fees.

Private Mortgage Insurance (PMI)   Several firms offer mortgage protection similar to FHA insurance to lenders under conventional loans which protects against the default of the mortgagor.

Impound Account   Also known as borrower's escrow account; a trust account kept by the lender for taxes and insurance when taxes and insurance are part of the mortgagor's payment to the mortgagee.

Points or Mortgage Discount Points   These are percentages of the loan amount. They are really additional prepaid interest to make a loan attractive to a lender by increasing its effective yield. Each point is considered to be equal to $\frac{1}{8}$ of one percent in interest. Points are a one-time charge at time of loan origination. While points are considered interest when paid by a buyer, points paid by a seller are considered to be sales costs.

LAWS RELATING TO REAL ESTATE FINANCING

Equal Credit Opportunity Act

The ECOA prohibits discrimination against any loan applicant on the basis of race, color, national origin, sex, marital status, or dependency upon public assistance.

Truth In Lending Law (Regulation Z)

Regulation Z, a part of the Federal Consumers Credit Protection Act of 1968, requires disclosure of credit costs in percentage as well as total finance charges. It is enforced by the Federal Trade Commission. If any credit terms are mentioned in advertising, all of the terms must be given—down payment, number of payments, amount of payments, and interest as an annual percentage rate (APR). The law makes bait-and-switch advertising a federal offense. All the facts must be included in a disclosure statement; however, the total dollar amount of finance charges need not be shown for first mortgages or purchase-money mortgages.

Rescission Right　　When the loan is for consumer credit secured by borrower's residence, there is a rescission right until midnight on the third business day following loan completion. Loans exempt from all Truth in Lending disclosure requirements are: business loans, construction loans, personal property loans over $25,000, and interest-free loans with four or less installments.

Real Estate Settlement Procedures Act

RESPA requires disclosure of loan costs for federally related real estate purchase loans of one to four residential units involving a new first mortgage. Federally related loans refer to loans made by a federally insured or regulated lender.

A HUD information booklet entitled *Settlement Costs* must be given to borrower within three business days of loan application.

The Uniform Settlement Statement must be given to the borrower on or before settlement. The purchaser has a right to review the statement on the business day prior to closing. There must be a justifiable service rendered for every charge. The buyer cannot be required to purchase title insurance from any particular company, and the lender is prohibited from accepting kickbacks for referring any service. The lender cannot charge for preparation of the disclosure statement. Limits are placed upon the amount of advanced taxes and insurance payments the lender can collect.

The law does not apply to business property, vacant land, dealers buying for resale, refinancing, junior loans, or loan assumptions where the lender charges less than $50.

Soldiers and Sailors Civil Relief Act

If a debt was incurred before a person entered military service, no foreclosure sale for nonpayment will be allowed until the person has been out of military service for more than three months, except by court order. Normally the foreclosing mortgagee or trustee files an affidavit that the debtor has not been in military service during the prior three months.

FINANCING PERSONAL PROPERTY

A security agreement is used under the Uniform Commercial Code to perfect a security interest in personal property. A financing statement is filed with the Secretary of State's office in the state where the property is located. The financing statement is good for five years. Continuation statements for additional five-year periods can be filed. To remove the lien, a termination statement is filed. A creditor, by filing a financing statement, could have a priority interest in a item such as an air conditioner, even though it was installed after a first mortgage was recorded.

CHAPTER 6 QUIZ: FINANCE

1. The term *hard money loan* refers to a:

   (A) loan with an extremely high rate of interest
   (B) loan that was difficult to obtain
   (C) cash loan, as opposed to seller financing
   (D) well-secured loan

2. The buyer under a VA loan informs the broker that he does not have the cash to cover the necessary closing costs. The broker should:

   (A) notify the seller
   (B) arrange for the buyer to borrow the necessary money
   (C) make a loan out of the commission
   (D) delay the closing until buyer can save the money

3. Which of the following terms in an advertisement would **NOT** subject the advertiser to federal Truth in Lending requirements?

   (A) No down payment
   (B) Low down payment
   (C) $1000 down
   (D) 25-year loan

4. A mortgage which is subordinate to other mortgages but includes the amount of the other mortgages is:

   (A) a subordinate loan
   (B) a wraparound mortgage
   (C) a purchase money mortgage
   (D) an open-end mortgage

5. At what point must a federally related lender provide a copy of the HUD information booklet to a borrower?

   (A) Within three business days of receiving the borrower's loan application
   (B) Upon the request of borrower
   (C) Upon closing
   (D) 48 hours prior to closing

6. A lender agreed to make a loan with the stipulation that the borrower maintain a set minimum balance in an account at the bank. This arrangement is known as:

   (A) usury
   (B) a compensating balance
   (C) a dragnet clause
   (D) implied interest

7. An owner can be relieved of primary responsibility for a mortgage by finding a buyer who is willing to:

   (A) take subject to the loan
   (B) assume the loan
   (C) subordinate the loan
   (D) give a wrap-around mortgage

8. Monthly payments on a VA loan may increase due to:

   (A) the lender's shortening the term of the loan
   (B) a rise in interest rates
   (C) a rise in taxes
   (D) a change in the loan principal

9. A builder purchased a lot with a very low down payment which he intended to pay off after he built and sold a house. He intended to obtain a construction loan to cover his building costs. Most likely the loan for the lot purchase had a:

   (A) release clause
   (B) dragnet clause
   (C) subordination clause
   (D) due-on-sale clause

10. A broker takes an offer of $48,000, contingent upon the buyer being able to obtain a VA loan with $4,500 down. The Certificate of Reasonable Value comes in at $42,500 and the seller refuses to reduce the price. The broker should:

    (A) loan the buyer $1,000
    (B) return the buyer's deposit
    (C) ask the seller to carry back a small second mortgage
    (D) complete the sale as agreed

11. A longer-term loan generally carries:

    (A) a higher interest rate
    (B) a lower interest rate
    (C) lower total loan costs
    (D) greater total loan costs

12. The owner's right to rescind within three business days when a consumer loan places a lien on his or her residence is provided by:

    (A) RESPA
    (B) the Truth in Lending Act
    (C) the Equal Credit Opportunity Act
    (D) the Uniform Commercial Code

13. A mortgage note is:

    (A) security for the loan
    (B) the primary evidence of the debt
    (C) a negotiable draft
    (D) the guarantee of payment

14. The disclosure requirements of the Truth In Lending Act apply to:

    (A) sellers of real estate providing credit
    (B) a personal loan for $30,000
    (C) business loans
    (D) a three-installment interest-free loan

15. A seasoned loan is a:

    (A) priority loan
    (B) long-term loan
    (C) loan that includes incentives for early payment
    (D) loan with a payment history

16. A veteran defaulted on an $87,000 VA-guaranteed loan. The maximum government liability is:

    (A) $87,000
    (B) $52,200
    (C) $27,500
    (D) $59,500

17. A defeasance clause in a mortgage provides for:

    (A) the right of the mortgagee to foreclose
    (B) the release of the mortgage upon payment of the note
    (C) mortgage protection against unrecorded liens
    (D) the assumption of the loan

18. The following is **NOT** a characteristic of FHA loans:

    (A) amortized
    (B) minimum property requirements
    (C) housing
    (D) guaranteed

19. Which of the following lenders is likely to provide the highest loan-to-value ratio loan for an owner-occupied residence?

    (A) A commercial bank
    (B) An individual lender
    (C) A mortgage broker
    (D) A federally chartered savings and loan institution

20. The Soldiers and Sailors Civil Relief Act is of most interest to:

    (A) widows and orphans
    (B) mortgagees
    (C) tax assessors
    (D) sellers

21. The loan most likely to change its interest rate over its life is:

    (A) a straight mortgage
    (B) an ARM
    (C) a construction loan
    (D) a second mortgage

22. The seller holds legal title to a sold real property under a:

    (A) trust deed
    (B) mortgage (lien theory)
    (C) land contract
    (D) security agreement

23. The liquidation of a loan in equal installments is:

    (A) acceleration
    (B) annuitization
    (C) compounding the interest
    (D) amortization

24. What loan type has changes in payment without any change in the interest rate?

    (A) SAM
    (B) GPM
    (C) VRM
    (D) ARM

25. Which loan type features a profit split between the borrower and lender when the property is sold?

    (A) SAM
    (B) GPM
    (C) GEM
    (D) ARM

26. The person hypothecating real property is:

    (A) selling it
    (B) renting it
    (C) giving up possession
    (D) keeping possession

27. A mortgage most commonly uses:

    (A) simple interest
    (B) compound interest
    (C) discounted interest
    (D) prepaid interest

28. An insurance company agreed to provide the developer financing for a shopping center at 13 percent interest plus an equity position. This arrangement is called:

    (A) a participation loan
    (B) a packaged loan
    (C) a variable loan
    (D) an open-end loan

29. An advertiser, in complying with Truth in Lending requirements, would state:

    (A) 12% interest
    (B) 12% straight interest
    (C) 12% annual interest
    (D) 12% annual percentage rate

30. The maximum a lender may charge for the statement required under RESPA is:

    (A) $50
    (B) one-half of one percent of the loan
    (C) $100
    (D) nothing

31. A mortgagee, in accepting a quitclaim deed from the mortgagor in lieu of foreclosure, would:

    (A) take the property clear of all liens
    (B) be subject to junior liens of record
    (C) wipe out the junior liens
    (D) still be subject to mortgagor's redemption rights

32. The rescission provisions of Truth In Lending apply to:

    (A) home-purchase loans
    (B) construction loans
    (C) business loans
    (D) consumer credit

33. If each percentage in interest yield is equal to 8 points, then a raise in yields from 12¼ percent to 12⅝ percent should cause a fixed-rate loan to increase:

    (A) 3 points
    (B) 1½ points
    (C) 6 points
    (D) 4½ points

34. Equal monthly payments on an amortized loan:

    (A) reduce the loan principal in equal monthly amounts
    (B) compound the interest
    (C) apply decreasing amounts to interest
    (D) apply increasing amounts to interest

35. An assignment-of-rents clause in a mortgage is for the benefit of the:

    (A) mortgagee
    (B) mortgagor
    (C) tenant
    (D) trustee

36. A deed of trust moves title from the:

    (A) mortgagor to mortgagee
    (B) trustor to trustee
    (C) trustor to beneficiary
    (D) beneficiary to trustor

37. An impound account is the property of the:

    (A) mortgagor
    (B) mortgagee
    (C) beneficiary
    (D) trustee

38. The Truth In Lending Law is enforced by:

    (A) HUD
    (B) OILSR
    (C) the Department of Real Estate
    (D) Federal Trade Commission

39. A buyer who wants an FHA loan should be directed to:

    (A) a mortgage loan broker
    (B) FHA
    (C) HUD
    (D) a conventional lender

40. A deed of reconveyance would be signed by the:

    (A) trustor
    (B) trustee
    (C) beneficiary
    (D) vendor

41. "Naked Legal Title" best describes the interest of the:

    (A) vendee under a land contract
    (B) trustee under a trust deed
    (C) beneficiary under a trust deed
    (D) trustor under a trust deed

42. What advantage might a land contract have to a buyer, compared to a mortgage?

    (A) lower down payment
    (B) amortized
    (C) longer term
    (D) more protection from foreclosure

43. Kickbacks from service providers are prohibited by:

    (A) RESPA
    (B) Truth In Lending
    (C) the Equal Credit Opportunity Act
    (D) FHA

44. Which of the following is NOT a violation of the Real Estate Settlement Procedures Act?

    (A) Directing the buyer to a particular lender
    (B) Accepting a kickback on a loan subject to RESPA

    (C) Requiring a particular title insurer
    (D) Acceptance of a fee or charge for services which were not performed

45. A VA loan does NOT involve:

    (A) a note
    (B) a mortgage
    (C) a loan trust account
    (D) an alienation clause

46. County records distinguish a first mortgage from a junior mortgage by:

    (A) the heading on the instrument
    (B) the recorder's declaration
    (C) the time and date of recording
    (D) information contained in the note

47. A subordination clause in a loan would be of greatest benefit to:

    (A) the mortgagor
    (B) the trustee
    (C) the beneficiary
    (D) the mortgagee

48. Which of the following is FALSE as to a VA loan?

    (A) The veteran cannot pay more than the Certificate of Reasonable Value amount.
    (B) The loan would be amortized.
    (C) The loan is not insured.
    (D) If it is for housing, it must be owner occupied.

49. Increasing the points on a loan in the absence of any economic change should have what effect on the loan?

    (A) Increase the risk
    (B) Reduce the interest
    (C) Increase the payments
    (D) Shorten the loan term

50. What would be violated by a bank's requirement that title insurance be obtained from a particular provider?

    (A) Realtor's Code of Ethics
    (B) Federal Fair Housing Act
    (C) Equal Credit Opportunity Act
    (D) Real Estate Settlement Procedures Act

GENERAL TEST

PLEASE PRINT THE FOLLOWING:
YOUR NAME

LAST · FIRST · MI

STREET ADDRESS

CITY · STATE · ZIP

TEST CENTER LOCATION (CITY, STATE)

TEST BOOKLET NO.

1ST THREE LETTERS OF LAST NAME

I.D. NUMBER FROM ADMISSION TICKET OR SCANNABLE APPLICATION

SOCIAL SECURITY NUMBER

TEST CENTER CODE

TEST DATE
JAN / YR.
FEB
MAR
APR
MAY
JUN
JUL
AUG
SEP
OCT
NOV
DEC

HAVE YOU EVER TAKEN THIS EXAMINATION BEFORE?   YES ○   NO ○

FOR WHICH LICENSE ARE YOU TAKING THIS EXAM?   BROKER ○   SALESPERSON ○

WHICH PART OF THE EXAMINATION ARE YOU TAKING?
GENERAL ○   STATE ○   BOTH ○

IN SIGNING BELOW I HEREBY AFFIRM THAT:
I AM THE UNDERSIGNED AND HAVE SIGNED MY CORRECT NAME ON THE SIGNATURE LINE BELOW.
IN ADDITION TO PASSING THE EXAMINATION FOR LICENSURE, I MUST MEET ALL STATE REQUIREMENTS.
I UNDERSTAND ALL EXAMINATION BOOKS ARE SECURE MATERIAL AND THAT NO BOOK OR PORTION THEREOF IS TO BE COPIED, TRANSMITTED TO ANY OTHER PERSON OR REMOVED FROM THE EXAMINATION ROOM.
I WILL NEITHER ASSIST NOR RECEIVE ASSISTANCE FROM ANOTHER CANDIDATE OR USE ANY NOTES, MANUALS OR OTHER AIDS.

SIGNATURE · DATE

PLEASE TURN TO REVERSE SIDE FOR STATE TEST.

ANSWERS

1. (C) Cash loans are generally at a higher interest rate than seller financing where cash does not change hands.

2. (A) While the seller can agree to pay the costs, secondary financing is not allowed at the time of purchase on VA or FHA loans. Broker also has a duty to notify the principal of any material facts.

3. (B) This is not a loan term. Since the others are, their use would require full disclosure of all of the terms.

4. (B) Or all-inclusive mortgage.

5. (A)

6. (B) Because the lender has the low-cost use of the borrower's money, the lender gets additional benefits from the loan.

7. (B) The buyer would become primarily liable, while the seller remains secondarily liable.

8. (C) Could also be increased insurance premiums. VA loans are fixed-rate loans.

9. (C) Making the purchase money loan secondary to a construction loan.

10. (B) Secondary financing is not allowed on FHA and VA loans, and the VA will not guarantee a loan greater than the CRV. Buyers are entitled to the return of the deposit if the CRV is less than the purchase price. The buyer could go through with the purchase by paying the difference in cash.

11. (D) Since more interest would be paid.

12. (B) Does not apply to purchase loans.

13. (B) The mortgage is the security for the note.

14. (A) Others are exempt.

15. (D)

16. (C) The amount of the guarantee (60 percent of the loan or up to $27,500).

17. (B)

18. (D) Insured, VA are guaranteed.

19. (D) Can make loans up to 95 percent of value if the portion of the loan over 80 percent is insured by a private mortgage insurer.

20. (B) Limits the right of foreclosure when mortgagor is in military service.

21. (B) Adjustable rate mortgage.

22. (C)

23. (D)

24. (B) Graduated payment mortgage. Lower payments for the first years, then gradual increase. A growing equity mortgage (GEM) would also have increased payments.

25. (A) Sharing appreciation mortgage.

26. (D) But giving a security interest to another, as in a mortgage.

27. (A) Interest is paid each month (usually for previous month), so the interest does not compound.

28. (A) Common on large projects; lender gets interest, plus is a limited partner sharing in the profits.

29. (D) Interest must be given as APR (Annual Percentage Rate).

30. (D) No charge is allowed.

31. (B) If the mortgagee had foreclosed, then all junior liens would have been removed.

32. (D) Consumer credit secured by borrower's residence.

33. (A) Since rate increase is ⅜ of a percentage point.

34. (C) And increasing amounts applied to principal.

35. (A) So mortgagor can't keep the rents during the foreclosure period.

36. (B) Who holds it in trust until the trustor pays the beneficiary.

37. (A) The borrower actually owns the prepaid insurance and taxes which are paid to the lender, who holds them in trust.

38. (D)

39. (D) Only a conventional lender can make FHA loans.

40. (B) Returns legal title from the trustee to the trustor.

41. (B) Vendee has *equitable,* not *legal* title.

42. (A) Sellers often sell with lower down payments on land contracts.

43. (A) Real Estate Settlement Procedures Act.

44. (A) The others are specifically prohibited.

45. (D) Since a VA loan is fully assumable.

46. (C) Recording determines priority.

47. (A) It allows the mortgagor to use the property as security for another loan, as if the prior loan were not there.

48. (A) Veteran can pay more than the Certificate of Reasonable Value amount, but the loan can't exceed the CRV.

49. (B) Since points are prepaid interest.

50. (D)

SEVEN
Mathematics of Real Estate

DECIMALS AND PERCENTAGES

To convert a decimal to a percentage, move the decimal point two places to the right: .6 becomes 60%.

To convert a percentage to a decimal, simply move the decimal point two places to the left: 60% = .6. Note: for examination purposes, your answers may be rounded off to the nearest whole number.

FINDING THE INTEREST

To determine the amount of interest earned, multiply the amount of the loan (principal) times the rate of interest times the time (period) of the loan:

$$\text{interest} = \text{principal} \times \text{rate} \times \text{time}$$

The interest earned on $20,000 for 1 year:

$$\text{interest} = 20{,}000 \times .06 \,[6\% \text{ as a decimal}] \times 1 = \$1200$$

Interest earned over six months would be:

$$\text{interest} = 20{,}000 \times .06 \times .5 \,[\tfrac{1}{2} \text{ year}] = \$600$$

FINDING THE PRINCIPAL

To find the principal amount when the annual amount of interest earned and the rate of interest is known, divide the interest earned by the interest rate:

$$\text{principal} = \frac{\text{interest earned}}{\text{rate of interest}}$$

If an investor received $1,200 in interest for one year on a six percent investment, the principal would be:

$$\text{principal} = \frac{\$1{,}200}{.06 \,[6\% \text{ as a decimal}]} = \$20{,}000$$

If the investor earned $100 in one month on a six percent investment, we could simply multiply the earnings by 12 to find the annual earnings of $1,200, and then use the formula above.

FINDING THE INTEREST RATE

To find the rate of interest when the annual amount of interest earned and the amount of the principal invested are known, divide the amount of interest earned by the principal:

$$\text{interest rate} = \frac{\text{interest earned}}{\text{principal}}$$

For a $1,200 return on a $20,000 investment for one year we would use the above formula:

$$\text{interest rate} = \frac{\$1,200}{20,000} = .06, \text{ or } 6\%$$

FINDING THE TIME

If we know the rate of interest, the amount of interest earned, and the principal amount, we can find the length of the investment by dividing the interest earned by the amount of the principal times the rate of interest:

$$\text{time} = \frac{\text{interest earned}}{\text{principal} \times \text{rate}}$$

Earnings of $1,200 on a $20,000 investment at six percent must have been invested for:

$$T = \frac{\$1,200}{20,000 \times .06} = \frac{\$1,200}{1200} = 1 \text{ year}$$

TAXES

Taxes on real estate are ad valorem (according to value). The tax rate is commonly expressed as a rate per $100 of valuation. A rate of 3.794 equals $3.79 and 4 mills (a mill is a tenth of a cent) per one hundred dollars of valuation.

If a property were assessed at one-half of its market value of $80,000 using the 3.794 rate per $100, we would find the taxes as follows:

$$\text{assessed valuation} = \frac{1}{2} \times \$80,000 = \$40,000$$

Since the tax rate in this case is per $100, we must find how many $100 are in $40,000. To do so we move the decimal point 2 places to the left and find it is 400.

We now multiply the rate times the number of $100 of evaluation to find the tax:

$$400 \times 3.794 = \$1,517.60$$

COMMISSION

The commission is a percentage of the selling price; it is determined by multiplying the selling price times the rate of commission.

A 6% commission on a selling price of $50,000 equals:

$$\$50,000 \times .06 \,[6\% \text{ as a decimal}] = \$3,000.00$$

SQUARE FOOTAGE

To find the square footage of a square or rectangle, we simply multiply the length (in feet) by the width (in feet). A 40′ × 140′ lot contains 5,600 square feet.

A right triangle is half of a rectangle. Therefore the square footage of a right triangle is one-half the length × width. The square footage of the 50′ × 60′ rectangle shown here is 3,000. Half of that number, 1,500 square feet, is the area of the triangle.

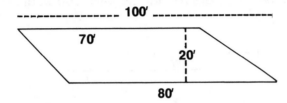

A trapezoid is a four-sided figure having two parallel sides:

To find the area of a trapezoid, you must find the rectangle and right angles. Breaking the trapezoid down to a rectangle and triangles, we get:

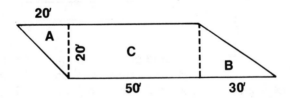

Triangle A contains ½ of 20′ × 20′ or   200 sq. ft.
Triangle B contains ½ of 20′ × 30′ or   300 sq. ft.
Rectangle C is 50′ × 20′, containing   1000 sq. ft.
Total area =   1500 sq.ft.

Square Yards   There are 9 square feet in a square yard:

Be sure to convert square feet to square yards or vice versa if the problem or answers use square feet and square yards.

PERIMETER

The perimeter is the outer boundary of an area. To find the perimeter of an area, the first step is to determine all of the dimensions. Assume you wished to find the perimeter of the following pool:

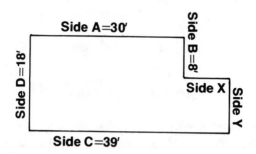

Side X would be nine feet, since Side A (30 feet) + X = 39 feet. Side Y would be 10 feet, since Side B (8 feet) + Y = 18 feet. Therefore, 30 feet (A) + 8 feet (B) + 9 feet (X) + 10 feet (Y) + 39 feet (C) + 18 feet (D) = 112 feet.

Assume a three feet walk was to be built around the perimeter of the pool and you needed to know the number of square feet for the walk. You would start by drawing the pool and walk:

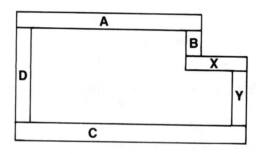

The walk on Side A would be 36' × 3' or	108 sq. ft.
The walk on Side B would be 8' × 3' or	24 sq. ft.
The walk on Side X would be 9' × 3' or	27 sq. ft.
The walk on Side Y would be 10' × 3' or	30 sq. ft.
The walk on Side C would be 45' × 3' or	135 sq. ft.
The walk on Side D would be 18' × 3' or	54 sq. ft.
Total sq. ft. of walk =	378 sq. ft.

CUBIC VOLUME

To find the cubic volume, multiply length by width by height:

A room 10' × 9' × 8' has 720 cubic feet.

A cubic yard contains 27 cubic feet (3' × 3' × 3'):

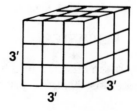

BOARD FEET

A board foot is 144 cubic inches. A 1 inch × 12 inch board 12 inches long (1 foot) equals 1 board foot:

$$1'' \times 12'' \times 12'' = 144 \text{ cubic inches.}$$

In computing board feet, you must make certain that all dimensions have been converted to inches.

To determine the number of board feet in a board two inches × six inches × nine feet long, first convert nine feet to inches.

$$9 \times 12 = 108'' \, [2'' \times 6'' \times 108'' = 1296 \text{ cubic inches} \, [1296 \div 144 = 9 \text{ board feet}$$

Since there are 144 cubic inches in a board foot, divide the total number of cubic inches by 144 to find the number of board feet.

To find the number of board feet in 48 boards 2″ × 6″ × 9′, multiply the number of board feet in one 2″ × 6″ 9′ board (9 board feet) times 48, for a total of 432 board feet.

FINDING ONE DIMENSION OF A RECTANGLE

To find one dimension of a rectangular-shaped parcel when one dimension and the total square area is known, divide the known dimension into the area (in square feet).

$$\text{unknown dimension} = \frac{\text{area in square feet}}{\text{known dimension}}$$

The diagram on the right shows a rectangular parcel having a width of 100′ and a total area of 1 acre. One acre = 43,560 square feet. Therefore we divide:

$$43,560 \div 100 = 435.6 \text{ feet}$$

SETTLEMENTS

It is often necessary to prorate taxes, insurance costs, rents, and interest in real estate closings, since the seller is liable for all costs up to and including the day of closing. All prorating is done on the basis of a 360-day year and a 30-day month.

On a loan assumption, to compute the daily prorated charge for a three-year policy of fire insurance that cost $421.20, divide the cost by three to find the annual charge:

$$421.20 \div 3 = \$140.40/\text{year}$$

To find the monthly charge, divide the annual charge by 12:

$$140.40 \div 12 = \$11.70/\text{month}$$

To find the daily charge, divide the month's charge by 30:

$$11.70 \div 30 = .39/\text{day}$$

If the seller had paid the insurance in advance for the year starting July 1, 1984, and the insurance policy was assumed by the buyer with a closing of September 10, 1984, then the seller would have been responsible for two months and ten days of the insurance cost:

$$
\begin{array}{ll}
2 \times 11.70 \text{ (cost per month)} & \$23.40 \\
10 \times .39 \text{ (cost per day)} & \underline{\quad 3.90} \\
& \$27.30
\end{array}
$$

The buyer would therefore owe the seller $421.20 (cost of the policy), less the amount used, $27.30:

$$
\begin{array}{r}
\$421.20 \\
-27.30 \\
\hline
\$393.90
\end{array}
$$

The buyer would be debited $393.90 on the closing statement and the seller would be credited with $393.90.

Prorating Interest   Interest on loans is usually paid in arrears, so a loan payment on 1 August would include the interest for the month of July. If a property settlement was scheduled for July 15 and a loan was being assumed, the buyer would be paying the entire month of July interest with the August first payment. The seller would therefore owe the buyer (be debited) 15 days interest and the buyer would be credited with it.

Percentage Returns   The net income is the gross income less all expenses. Payment on the principal is not an expense and should never be deducted in computing the net.
    Whenever a problem involves a percentage return, divide the net by whatever you want a percentage return on:

$$
\begin{array}{l}
\text{total price} = \text{net} \div \text{total price} \\
\text{down payment} = \text{net} \div \text{down payment} \\
\text{owner's equity} = \text{net} \div \text{owner's equity}
\end{array}
$$

If the net income was $1,200 and the down payment was $6,000, the percentage return on the down payment is:

$$
1,200 \div 6,000 = .20 \text{ or } 20\%
$$

SOLVING FOR AN UNKNOWN

In solving for unknowns you will be using basic algebra. What is important to remember is that if you have a percentage and you are looking for the whole number you can simply turn the percentage to a decimal and divide it by itself. When you divide on one side of an equation you must then do the same on the other side.
    Assume a seller wanted $23,500 after a 6% commission was paid out of the sales price. The sales price then must be:

$$
\$23,500 = 94\% \text{ of sales price}
$$
(because 6% is the commission).
$$
\$23,500 = .94 \text{ of the sales price (changed to decimal)}.
$$

$$\frac{\$23,500}{.94} = \frac{.94}{.94}$$

To make the sales price stand by itself we divide .94 by itself. Since we did this on one side of the equation we must do it on both sides.

$$\frac{\$23,500}{.94} = \text{sales price}$$

$$\$25,000 = \text{sales price}$$

Another example of solving for an unknown involves property selling for $80,000, which is 40 percent more than it cost the seller. What did the seller originally pay?

$$\$80,000 = 140\% \text{ of cost } \%(\text{since it sold for 40\% more than its cost or,}$$
$$100\% \text{ of its cost plus 40\%})$$

$$\$80,000 = 1.4 \text{ times cost (percentage changed to a decimal)}$$

$$\frac{\$80,000}{1.4} = \frac{1.4 \text{ cost}}{1.4}$$

(we divide the decimal by itself to find 1 cost)

$$\frac{\$80,000}{1.4} = \text{cost}$$

Since we divided on one side of the equation, we must do the same thing on the other side:

$$\$57,142.86 = \text{cost}$$

CHAPTER 7 QUIZ: MATHEMATICS OF REAL ESTATE

1. Which of the following boards contains more than one board foot?

    (A) 1" × 6" × 24"
    (B) 24" × 3" × 2"
    (C) 6" × 6" × 6"
    (D) 17" × 4" × 2"

2. The investment necessary for a yield of $500 per month at 6 percent interest is:

    (A) $60,000
    (B) $120,000
    (C) $8,333.33
    (D) $100,000

3. A rectangular shaped parcel contains 14 acres. Its width is 800 feet. The depth of the parcel is:

    (A) 762.3 feet
    (B) 3111.42 feet
    (C) 131.18 feet
    (D) 913.11 feet

4. To leave the owner $90,000 after a 6 percent commission is paid, the list price would be:

    (A) $96,000.00
    (B) $95,400.00
    (C) $95,744.68
    (D) $95,905.66

5. L sold a note to M at a 14 percent discount. L received $9,800.00. The amount due on the note was:

    (A) $11,172.00
    (B) $11,395.35
    (C) $10,800.00
    (D) $12,558.13

6. The next monthly interest payment on a loan balance of $17,835 is $132.28. The interest rate on the loan is:

    (A) 13.48%
    (B) 8.9%
    (C) 7.4%
    (D) 6.78%

7. On a 70 feet × 70 feet rectangular lot, the side yard building setbacks are 10 feet, the front yard setback is 25 feet, and the rear setback is 20 feet. The maximum size possible for one-story structure would be:

    (A) 4,900 sq. ft.
    (B) 1,200 sq. ft.
    (C) 1,000 sq. ft.
    (D) 1,250 sq. ft.

8. In the triangular parcel shown below, there are five acres between A and B streets. What is the distance between the streets?

    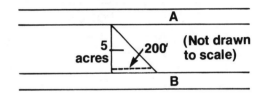

    (A) 2,178 feet
    (B) 1,304.54 feet
    (C) 800 feet
    (D) 1,625.5 feet

9. How many cubic feet of space are contained in the building shown?

    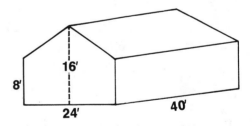

    (A) 12,800
    (B) 11,520
    (C) 9,600
    (D) 11,820

10. If a monthly interest payment was $957.52 at 12 percent interest, what was the principal due at the time of payment?

    (A) $7,979.33
    (B) $95,752.00
    (C) $76,812.37
    (D) $11,490.24

11. A house purchased four years ago for $50,000 has increased in value by 10 percent each year. The house is now worth:

(A) $70,000
(B) $90,000
(C) $73,205
(D) $66,550

12. Use the following illustration to answer the question below:

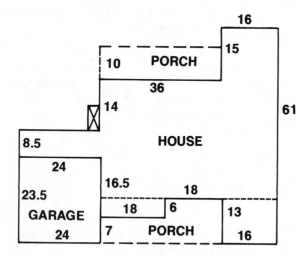

How many square feet are contained in the living area of the dwelling only?

(A) 2,236 sq. ft.
(B) 2,272 sq. ft.
(C) 2,476 sq. ft.
(D) 2,542 sq. ft.

13. A property with a gross annual income of $20,000 was purchased for $120,000. The only expense is the 11 percent interest payment on a $100,000 straight mortgage. The owner's percentage return on equity would be:

(A) 22.2%
(B) 16.6%
(C) 45%
(D) 20%

14. Which of the following areas is largest?

(A) one-fifth of a township
(B) 5 sections
(C) 1 mile × 7 miles
(D) 5,000' × 35,000'

15. Property was sold on December 10. The seller had paid the property tax of $334.80 for the calendar year of the sale. On a closing statement, the taxes would be shown as:

(A) credit buyer $18.60
(B) debit buyer $17.67
(C) credit seller $18.60
(D) credit seller $19.53

16. A 50-acre rectangular industrial site fronting on a highway is 1,000' deep. Assuming a sale price of $3,000 per acre, the price per front foot would be:

(A) $150.00
(B) $3,443.52
(C) $74.93
(D) $68.87

17. A fully rented ten-unit apartment building has rents of $500 per month. A ten percent rent increase brings a ten percent vacancy factor. The gross income:

(A) remains the same
(B) increases 1%
(C) increases 9%
(D) decreases 1%

18. An investor purchased two lots for $9,500 each. He subdivided them into three lots that he sold for $8,200 each. His percentage of profit on his cost was:

(A) 86.31%
(B) 29.47%
(C) 22.76%
(D) 13%

19. A six foot wide sidewalk is to be constructed inside the perimeter (on the lot line) of two adjacent sides of a 60′ × 100′ corner lot. The sidewalk will contain:

    (A) 1,600 sq. ft.
    (B) 960 sq. ft.
    (C) 924 sq. ft.
    (D) 900 sq. ft.

20. A six foot wide sidewalk is to be constructed outside the perimeter (on the lot line) of two adjacent sides of a 60′ × 100′ lot. The sidewalk would contain:

    (A) 960 sq. ft.
    (B) 996 sq. ft.
    (C) 1,032 sq. ft.
    (D) 1,660 sq. ft.

21. How much concrete is needed in a 30 foot driveway 18 feet wide and 4 inches thick?

    (A) 540 cubic yards
    (B) 180 cubic yards
    (C) 20 cubic yards
    (D) 7 cubic yards

22. One-sixtieth of a township is what percentage of a section?

    (A) 60
    (B) 166
    (C) 58
    (D) 62

23. An apartment has a gross income of $87,500. Annual expenses are depreciation $8,500, principal payments $7,200, interest on the loan $26,800, taxes $5,100 and other operating costs of $14,100. The annual cash flow is:

    (A) $25,800
    (B) $41,500
    (C) $79,000
    (D) $34,300

24. L purchased a lot for $9,000. He listed the lot for sale at 40 percent more than he paid. Because he could not find a buyer, he reduced his price by 30 percent. He found a buyer at the reduced price. After paying a seven percent commission, what was the profit or loss?

    (A) profit of 3 percent
    (B) loss of $180
    (C) loss of $794
    (D) profit of $207

25. The distance between the S.E. corner of section 13 of T3NR2E and the N.W. corner of section 30 of T2NR3E in the same county would be:

    (A) 7 miles
    (B) 12 miles
    (C) 9 miles
    (D) 14 miles

26. How many acres is 348,480 square yards?

    (A) 8
    (B) 2.66
    (C) 24
    (D) 72

27. Builder's blueprints frequently use the scale of ¼ inch = 1 foot. If such a plan indicated a family room 10½ inches by 3½ inches, what would floor tile cost at $3.80 per square yard?

    (A) $2,234.40
    (B) $744.80
    (C) $311.16
    (D) $248.25

28. How many cubic yards of concrete are required for a footing 168′ long, 18″ wide, and 6″ deep?

    (A) 126
    (B) 4.67
    (C) 13.75
    (D) 14

29. A 90' × 60' building needs floor covering. 60 percent of the building will be carpeted at a cost of $16 per square yard and the remainder will be tiled at a cost of $8 per square yard. The cost of the floor covering will be:

(A) $5,760
(B) $7,680
(C) $23,040
(D) $2,560

30. A rectangular lot with 80' of frontage has adjoining rectangular lots 160 feet deep on each side. One of these side lots contains 12,800 square feet and the other has 9,600 square feet. The combined front footage of the three lots equals:

(A) 200 feet
(B) 220 feet
(C) 250 feet
(D) 140 feet

31. A father willed his estate as follows: 54 percent to his wife, 18 percent to his daughter, 16 percent to his son and the remainder to his church. The church received $79,000. The daughter received:

(A) $658,333
(B) $105,333
(C) $118,500
(D) $355,500

32. A railroad divided three sections into 20-acre parcels and sold 16 of the parcels for $4,000 each. The remainder sold for $5,000 each. The total sale price was:

(A) $84,000
(B) $64,000
(C) $264,000
(D) $464,000

33. A $100,000 loan at 12 percent could be amortized with monthly payments of $1,200.22 on a 15-year basis, or payments of $1,028.63 on a 30-year basis. The 30-year loan results in total payments of what percent of the 15-year total payments?

(A) 158%
(B) 171%
(C) 146%
(D) 228%

34. An income property sold for $400,000 to an investor who planned on a nine percent return on the investment. If the investor had wanted a 12 percent return, what would she have paid for the property?

(A) $400,000
(B) $300,000
(C) $360,000
(D) $330,000

35. A three-year insurance policy which cost $144 was taken out by the seller four months and three days prior to closing. The policy, which was assumed by the buyer, would be shown as a:

(A) $16.40 buyer credit
(B) $122.60 buyer credit
(C) $16.40 seller credit
(D) $127.60 seller credit

36. The owner of a commercial building worth $107,000 owes $82,000. With net income of $10,000, the return on equity is closest to:

(A) 8.2%
(B) 20%
(C) 40%
(D) 10.65%

37. Five condominiums were sold at $82,500, $97,600, $112,500, $132,800, and $148,000. Together the units have annual property maintenance expenses of $3,850, which the owners share on a prorata basis, based on the cost of their units. The lowest-priced unit had a monthly assessment of:

(A) $14.39
(B) $55.38
(C) $46.16
(D) $39.14

38. A $90,000 mortgage on a $100,000 house has amortized monthly payments on a 13½%, 30-year loan of $1,030.88. Financing costs will increase the real price of the house by:

(A) 312%
(B) 281%
(C) 69%
(D) 187%

39. An eight percent term loan of $800 is paid off with an interest cost of $42.60. The loan was paid off in:

   (A) 6 months
   (B) 7 months
   (C) 8 months
   (D) 9 months

40. The last month's interest on a 12 percent amortized loan was $923.18. The balance due was:

   (A) $92,318.00
   (B) $7,693.00
   (C) $110,781.00
   (D) $1,178.16

41. A rectangular property sold for $6,400, or 40¢ per square foot. The parcel had a depth of 200 feet. What price did the buyer pay per front foot?

   (A) $16
   (B) $80
   (C) $40
   (D) $32

42. The quarterly interest payment on a $9,600 term loan at eight percent would be:

   (A) $63.33
   (B) $760
   (C) $192
   (D) $256

43. A property which is said to offer a 7.5 percent return has a monthly net of $810. The property is likely listed at:

   (A) $10,800
   (B) $9,720
   (C) $129,600
   (D) $138,400

44. You sold a lot for 30% more than you paid for it. You invest money at 14% which gives you $820 per year in interest. What did you originally pay for the lot?

   (A) $5,857
   (B) $4,505
   (C) $9,837
   (D) $5,123

45. An apartment has an annual gross income of $64,000. The net income is 30% of the gross. An investor who wants an 11 percent return on the purchase price would pay no more than:

   (A) $581,818
   (B) $831,168
   (C) $174,545
   (D) $192,000

46. A 40' × 60' rectangular building which is 8' high sells for $1.40 per cubic foot. What is the price per square foot?

   (A) $11.20
   (B) $14.00
   (C) $5.71
   (D) $16.38

47. How many board feet are there in a beam 18" × 12" × 36'?

   (A) 54 board feet
   (B) 432 board feet
   (C) 648 board feet
   (D) 1296 board feet

48. C purchased six acres of land for $1,800 per acre and divided them into 14 lots which he sold for $1,150 each. His return on the purchase price is most nearly:

   (A) 49%
   (B) 25%
   (C) 18%
   (D) 21%

49. Use the following illustration to answer the question below:

In Section 13, the North one-half sells for $200 per acre, the South one-half sells for $300 per acre. The shaded portion belongs to farmer J. For her to own all of Section 13 she would need:

(A) $56,000
(B) $80,000
(C) $68,000
(D) $104,000

50. B sells a lot for $38,600, or 16 percent over her cost. What is her profit after she pays a six percent commission?

(A) $33,276
(B) $5,324
(C) $2,316
(D) $3,008

GENERAL TEST

PLEASE PRINT THE FOLLOWING:
YOUR NAME

LAST   FIRST   MI

STREET ADDRESS

CITY   STATE   ZIP

TEST CENTER LOCATION (CITY, STATE)

TEST BOOKLET NO.

1ST THREE LETTERS OF LAST NAME

I.D. NUMBER
FROM ADMISSION TICKET OR SCANNABLE APPLICATION

SOCIAL SECURITY NUMBER

TEST CENTER CODE

TEST DATE

JAN   FEB   MAR   APR   MAY   JUN   JUL   AUG   SEP   OCT   NOV   DEC

YR.

HAVE YOU EVER TAKEN THIS EXAMINATION BEFORE?   YES ○   NO ○

FOR WHICH LICENSE ARE YOU TAKING THIS EXAM?   BROKER ○   SALESPERSON ○

WHICH PART OF THE EXAMINATION ARE YOU TAKING?
GENERAL ○   STATE ○   BOTH ○

IN SIGNING BELOW I HEREBY AFFIRM THAT:
I AM THE UNDERSIGNED AND HAVE SIGNED MY CORRECT NAME ON THE SIGNATURE LINE BELOW.
IN ADDITION TO PASSING THE EXAMINATION FOR LICENSURE, I MUST MEET ALL STATE REQUIREMENTS.
I UNDERSTAND ALL EXAMINATION BOOKS ARE SECURE MATERIAL AND THAT NO BOOK OR PORTION THEREOF IS TO BE COPIED, TRANSMITTED TO ANY OTHER PERSON OR REMOVED FROM THE EXAMINATION ROOM.
I WILL NEITHER ASSIST NOR RECEIVE ASSISTANCE FROM ANOTHER CANDIDATE OR USE ANY NOTES, MANUALS OR OTHER AIDS.

SIGNATURE   DATE

Questions 1–80, each with answer choices A B C D.

ANSWERS

1. (C) There are 144 cubic inches in a board foot. 6″ × 6″ × 6″ = 216 cubic inches, or 1½ board feet. *A* and *B* are exactly 1 board foot, not "more than."

2. (D) $500 per month = $6,000 per year.

   .06 of investment = $6,000 per year

   $$\frac{.06X}{.06} = \frac{\$6000}{.06} = \$100,000$$

3. (A) 14 × 43,560 (number of square feet in acre) = 609,840 square feet. To find one dimension of rectangle, divide known dimension into area:

   $$609,840 \div 800 = 762.3$$

4. (C) $90,000 = what is left after 6% of sale price is removed:

   .94% X (sales price) = $90,000

   $$\frac{.94X}{.94} \quad \frac{90,000}{.94}$$

   $$90,000 \div .94 = \$95,744.68$$

5. (B) Since the note was discounted 14% less than face value, it sold for 86% of its value:

   .86X (value) = $9800

   $$\frac{.86X}{.86} = \frac{9800}{.86} = 11395.35$$

6. (B)

   $$\text{Interest Rate} = \frac{\text{Interest earned}}{\text{Principal}}$$

   $$\text{Interest Rate} = \frac{\$132.28 \times 12 \,(\text{for 1 year})}{\$17,835.00}$$

   $$\text{Interest Rate} = \frac{\$1587.36}{\$17,835.00}$$

   $$1587.36 \div 17,835 = .089$$

   Another way to do the problem:

   $$1\% \text{ of } 17,835 = \$178.35 \text{ per year}$$

   $$178.35 \div 12 = 14.86 \text{ per month}$$

How many 1% are there in 132.28?

$$132.28 \div 14.86 = 8.9\%$$

7. (D) 50 feet wide (10 foot setbacks on each side) × 25 feet deep (front setback of 25 feet + rear setback of 20 feet = 45 feet, and 70 feet − 45 feet = 25 feet) = 1250 sq. ft.

8. (A) If there are five acres in the triangle, there would be 10 acres in a rectangle. If we know one dimension of a rectangle (200 feet) and we know the total area (10 acres), we can find the unknown dimension by dividing the known dimension into the total area:

$$10 \times 43,560 = \text{the sq. ft. in 10 acres}$$

$$435,600 \div 200 = 2,178$$

9. (B) To find cubic feet, we multiply length by width times depth:

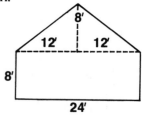

$8' \times 24' = 192$ sq. ft.
Since we have 2 right triangles, each 12' × 8', we have the equivalent of one rectangle 12' × 8' = 96 sq. ft.
192 + 96 = 288
288 × 40 (depth) = 11,520 cubic ft.

10. (B)

$$\text{Principal} = \frac{\text{Interest earned}}{\text{Rate of interest}}$$

$$\text{Principal} = \frac{957.52 \times 12 \text{ (annual interest)}}{.12}$$

$$\text{Principal} = \frac{11,490.24}{.12}$$

$$\text{Principal} = \$95,752.00$$

The problem could also be expressed as:

$$957.52 \times 12 = 11,490.24 \text{ annual interest}$$

$$.12 \text{ of } X \text{ (principal)} = 11,490.24$$

$$\frac{.12X}{.12} = \frac{11,490.24}{.12}$$

$$X = \$95,752.00$$

11. (C)

First year increase $50,000
× .10
$ 5,000

Second year increase $55,000
× .10
$ 5,500

Third year increase $60,500
× .10
$ 6,050

Fourth year increase $66,550
× .10
$ 6,655

$6,655 + 66,550 = $73,205.

12. (C) We must break the structure down into rectangles:

A is 8.5 feet × 24 feet or   204 sq. ft.
B is 33 feet × 52 feet or 1716 sq. ft.
C is 6 feet × 18 feet or   108 sq. ft.
D is 13 feet × 16 feet or   208 sq. ft.
E is 15 feet × 16 feet or   240 sq. ft.
Total 2476

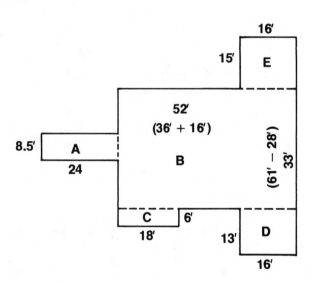

13. (C) For percentage return, we always divide into the net: net ÷ equity.

Equity = $20,000 ($120,000 less $100,000 Mtg)
Net = $20,000 gross less $11,000 (11% of $100,000) or $9,000.
$9,000 ÷ 20,000 = 45%

14. (A) Since there are 36 sections in a township, one-fifth of a section = 7.2 sections, or 7.2 square miles.

15. (C) Prorations are based on twelve 30-day months, or 360 days each year. 334.80 ÷ 360 = $.93 per day. The seller has paid until the end of the year but closing is on the tenth of December. Seller is responsible through the tenth, so the seller is entitled to .93 × 20, or $18.60 credit, and the buyer should be debited for that amount.

16. (D) First we must find the frontage. To do so we divide known dimensions into the total area:

$$\frac{43,560 \times 50}{1000} = 2,178$$

Price paid was 3000 × 50, or $150,000.

150,000 ÷ 2,178 = $68.87/front foot

17. (D) Income was $500 × 10 = $5000. Raising the rents ten percent brings rent to $550, but the 10% vacancy leaves only nine units rented: $550 × 9 = $4,950. $4,950 is $50, or one percent, less than the previous $5,000 gross.

18. (B) To find a percentage return we divide into the net.

He paid $9500 × 2 = $19,000
He sold $8200 × 3 = $24,600
Net = $5,600
$5,600 ÷ 19,000 = 29.47%

19. (C) 100' × 6' + 54' × 6' = 924 square feet. (We don't want to count the corner area twice)

20. (B) 100 × 6 + 60 × 6 + 6 × 6. We don't want to miss the corner.

21. (D) 18' × 30' = 540 square feet. 4 inches thick is one-third of a foot, so the driveway would take one-third of 540 cubic feet: 540 ÷ 3 = 180 cubic feet.

Since there are 27 cubic feet in a cubic yard, 180 ÷ 27 = 6.6 yards (but you would need seven yards).

22. (A) There are 36 sections in a township, so one-sixtieth of the township equals one-sixtieth of the 36 sections: 36 ÷ 60 = .60 = 60%.

23. (D) Because cash flow is net spendable, we deduct all cash expenses. Since depreciation is not a cash expense, it is not deducted.

24. (C)   Paid $9,000 × 1.40 (listed at 40% more than paid) =
$12,600 (list price) × .30 = $3,780 reduction.
12,600 −3,780 = $8,820 (sale price) × .07 commission = $617.40 commission
$8820 − $617.40 = $8,202.60
Loss of $794.40

25. (A)

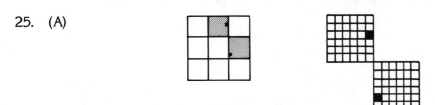

26. (D) 348,480 square yards × 9 (number of square feet in a square yard) = 3,136,320 square feet

Divide by number of square feet in an acre:

3,136,320 ÷ 43,560 = 72 acres

27. (D) Each inch would equal 4 feet, so 10½ inches = 42' and 3½ inches = 14':

42 × 14 = 588 square feet

There are 9 square feet in a square yard, so:

588 ÷ 9 = 65.33 yards.
65.33 × 3.80 = 248.25

28. (B) A cubic foot is 12" × 12" × 12". The footing is 1½' wide and ½' thick. Each linear foot of footing contains ¾ of a cubic foot of concrete (if it were 1' thick it would contain 1½ cubic feet per linear foot).

168 × .75 = 126 cubic feet
126 ÷ 27 = 4.66 cubic yards

29. (B)   90' × 60' = 5400 square feet
5,400 ÷ 9 = 600 square yards
60% of 600 = 360
360 × $16 = $5760
40% of 600 = 240
240 × $8 = $1920
Total = $7680

30. (B) The two side lots have 12,800 and 9,600 square feet or a total of 22,400 square feet. The depth is 160'. Frontage is 22,400 ÷ 160 = 140'. With the 80' of the central lot, the combined total is 220'.

31. (C) The church received 12 percent of his estate.

$$12\% \text{ of estate} = \$79,000$$

$$\frac{.12X}{.12} = \frac{\$79,000}{.12} = \$658,333.33 \text{ (value of estate)}$$

Daughter's share is 18% of $658,333.33, or $118,499.99

32. (D) There are 640 acres in a section, so three sections = 1,920 acres.

$$1,920 \div 20 = 96 \text{ 20-acre parcels}$$

16 sold at $4,000 each = $ 64,000
80 sold at $5,000 each = $ 400,000

Total = $464,000

33. (B)
$1200.22 × 12 (months) = $14,402.64 × 15 years = total payments of $216,039.60
$1028.63 × 12 = $12,343.56 × 30 years = $370,306.80
370,306 ÷ 216,039 = 171.4%

34. (B) Since she made nine percent at $400,000, the net income was .09 × $400,000 or $36,000. A 12% return = 36,000 ÷ .12 = $300,000

35. (D) $144 for 36 months = $4 per month. Based on a 30-day month, the cost is .133 per day. The used portion of the policy (4 months + 3 days) = $16.40. The unused portion of $127.60 should be credited to the seller and debited from the buyer.

36. (C) The equity is $25,000:

$$\$107,000 \text{ value} - 82,000 \text{ loan} = \$25,000$$

To find percentage return we divide into the net:

$$10,000 \div 25,000 = .40 \text{ or } 40\%$$

37. (C) Total cost of all five = $573,400:

$82,500 ÷ 573,400 = 14.387% of total
3,850 × .14387 = 553.89 yearly share
553.89 ÷ 12 = $46.16 monthly share

38. (B) $1030.88 × 12 (per year) × 30 = $371,116.80
Principal   −90,000.00
Interest = $281,116.80

$$281,116.80 \div 100,000 = 2.81, \text{ or } 281\%$$

39. (C) A term loan is interest payments only.

$$\text{Time} = \frac{\text{Interest earned}}{\text{Principal} \times \text{rate}}$$

$$\text{Time} = \frac{42.60}{800 \times .08}$$

$$\text{Time} = \frac{42.60}{64}$$

Time = .666 years or 8 months.

40.   (A) 12% per annum is one percent per month. $923.18 is one percent of $92,318.

$$\text{OR Principal} = \frac{\text{Interest earned}}{\text{Rate of interest}}$$

$$\text{Principal} = \frac{923.18 \times 12\,(1\text{ year})}{.12}$$

$$\text{Principal} = \frac{11078.16}{.12} = \$92,318$$

41.   (B)   6,400 ÷ .40 = 16,000 square feet.
16,000 ÷ 200 = 80' wide
6,400 ÷ 80 = $80 per front foot

42.   (C) $9600 × 8% = $768 per year
768 ÷ 4 = $192 (quarterly payment)

43.   (C)   810 × 12 = $9720 (annual net)

9720 = 7.5% value

$$\frac{9720}{.075} = \frac{.075X}{.075}$$

9,720 ÷ .075 = $129,600

44.   (B)   14%X = $820
$$\frac{.14X}{.14} = \frac{820}{.14}$$

820 ÷ .14 = $5857

5857 = 130% of the cost
$$\frac{5857}{1.3} = \frac{1.3X}{1.3}$$

$5857 ÷ 1.3 = $4505.38

45.   (C) Net is 30% of 64,000 or $19,200.

$19,200 ÷ .11 = $174,545.

46. (A)
$$40' \times 60' \times 8' = 19{,}200 \text{ cubic feet}$$
$$19{,}200 \times \$1.40 = \$26{,}880$$
$$\text{Total sq. ft.: } 40' \times 60' = 2{,}400$$
$$26{,}880 \div 2400 = \$11.20$$

47. (C) $18'' \times 12'' \times 432'' \, (36' \times 12) = 93{,}312$ cubic inches

$$93{,}312 \div 144 = 648 \text{ board feet}$$

You might be able to conceptualize that each foot in length contains 18 board feet.

48. (A)
$$\$1150 \times 14 = \$16{,}100 \text{ sale price}$$
$$\$1800 \times 6 = \$10{,}800 \text{ purchase price}$$
$$\$16{,}100 - \$10{,}800 = \$5{,}300 \text{ profit}$$

To find the percentage return on the purchase price, divide purchase price into the net:

$$\$5{,}300 \div 10{,}800 = .49, \text{ or } 49\%$$

49. (C) Each square shown is ¼ of ¼ Section or 40 acres. Since a right triangle contains ½ of a rectangle the triangle in the Northwest corner contains 20 acres and the one in the Northeast corner contains 80 acres. Total of 100 acres in the North at $200/acre or $20,000. The two triangles in the South half each contain 80 acres or 160 total at $300 per acre or $48,000. $20,000 + $48,000 = $68,000.

50. (D)
$$38{,}600 = 116\% \text{ of cost}$$

$$\frac{38{,}600}{1.16} = \frac{1.16}{1.16} \text{ cost}$$

$$\text{Cost} = \$33{,}275.86$$

$$
\begin{array}{ll}
\$38{,}600.00 & \text{sale price} \\
-\ 33{,}275.86 & \text{cost} \\
\hline
\$\ 5{,}324.14 & \text{gross profit} \\
-\ 2{,}316.00 & (6\% \text{ of } \$38{,}600) \\
\hline
\$\ 3{,}008.14 & \text{profit}
\end{array}
$$

EIGHT
REVIEW TESTS

TEST A

1. Which of the following would **NOT** be a cost disclosed under the Real Estate Settlement Procedures Act?

    (A) An appraisal fee
    (B) Costs for a credit report
    (C) Loan points
    (D) Costs for the RESPA report

2. Which method would be used by real estate brokers in estimating the value of a single-family residence?

    (A) Cost approach
    (B) Income approach
    (C) Market comparison approach
    (D) Gross multiplier

3. Failing to assert a right within a reasonable period of time might lead a court to determine that the right to assert it is lost because of:

    (A) laches
    (B) novation
    (C) rescission
    (D) reformation

4. An appraiser received figures from a CPA on past rent receipts and operating expenses. The appraiser should:

    (A) use the figures to determine the net
    (B) adjust the figures for future occurrences
    (C) use the figures but add depreciation as an expense
    (D) use the figures provided after their verification

5. Which of the following would **ALWAYS** be found by searching county records?

    (A) Encroachments
    (B) Rights of parties in possession
    (C) Inaccurate surveys
    (D) Mechanics' liens

6. An election of remedies is commonly found in:

    (A) purchase agreements
    (B) options
    (C) settlement statements
    (D) unilateral contracts

7. An individual who owns a living unit and the land under it, plus a share in a common recreation area owns part of a:

    (A) standard subdivision
    (B) planned development project
    (C) cooperative
    (D) condominium

8. A limited partner is **ALWAYS:**

    (A) an active partner
    (B) liable for debts beyond the investment
    (C) limited as to profits received
    (D) limited as to liability

9. *Definite duration* refers to:

    (A) a life estate
    (B) an estate for years
    (C) an estate at will
    (D) a periodic tenancy

10. What advantage does a real estate investor have over an investor in stocks?

    (A) Appreciation
    (B) Capital gains
    (C) Liquidity
    (D) Depreciation

11. An appraiser has the most difficulty in determining the:

    (A) cost new
    (B) cost basis
    (C) net income
    (D) accrued depreciation

12. During a tight money market, the highest cash yield would most likely be from investing in:

    (A) a money market account
    (B) existing well-secured second mortgages
    (C) income property
    (D) a mutual stock fund

13. A broker allowed a person to appear to act as her agent. She cannot now deny the agency because of:

    (A) ratification
    (B) estoppel
    (C) subrogation
    (D) reformation

14. What is ground rent?

    (A) A separate rent for the land and improvements
    (B) A rental of unimproved land, with improvements by lessee
    (C) That portion of the rent attributable to the land alone
    (D) A lease where lessee pays a net amount for the land plus all expenses

15. A broker's client is customarily:

    (A) the owner of listed property
    (B) a prospective purchaser
    (C) an owner of a property the broker hopes to list
    (D) the owner of a property listed by another which the broker has sold

16. Who would most likely discount a mortgage?

    (A) Mortgagor
    (B) Mortgagee
    (C) A subsequent purchaser
    (D) A private insurer

17. Which of the following parcels of land is the **SMALLEST?**

    (A) 2,640' × 165'
    (B) 660' × 660'
    (C) 5,280' × 80'
    (D) 1,320' × 330'

18. A subdivider who does not have a real estate license hires a broker to sell his property. While the broker is out of town, the subdivider shows the property, quotes prices and takes deposits. His actions:

    (A) place the broker in jeopardy, since he is acting as an unlicensed salesperson
    (B) cannot be compensated by the broker
    (C) have made him subject to disciplinary action by the Department of Real Estate
    (D) were entirely proper

19. A former use continuing in contravention of new zoning is:

    (A) a variance
    (B) incentive zoning
    (C) a nonconforming use
    (D) illegal

20. Which of the following would command the highest loan-to-value-ratio loan?

    (A) A single-family residence
    (B) Agricultural land
    (C) Residential lot
    (D) Commercial property

21. What is the front footage of a rectangular lot with 200' on one side and an apartment worth $193,600, which is equivalent to $4.40 per square foot for the lot?

    (A) 110'
    (B) 220'
    (C) 400'
    (D) 880'

22. Which of the following is **NOT** a specific lien?

    (A) An unrecorded property tax lien
    (B) A mechanic's lien
    (C) A judgment lien
    (D) A blanket mortgage

23. Broker A listed widow B's property for an eight percent commission. After the sale, widow B discovered that broker A had been listing similar property at a six percent commission. Based on these facts:

(A) broker A has done nothing wrong
(B) broker A can lose his license
(C) widow B can recover from the state Recovery Fund
(D) widow B is entitled to a refund

24. A tenant on a long-term commercial lease wants to go out of business. Since the rent is worth much more than the current tenant is paying, she should consider:

(A) assigning the lease
(B) subletting the property
(C) asking the owner to rescind the lease
(D) surrendering the premises

25. A broker would not have to show he was the procuring cause in:

(A) an exclusive right to sell listing
(B) an exclusive agency listing
(C) an open listing
(D) a net listing

26. A corporate officer's authority to make an offer can be checked in the:

(A) corporate charter
(B) corporation code
(C) corporate bylaws
(D) state Department of Corporations regulations

27. $142 is paid over an eight-month period on a $2,400 straight note. What is the interest rate?

(A) Between 7½% and 8%
(B) Between 8% and 8½%
(C) Between 8½% and 9%
(D) Between 9% and 9½%

28. Which of the following is NOT an encumbrance on real property?

(A) Lease
(B) Easement
(C) Homestead right
(D) Restrictive covenant

29. Which of the following is an example of down zoning?

(A) Height limitations
(B) Zoning from single-family to multiple-family use
(C) Zoning from multiple-family to single-family use
(D) Zoning designed to encourage redevelopment

30. A broker purchased her own listing because she knew of a purchaser who would pay more than the listing price. The broker:

(A) may never purchase one of her own listings
(B) has done nothing wrong if she never misrepresented the value
(C) acted properly if she revealed the offer was hers
(D) is liable to the owner for the profit made

31. Even though the agreement does not specify it, a homeseller can generally remove:

(A) sprinkler heads that unscrew from the underground system
(B) prize rose bushes
(C) the freestanding fireplace screen
(D) the almost-new garbage disposal

32. The primary purpose of real estate licensing statutes is to:

(A) have well trained professionals
(B) protect brokers against incompetent salespeople
(C) avoid cutthroat competition
(D) protect the public

33. The capitalization rate does not provide for:

(A) depreciation
(B) property taxes
(C) return on the investment
(D) return of the investment

34. An exclusive agency may NOT be terminated:

(A) before its expiration date
(B) by the principal when the broker is making the principal's payments to avoid foreclosure
(C) if the broker has been using diligent effort
(D) unilaterally by agent or principal

35. To fence the North ½ of the North ½ of the SE ¼ of a Section would take how much fencing?

   (A) 1 mile
   (B) 1¼ mile
   (C) 2 miles
   (D) 3,960 feet

36. Which of the following is an example of blockbusting?

   (A) Refusal to sell or rent to prospects because of race
   (B) Refusal to lend within a designated area
   (C) Soliciting listings based on a fear of racial change in the area
   (D) Directing people to areas based on race

37. Estimating total land value and adding the value of the improvements:

   (A) tends to set the upper limit of value
   (B) tends to set the lower limit of value
   (C) is not appropriate for newer construction
   (D) is the best method for appraisal of residential property

38. Which of the following may a broker properly disclose to a prospective purchaser without permission?

   (A) Why the seller must conclude a sale
   (B) Why the property is not desirable
   (C) What the owner will actually accept
   (D) What the owner originally paid

39. An investment property worth $180,000 was purchased seven years ago for $142,000. At the time of purchase, the land was valued at $18,000. Assuming a 30-year life for straight-line depreciation, what is the present book value of the property?

   (A) $139,140
   (B) $95,071
   (C) $113,071
   (D) $132,426

40. A broker is prohibited from accepting a listing from a minor because:

   (A) a minor cannot appoint an agent
   (B) of the Statute of Frauds
   (C) of the Statute of Limitations
   (D) of laches

41. If $192.50 is paid over a five-month period on a $3,000 straight mortgage, the interest rate is:

   (A) more than 8 percent, but less than 10 percent
   (B) more than 10 percent, but less than 12 percent
   (C) more than 12 percent, but less than 14 percent
   (D) more than 14 percent, but less than 16 percent

42. The Federal Fair Housing Act is enforced by bringing complaints to:

   (A) Federal Housing Administration
   (B) HUD
   (C) U.S. Court of Appeals
   (D) U.S. Department of Commerce

43. Treatment of nonconforming uses under new zoning does not include:

   (A) a prohibition on expansion
   (B) a prohibition on rebuilding
   (C) a time period for cessation
   (D) immediate closure

44. A farmer died owning the farm as a joint tenant with his son. The farmer had personal debts of over $25,000 and no assets other than his share of the farm. Which of the following is true?

   (A) The farmer's creditors can reach the farm.
   (B) The son is liable for the debts, since he is the heir.
   (C) The son is liable for the debt because he is the son.
   (D) The son owns the farm and has no obligation for his father's debt.

45. Which of the following is NOT done under the police power of the state?

   (A) Control land use
   (B) Control rents
   (C) Collect taxes
   (D) Condemn as unfit for occupancy

46. Which sections are contiguous to Section 7 in a township?

    (A) 12 and 17
    (B) 6 and 19
    (C) 8 and 16
    (D) 8 and 14

47. How would you best describe blackened area within the section shown?

    (A) NE ¼ of NE ¼ of SW ¼
    (B) N ½ of E ½ of NE ¼
    (C) SW ¼ of NE ¼ of NE ¼
    (D) SW ¼ of NW ¼ of NW ¼

48. "It would not be an appurtenance" describes which of the following?

    (A) Easement rights
    (B) Mineral rights
    (C) Water rights
    (D) Trade fixtures

49. Which of the following is **FALSE** regarding an option?

    (A) Consideration is necessary for a valid option.
    (B) Optionee has a legal right of use until the option expires.
    (C) An option is assignable unless prohibited.
    (D) Optionee has the option to refrain from exercising the option.

50. If the number 12 on a clock were placed facing North, then the description N60°W would be:

    (A) 2 o'clock
    (B) 10 o'clock
    (C) 6 o'clock
    (D) 9 o'clock

51. A commercial property was purchased for $85,000 and has depreciated down to $28,000. If it is sold for $75,000, there is a:

    (A) $10,000 taxable loss
    (B) $47,000 taxable gain
    (C) $18,800 taxable gain
    (D) $28,200 taxable gain

52. A major distinction between a planned unit development and a condominium is:

    (A) fee simple ownership
    (B) ownership of land
    (C) common area ownership
    (D) transferability of interests

53. Real estate title information is best found in the records of the:

    (A) secretary of state
    (B) county recorder
    (C) tax assessor
    (D) vendor

54. Which of the following is **NOT** required of all valid contracts?

    (A) In writing
    (B) Mutual agreement
    (C) Lawful object
    (D) Competent parties

55. G leased a commercial building to S for ten years. After six months, S moved out without notice. G advertised for a tenant. G's actions most likely relate to:

    (A) liquidated damages
    (B) mitigation of damages
    (C) punitive damages
    (D) severance damages

56. The recording of instruments which transfer or encumber real property has all of the following effects **EXCEPT**:

    (A) giving notice of the contents of the instrument
    (B) creating the presumption of delivery
    (C) preventing the creation of any priority liens
    (D) giving priority over subsequently recorded instruments

57. A voidable contract is:

    (A) unenforceable
    (B) illegal
    (C) void
    (D) valid until voided

58. Replacement cost is for:

    (A) the identical structure
    (B) the identical structure using modern materials
    (C) an equally desirable property with the same utility value
    (D) the most economical structure having the same utility value

59. A 660' × 660' parcel contains what percentage of the land contained in a 1320' × 1320' parcel?

    (A) 50
    (B) 25
    (C) 33⅓
    (D) 42½

60. A broker has just received a full-price offer on one of her own listings. Minutes later she receives an identical offer from another office. How should she proceed with the presentation of the offers?

    (A) The broker should present them in the order they were received.
    (B) All offers should be presented at the same time.
    (C) The broker should present the first offer, but inform the owner about the duplicate offer.
    (D) The broker should recommend acceptance of the first offer as the primary offer and the second offer as a backup offer in case there are any problems with the first buyer.

61. A lender might make an FHA or VA loan rather than a conventional loan because of:

    (A) the lower risk
    (B) the higher interest
    (C) the longer investment period
    (D) the federal tax benefits

62. Which of the following statements as to depreciation is **NOT** true?

    (A) Not all capital assets can be depreciated.
    (B) Depreciation can consider the life of the property.
    (C) Depreciation can be deferred and taken in a higher-income year.
    (D) An asset which has been appreciating can be depreciated.

63. Ripping down a hotel to build an office building is an example of the principle of:

    (A) highest and best use
    (B) conformity
    (C) progression
    (D) change

64. An option does not become a binding contract upon both parties until the:

    (A) consideration is paid
    (B) option is signed by both parties
    (C) expiration of the option period
    (D) option is exercised

65. A rectangular lot has 90' frontage and is 140' deep. The building setbacks are 15' front, 30' rear and 10' on the sides. The maximum square footage of a three-story building would be:

    (A) 13,500 square feet
    (B) 12,600 square feet
    (C) 6,650 square feet
    (D) 19,950 square feet

66. A limited partner may **NOT**:

    (A) demand an accounting
    (B) participate in management
    (C) share in the profits
    (D) retain limited liability

67. A broker is instructed not to show a property while the owner, a white, is away. While the owner is out of town, a black couple requests to be shown the property. The broker should:

    (A) show the property
    (B) refuse to show the property
    (C) ask HUD for an exception to the Fair Housing Act
    (D) inform the prospects that the home is not available

68. A party would **NOT** receive constructive notice by:

    (A) finding a stranger in possession
    (B) discovering that a stranger has a recorded deed
    (C) knowing a stranger has an unrecorded deed
    (D) seeing utility poles on the property

69. A verbal agreement between brokers to split commissions is:

    (A) enforceable
    (B) void because of the Statute of Frauds
    (C) legal but unenforceable
    (D) voidable

70. A property is bought based on fraudulent statements by the listing broker. The sales contract is:

    (A) void
    (B) voidable
    (C) valid
    (D) illegal

71. A corporate seal on a deed:

    (A) guarantees the title
    (B) creates a presumption of delivery
    (C) creates a presumption of authority
    (D) indicates corporate board approval

72. A written agreement whereby the seller agreed to convey title to a house for $80,000 and the buyer agreed to purchase the house for $80,000, with the sale to be completed within 30 days, is:

    (A) an express unilateral executory contract
    (B) an express bilateral executory contract
    (C) an express bilateral executed contract
    (D) a valid bilateral implied executory contract

73. What authority is responsible for compliance with federal disclosure requirements in interstate land sales?

    (A) Federal Trade Commission
    (B) Real Estate Commissioner of each state
    (C) Department of Housing and Urban Development
    (D) U.S Attorney General

74. What do topographical lines on maps indicate?

    (A) Rivers
    (B) Contours
    (C) Longitude and latitude
    (D) Roads

75. Which of the following acts is **NOT** an example of constructive eviction?

    (A) Discontinuing required utilities
    (B) Making modifications that make the property unsuitable for the purpose it was rented for
    (C) Making constant unnecessary repairs which interfere with the tenant's quiet enjoyment of the premises
    (D) Serving the tenant with an unlawful detainer action

76. The most likely action for a vendor to take when the vendee under a land contract defaults is to:

    (A) file a lis pendens
    (B) file a quiet title action
    (C) sue for damages
    (D) order the trustee to foreclose

77. A buyer discovers that the neighbor's fence is 3 feet inside her property line, and the neighbor refuses to move it. The buyer's best action is to:

    (A) sue the broker for misrepresentation
    (B) sue the broker and neighbor for not disclosing the true boundary
    (C) move the fence themselves
    (D) sue the neighbor for corrective action

78. A tight money market would **NOT** result in an increase in:

    (A) interest rates
    (B) buyer points on conventional loans
    (C) buyer points on VA-purchase loans
    (D) down-payment requirements

79. Which remedy would be most effective for a property owner whose request for rezoning has been refused by the city planning commission?

    (A) Asking the court for a writ requiring the planning commission to approve the request
    (B) A suit against the planning commission for damages
    (C) Disregarding the planning commission because they acted arbitrarily
    (D) Appealing to the city council or zoning appeals board

80. At closing the lender requests $280 which will be kept in a trust fund. This money is:

    (A) a security deposit
    (B) for taxes and insurance
    (C) to insure against default
    (D) to cover points

GENERAL TEST

PLEASE PRINT THE FOLLOWING:
YOUR NAME

LAST   FIRST   MI

STREET ADDRESS

CITY   STATE   ZIP

TEST CENTER LOCATION (CITY, STATE)

TEST BOOKLET NO.

1ST THREE LETTERS OF LAST NAME	I.D. NUMBER FROM ADMISSION TICKET OR SCANNABLE APPLICATION	SOCIAL SECURITY NUMBER	TEST CENTER CODE	TEST DATE

TEST DATE: JAN, FEB, MAR, APR, MAY, JUN, JUL, AUG, SEP, OCT, NOV, DEC / YR.

HAVE YOU EVER TAKEN THIS EXAMINATION BEFORE?   YES ○   NO ○

FOR WHICH LICENSE ARE YOU TAKING THIS EXAM?   BROKER ○   SALESPERSON ○

WHICH PART OF THE EXAMINATION ARE YOU TAKING?
GENERAL ○   STATE ○   BOTH ○

IN SIGNING BELOW I HEREBY AFFIRM THAT:
I AM THE UNDERSIGNED AND HAVE SIGNED MY CORRECT NAME ON THE SIGNATURE LINE BELOW.
IN ADDITION TO PASSING THE EXAMINATION FOR LICENSURE, I MUST MEET ALL STATE REQUIREMENTS.
I UNDERSTAND ALL EXAMINATION BOOKS ARE SECURE MATERIAL AND THAT NO BOOK OR PORTION THEREOF IS TO BE COPIED, TRANSMITTED TO ANY OTHER PERSON OR REMOVED FROM THE EXAMINATION ROOM.
I WILL NEITHER ASSIST NOR RECEIVE ASSISTANCE FROM ANOTHER CANDIDATE OR USE ANY NOTES, MANUALS OR OTHER AIDS.

SIGNATURE   DATE

Questions 1–80, each with answer choices A B C D

PLEASE TURN TO REVERSE SIDE FOR STATE TEST.

ANSWERS: TEST A

1. (D) The lender cannot charge for the RESPA disclosure statement.

2. (C) Brokers make a competitive market analysis using this method. It is the best method for single-family residences.

3. (A) If, because of the delay, another party acted to their detriment, it would not be equitable to allow enforcement of the right.

4. (B) The appraiser must forecast future income and expenses. Depreciation is normally considered in the capitalization rate.

5. (D) Mechanics' liens must be recorded to have any effect. Others would be discovered by checking the property.

6. (A) The parties agree to the remedy in the event of breach. Liquidated damages in the amount of the deposit or the right to sue for actual damages.

7. (B) Condominium owners do not own the land.

8. (D) A limited partner cannot be active and has limited liability.

9. (B) Since it is a lease for a definite period.

10. (D) Real property improvements can be depreciated to shelter other income from taxation.

11. (D) Must determine both the economic life and the effective age of the property.

12. (B) They could be purchased at a discount to offer an exceptional yield.

13. (B) She is barred from now denying the existence of the agency. Ratification is forming an agency by approving an unauthorized act.

14. (C)

15. (A) The broker represents the principal (client).

16. (B) The mortgagee discounts the mortgage by selling it on the secondary mortgage market for less than the face amount.

17. (C) $2640' \times 165' = 435,600$ sq. ft. = 10 acres
    $660' \times 660' = 435,600$ sq. ft. = 10 acres
    $5280' \times 80' = 422,400$ sq. ft. = 9.7 acres
    $1320' \times 330' = 435,600$ sq. ft. = 10 acres

18. (D) A person need not be licensed to sell his or her own property.

19. (C) Zoning cannot be retroactive, so nonconforming use is allowed to continue.

20. (A) Up to 95 percent of appraised value from a federal savings & loan.

21. (B) 193,600 ÷ 4.40 = 44000 sq. ft.
44,000 ÷ 200 = 220′

22. (C) A judgment lien is a general lien covering all of the debtor's property in the county where recorded.

23. (A) Commission is negotiable between owner and broker.

24. (B) This way she could make money on a rental differential.

25. (A) He has earned the commission no matter who sold it. In the others the problem of procuring cause could arise.

26. (C) Bylaws show corporate authority of officers.

27. (C)

$$\text{Interest Rate} = \frac{\text{Interest Earned}}{\text{Principal}}$$

$$142 \div 8 = {}^\$17.75 \text{ per month}$$

$${}^\$17.75 \times 12 = {}^\$213/\text{year}$$

$$\text{Rate} = \frac{213}{2400} = 8.875\%$$

28. (C) Homestead rights do not encumber use or title.

29. (C) To a less-intensive use.

30. (D) She violated her fiduciary responsibility. She had a duty to inform the owner about the buyer. She also made a secret profit.

31. (C) This is personal property. The other items are clearly fixtures.

32. (D)

33. (B) This is an expense that reduces the net.

34. (B) While normally either principal or agent can terminate at will (although possibly subject to damages), an exception is an agency coupled with an interest.

35. (B) The SE ¼ has ½ mile on each side. The North ½ would therefore be ¼ miles by ½ mile. The North ½ of that would be ⅛ of a mile wide. So 2 sides at ⅛ mile each = ¼ mile and 2 sides at ½ mile = 1 mile.

36. (C) B is redlining and D is steering.

37. (A) This is the reproduction cost approach.

38. (B) Broker must disclose all detrimental facts. Others breach confidentiality of the agency.

39. (C) Book value is cost less depreciation. We only depreciate improvements, so:

$$\$142,000 - \$18,000 \text{ land} = \$124,000.$$
$$100\% \div 30 \text{ years} = 3.333\% \text{ per year}$$
$$3.333 \times 7 \text{ years} = 23.33\%$$
$$23.33\% \times \$124,000 = \$28,929 \text{ depreciation}$$
$$\$124,000 - 28,929 = \$95,071$$
$$\$95,071 + \$18,000 \text{ (land)} = \$113,071.$$

40. (A) A person cannot appoint an agent to do what the person cannot legally do himself or herself.

41. (D)

$$\text{Interest rate} = \frac{\text{Interest earned}}{\text{Principal}}$$

$$\$192.50 \text{ earned for 5 months}$$
$$\$192.50 \div 5 = \$38.50 \text{ per month}$$
$$\$38.50 \times 12 \text{ months} = \$462 \text{ (1 year's return)}$$

$$\text{Rate} = \frac{462}{3000} = 15.4\%$$

42. (B) Or filing a civil action in the Federal District Court or contacting the U.S. Attorney General.

43. (D) Zoning is never retroactive. Others are acceptable limitations.

44. (D) Property in joint tenancy passes free of the debts of the former joint tenant.

45. (C) Tax authority is separate from police power, as is eminent domain.

46. (A) Section 12 is West in the adjoining township and Section 17 touches on its Southeast corner.

47. (C)

48. (D) Trade fixtures do not go with the land. They remain the personal property of the lessee.

49. (B) Optionee has no rights of use or of title until the option has been exercised.

50. (B) Since there are 360° in a circle, there would be 30° for each hour.

51. (B) Gain is the difference between sale price ($75,000) and cost base ($28,000).

52. (B) A condominium owner does not own the land under the unit.

53. (B) County recorder keeps all records of recorded title transfers and liens. (Most states)

54. (A) Only contracts specified by the Statute of Frauds need be in writing. There can be valid verbal contracts.

55. (B) Using reasonable efforts to reduce damages caused by the breach.

56. (C) Taxes are a lien which take priority regardless of what has been recorded.

57. (D) Only one party can void the contract.

58. (C) Because construction methods and styles change.

59. (B) It is ¼ of a 40-acre parcel.

60. (B) And any recommendation should be based upon the best interests of the client.

61. (A) Because of FHA insurance or VA guarantee.

62. (C) Depreciation not taken is lost.

63. (A) That use which provides the greatest net.

64. (D) Until it is exercised, optionee is not bound to buy.

65. (D) Buildable area is 95' × 70', or 6650 square feet × 3.

66. (B) Must be an inactive partner to retain limited liability.

67. (B) Broker must obey legal instructions of owner. Instructions were reasonable and not racially restrictive.

68. (C) This is actual notice.

69. (A) An exception to the Statute of Frauds.

70. (B) At the option of the buyer.

71. (C) Burden of proof is on the corporation to show that there was no authority.

72. (B) Stated (express) promise for a promise (bilateral) not yet performed (executory).

73. (C) Office of Interstate Land Sales Registration (OILSR) (Part of HUD).

74. (B) Lines close together indicate a steep slope; far apart means level.

75. (D) This is actual, not constructive, eviction.

76. (B) To determine the rights of the parties.

77. (D) To remove their encroachment.

78. (C) Sellers pay the points on VA loans.

79. (D) You must exhaust your administrative remedies before you can go to the courts.

80. (B) An impound account for taxes and insurance.

TEST B

1. Functional obsolescence can be created by:

   (A) deterioration of the driveway
   (B) an overimprovement
   (C) a land use not in conformance with the area
   (D) forces outside the property itself

2. *Tacking on* would most likely refer to:

   (A) an addition to a structure
   (B) an additional party to a document
   (C) obtaining an easement by prescription
   (D) an amendment to a purchase contract

3. The Statute of Frauds does **NOT** cover:

   (A) leases over one year
   (B) agreements that cannot be performed within one year
   (C) commission agreements between brokers
   (D) a promise to be liable for the debts of another

4. To find the square footage of a square 40-acre parcel, multiply:

   (A) 40' × 5,280'
   (B) 2,640' × 2,640'
   (C) 1,320' × 1,320'
   (D) 5,280' × 5,280' × 40'

5. The broker most certain to earn a commission has:

   (A) received an acceptance of an offer
   (B) notified the buyer of the seller's acceptance
   (C) received an offer substantially in accordance with the listing
   (D) received a full price offer on an open listing

6. In 1968, a 1,500-square-foot house was built for $25 a square foot. Since then the construction cost index has increased from 1.748 to 3.436. What would it cost to build the same house today?

   (A) $75,000
   (B) $73,710
   (C) $76,350
   (D) $40,350

7. A listing cannot be terminated by the principal when:

   (A) the agent has not breached the agreement
   (B) the listing has not expired
   (C) an offer has been received
   (D) the agent has an interest coupled with the agency

8. The Federal Fair Housing Act does **NOT:**

   (A) prohibit steering
   (B) provide minimum housing standards
   (C) prohibit blockbusting
   (D) prohibit sex discrimination

9. How long does a purchaser have to rescind a purchase subject to the Interstate Land Sales Act?

   (A) 48 hours after receipt of property report
   (B) within 7 days of closing
   (C) within 14 days of closing
   (D) until the buyer has approved the property report

10. A broker with an open listing can help protect her commission by:

    (A) notifying the other brokers in the area of her prospect's name
    (B) notifying the owner in writing that she is negotiating with a particular prospect
    (C) notifying the prospect that any purchase must be made through her
    (D) registering her prospect with the local real estate board

11. In using the market comparison approach, the appraiser assumes:

    (A) anticipated future income is more important than present income
    (B) no two properties are identical
    (C) the cost to reproduce now is more important than the original cost
    (D) risk will affect the capitalization rate

12. A five-acre rectangular parcel is divided into six equal lots, each having a depth of 250'. The width of each lot is approximately:

    (A) 871.2'
    (B) 145.2'
    (C) 174.24'
    (D) 208.7'

13. What provision characterizes a purchase-money mortgage?

    (A) It takes precedence over liens that are against the purchaser at time of sale.
    (B) Secondary financing is outlawed.
    (C) It has priority over all other liens.
    (D) It is always a first mortgage.

14. Recording does **NOT** give:

    (A) constructive notice
    (B) actual notice
    (C) a presumption of delivery
    (D) priority as to the interest

15. Checking a bank statement against records is known as:

    (A) balancing the books
    (B) reconciling
    (C) invoicing
    (D) recording

16. Cost base is **NOT** affected by:

    (A) purchase costs
    (B) improvements
    (C) interest expense
    (D) broker's commission

17. The broker least affected by a tight-money market specializes in:

    (A) trades
    (B) commercial property
    (C) single-family homes
    (D) second homes

18. Which of the following loans is certainly assumable?

    (A) One insured by FHA
    (B) One insured by PMI
    (C) A conventional loan
    (D) One made through a mortgage loan broker

19. A datum plane is used by:

    (A) appraisers
    (B) bankers
    (C) surveyors
    (D) carpenters

20. A right to buy only if the owner decides to sell is:

    (A) a right of option
    (B) a right of first refusal
    (C) an unaccepted offer
    (D) a nontransferable right

21. In lieu of a loan, a lender purchased a property and leased it back to the seller, who was given a right to repurchase. This arrangement is:

    (A) illegal
    (B) an all-inclusive deed of trust
    (C) a sale-lease back
    (D) usury

22. A broker should not tell a prospective purchaser:

    (A) about property defects he was told about by a neighbor
    (B) about zoning that makes the present use non-conforming
    (C) that people of a different race live next door
    (D) that the area has been designated for urban renewal

23. Witnessing a document is known as:

    (A) attestation
    (B) acknowledgment
    (C) verification
    (D) affirmation

24. A state homestead exemption protects a homeowner against:

    (A) a tax lien
    (B) a mechanic's lien
    (C) a second mortgage
    (D) an unsecured creditor about to obtain a judgment

25. Which of the following is an estate of inheritance?

    (A) Joint tenancy
    (B) Life estate
    (C) Fee simple estate
    (D) General partnership interest

26. Which of the following is a freehold interest?

    (A) Life estate
    (B) Estate for years
    (C) Estate at will
    (D) Periodic tenancy

27. A broker member of the National Association of Real Estate Brokers is:

    (A) a Realtor®
    (B) a Realtist
    (C) an associate broker
    (D) an associate member

28. Before a tenant can move into a newly completed building:

    (A) the builder must supply lien waivers
    (B) the lender must approve
    (C) an occupancy permit must be obtained
    (D) all work must be completed

29. An offer that fails to specify a definite period for acceptance:

    (A) must be accepted immediately or it lapses
    (B) cannot be accepted because it lacks definiteness
    (C) is valid for a reasonable period of time
    (D) remains valid for the statutory limit

30. A straight nine percent loan at 75 percent of a property's appraised value earned first year's interest of $9,840. What was the property's valuation?

    (A) $109,333
    (B) $145,777
    (C) $82,000
    (D) $96,840

31. An easement in gross:

    (A) is attached to a person, not a property
    (B) is always a negative easement
    (C) must have a definite termination date
    (D) is an appurtenant easement

32. What is the greatest number of properties that can be covered by a mortgage without having a blanket encumbrance?

    (A) one
    (B) two
    (C) three
    (D) four

33. The recapture rate refers to the:

    (A) rate of depreciation
    (B) rate at which an investment is returned
    (C) prime rate
    (D) capitalization rate

34. A property is listed by broker A at $92,500 with $30,000 down. Broker T brought in a full-price cash offer which the owner rejected. Broker T is entitled to:

    (A) the full commission
    (B) half the commission
    (C) the commission split agreed upon
    (D) nothing

35. An easement in gross on the servient tenant's property would:

    (A) be lost upon sale of the property
    (B) be included in every deed
    (C) go with the real property
    (D) be lost by one year of nonuse

36. An agency agreement **CANNOT** be created by:

    (A) a verbal agreement
    (B) implication
    (C) ratification
    (D) action of law

37. A buyer wishes to give a post-dated check with an offer. The broker should:

    (A) wait until it can be determined if the check is good before presentation of the offer
    (B) treat the check as any other check
    (C) inform the seller as to the form of the deposit
    (D) refuse to accept the offer

38. Interest acquired by adverse possession is:

    (A) a dominant tenement
    (B) personal in nature to the holder
    (C) a life interest
    (D) a fee

39. A newspaper advertisement by a broker is:

    (A) an irrevocable offer
    (B) a revocable offer
    (C) an invitation to negotiate
    (D) a firm offer

40. A property manager should **NOT** be compensated:

    (A) for rentals
    (B) for a percentage of the gross
    (C) for supervising repairs
    (D) by receiving discounts on material and services

41. A legal process used to clear a title is a:

    (A) quitclaim deed
    (B) quiet title action
    (C) action in personam
    (D) writ of mandamus

42. Which of the following is most likely a lien?

    (A) An easement
    (B) A homestead declaration
    (C) A debt to a carpenter
    (D) A fixture

43. As property tax increases, the value of rent-controlled property:

    (A) increases by the amount of the tax increase
    (B) increases by a greater amount than the tax increases
    (C) decreases by the amount of the tax increase
    (D) decreases by a greater amount than the tax increases

44. A child was injured when he entered an abandoned house. If the owner was held liable for the injury, it was probably considered:

    (A) an encroachment
    (B) an attractive nuisance
    (C) a license
    (D) an implied easement

45. An indefeasible contract:

    (A) has been executed
    (B) provides for exceptions
    (C) is unenforceable
    (D) cannot be voided

46. Both FHA and VA loans cover:

    (A) rental and owner-occupied housing
    (B) business and home loans
    (C) farm and business loans
    (D) single-family and multifamily housing

47. To have any validity, a deed requires:

    (A) recording
    (B) signature of grantee
    (C) a legal description
    (D) delivery

48. FNMA is primarily involved in:

    (A) low-cost housing
    (B) secondary financing
    (C) the secondary mortgage market
    (D) government-assisted housing

49. Which of the following statements applies to all appurtenances?

    (A) They go with the land.
    (B) They are joined by accession.
    (C) They once were personal property.
    (D) They are easements.

50. A disadvantage of a cooperative is:

    (A) inability to mortgage unit
    (B) higher taxes
    (C) personal liability of owners in the event of foreclosure
    (D) the inability to realize appreciation because a cooperative is non-profit

51. In the absence of any agreement in the sale contract, which of the following would most likely be considered personal property?

    (A) Wall-to-wall carpeting
    (B) An ornamental hedge
    (C) Fuel in an oil tank
    (D) Custom-made window shades

52. In a 40' × 40' rectangular shell building, the cost of the floor was $1.13/sq. ft.; the cost of the flat roof was $1.96/sq. ft.; and the cost of the 10' high walls was $2.38/sq. ft. What was the total cost per square foot?

    (A) $87.52
    (B) $8.75
    (C) $5.47
    (D) $3.84

53. Title to personal property is transferred by a:

    (A) bill of sale
    (B) security agreement
    (C) packaged mortgage
    (D) bargain & sale deed

54. Which of the following restrictive covenants is most likely to be enforceable?

    (A) Prohibits sales to blacks
    (B) Prohibits resales for 20 years
    (C) Prohibits use for anything other than single-family dwellings
    (D) Absolutely prohibits any resales

55. A tenancy by the entirety differs from a joint tenancy as to:

    (A) survivorship
    (B) termination by conveyance of one owner
    (C) ability to will an interest
    (D) right of possession

56. How does an increase in interest rates without a corresponding increase in rents affect real property investments?

    (A) Values increase
    (B) Down payments decrease
    (C) Equities decrease
    (D) Capitalization rates decrease

57. An $1,800 loan is repaid with $600-payments every six months plus nine percent annual interest. What is the total interest paid?

    (A) $243
    (B) $162
    (C) $216
    (D) $81

58. The following municipal function is NOT an exercise of police power:

    (A) rent control
    (B) construction codes
    (C) real estate taxation
    (D) health codes

59. The disclosure requirements of the Truth in Lending Act apply to:

    (A) sellers of real estate providing credit
    (B) a personal loan for $30,000
    (C) business loans
    (D) a three-installment no-interest loan

60. A piece of property is valued at $300,000, using a six percent capitalization rate. If the prospective investor wants an eight percent return, the value of the property becomes:

    (A) $290,000
    (B) $270,000
    (C) $225,000
    (D) $210,000

61. Using all three methods of appraisal for a property and assigning different weights to each method is known as:

    (A) averaging
    (B) correlation
    (C) bond of investment method
    (D) the Ellwood method

62. Which of the following contracts does NOT have to be in writing?

    (A) Promise to pay a debt of another
    (B) One-year lease starting immediately
    (C) Six-month lease starting in 7 months
    (D) Contract for the sale of real property valued less than $500

63. In a tight-money market, which lender would be likely to offer the lowest interest rate?

    (A) An insurance company
    (B) A private lender
    (C) A savings & loan association
    (D) The seller

Real Estate Exam Guide

64. Ownership as a tenant in common, coupled with an exclusive right of occupancy for a stated period of time, describes a:

   (A) timeshare
   (B) cooperative
   (C) planned unit development
   (D) condominium

65. Mr. F lost his home because of execution on a judgment by Mrs. K, who was injured in Mr. F's swimming pool. The judgment was a:

   (A) mechanic's lien
   (B) specific lien
   (C) general lien
   (D) voluntary lien

66. A cost of real property ownership is:

   (A) amenity value
   (B) psychic income
   (C) interest lost on owner's equity
   (D) appreciation

67. A grantor of a life estate has:

   (A) a fee simple
   (B) a remainder interest
   (C) a reversionary interest
   (D) a leasehold interest

68. Which of the following would be of LEAST interest to an investor in a sale leaseback?

   (A) Credit of lessee
   (B) Value of property
   (C) Seller's book value
   (D) Length of lease

69. A valid deed can be made to:

   (A) a person using a fictitious name
   (B) a fictitious person
   (C) either H or T
   (D) H for property, the exact description and nature of which is to be determined by later agreement.

70. Which of the following would NOT terminate an easement?

   (A) Nonuse of a prescriptive easement for six months
   (B) Express agreement of the parties
   (C) Adverse possession of the dominant tenement by the holder of the servient tenement
   (D) Destruction of the servient tenement

71. A duplex that rents for $275 per unit is in the same area as a slightly smaller duplex in similar condition which rents for $240 per unit and just sold for $67,200. Using this data only, the larger duplex has a value of:

   (A) $67,200
   (B) $70,000
   (C) $77,000
   (D) $77,500

72. In an exclusive listing, the broker's promise to use diligence makes the listing:

   (A) a unilateral contract
   (B) a bilateral contract
   (C) voidable
   (D) an illusory contract

73. To fence the N ½ of the S ½ of the N ½ of a Section would take how much fencing?

   (A) 1¼ miles
   (B) 2¼ miles
   (C) 3 miles
   (D) 3¼ miles

74. Company A is selling 500 lots improved with small homes by direct mail in interstate commerce. In accordance with the Interstate Land Sales Act, the purchasers:

   (A) have 48 hours to rescind
   (B) can rescind if they had not seen the property prior to purchase
   (C) cannot rescind because there are fewer than 1,000 units
   (D) cannot rescind because the Act does not apply

75. A mortgage assumption on a settlement statement would appear as:

    (A) a balance factor
    (B) a credit to the seller
    (C) a debit to the buyer
    (D) a credit to the buyer

76. The market comparison method has the least validity:

    (A) when used for commercial property
    (B) in a thin market
    (C) in a period of rapid change
    (D) when applied to raw land

77. A broker wants to advertise a property in a black neighborhood in a paper aimed at a black readership. To do so, the broker must:

    (A) indicate compliance with the fair housing laws
    (B) also advertise properties in white neighborhoods in the same paper
    (C) include the equal housing opportunity logo in the ads.
    (D) identify the location in the ad

78. What is the function of a real estate appraiser?

    (A) To set market value
    (B) To determine market value
    (C) To estimate market value
    (D) To establish the cost

79. A broker accepted 20 acres of land valued at $4,000 in lieu of a cash commission for a sale. Immediately after the closing, the broker accepted an offer of $200,000 for the land. Which of the following statements is correct?

    (A) The broker has made a secret profit.
    (B) The broker must return the property.
    (C) The broker must turn over the profit.
    (D) The broker has not done anything wrong.

80. A prospective buyer knows the owner is considering an offer. She asks the broker the amount of the offer so she can exceed it. The broker should:

    (A) tell her as it is in the owner's best interests
    (B) tell her, as a broker must reveal to a buyer everything he or she knows about a property
    (C) notify the owner of the request
    (C) notify the owner of the request
    (D) tell her that any offers you have do not concern her

GENERAL TEST

PLEASE PRINT THE FOLLOWING:
YOUR NAME

LAST   FIRST   MI

STREET ADDRESS

CITY   STATE   ZIP

TEST CENTER LOCATION (CITY, STATE)

TEST BOOKLET NO.

1ST THREE LETTERS OF LAST NAME

I.D. NUMBER FROM ADMISSION TICKET OR SCANNABLE APPLICATION

SOCIAL SECURITY NUMBER

TEST CENTER CODE

TEST DATE

JAN FEB MAR APR MAY JUN JUL AUG SEP OCT NOV DEC

YR.

HAVE YOU EVER TAKEN THIS EXAMINATION BEFORE?   YES ○   NO ○

FOR WHICH LICENSE ARE YOU TAKING THIS EXAM?   BROKER ○   SALESPERSON ○

WHICH PART OF THE EXAMINATION ARE YOU TAKING?
GENERAL ○   STATE ○   BOTH ○

IN SIGNING BELOW I HEREBY AFFIRM THAT:
I AM THE UNDERSIGNED AND HAVE SIGNED MY CORRECT NAME ON THE SIGNATURE LINE BELOW.
IN ADDITION TO PASSING THE EXAMINATION FOR LICENSURE, I MUST MEET ALL STATE REQUIREMENTS.
I UNDERSTAND ALL EXAMINATION BOOKS ARE SECURE MATERIAL AND THAT NO BOOK OR PORTION THEREOF IS TO BE COPIED, TRANSMITTED TO ANY OTHER PERSON OR REMOVED FROM THE EXAMINATION ROOM.
I WILL NEITHER ASSIST NOR RECEIVE ASSISTANCE FROM ANOTHER CANDIDATE OR USE ANY NOTES, MANUALS OR OTHER AIDS.

SIGNATURE   DATE

1–20 A B C D
21–40 A B C D
41–60 A B C D
61–80 A B C D

PLEASE TURN TO REVERSE SIDE FOR STATE TEST.

ANSWERS: TEST B

1. (B) An overimprovement is built-in obsolescence: for example, making a unit so luxurious that the rental cannot compensate for the expenditure.

2. (C) A new owner can add the previous owner's adverse use to obtain the statutory period of use.

3. (C) The others must be in writing.

4. (C) It is ¼ mile on each side (¼ of a ¼ section).

5. (B) An offer can be revoked by offeror prior to notification of acceptance.

6. (B) $$3.436 \div 1.748 = 1.9657,$$
    or a 196.57 increase in cost
    $$\$25 \times 1.9657 = \$49.14 \text{ per square foot}$$
    $$\$49.14 \times 1500 = \$73,710$$

7. (D) Otherwise an agent can be terminated, although it might expose a party to damages.

8. (B) Others are prohibited.

9. (B)

10. (B) To establish "procuring cause."

11. (B) The others deal with different methods.

12. (B)   Total area ÷ known dimension = other dimension:
    $$(5 \times 43,560) \div 250 = 871.2$$
    Divided by 6 lots = 145.2

13. (A) Buyer's creditors have a subordinate interest to the purchase-money mortgagee.

14. (B) It gives constructive notice.

15. (B)

16. (C) This is a deductible expense that has no effect on cost base.

17. (A) Since financing is not required.

18. (A) FHA loans are assumable.

19. (C) This is a surveyor's reference point for elevations.

20. (B) Before an owner can sell to another (if the owner wishes to) the offer must first be made to holder of a right of first refusal.

21. (C) The courts in some states regard it as a mortgage, as title was really given as security for a loan, evidenced by the right to repurchase.

22. (C) Broker must tell the prospective buyer anything detrimental about the property he knows of, but this is not detrimental. To tell the prospective buyer could be steering, which is illegal.

23. (A)

24. (D) The homestead exemption offers protection only against unsecured liens recorded after the homestead exemption.

25. (C) A fee simple can be inherited. Heirs of partners are only entitled to value of former partner's share of assets, and do not become partners.

26. (A) This is a freehold interest; the others are nonfreehold estates.

27. (B) An organization of black brokers formed in 1947. Realtors® are broker members of the National Association of Realtors®.

28. (C) From the building department.

29. (C) Or until voided by the offeror.

30. (B) A straight loan is interest only, so: $9840 = 9 percent of loan.

$$\frac{9840}{.09} = \frac{.09X}{.09}$$

$$X = \$109,333.$$

But, $109,333 = 75\% appraisal.

$$\$109,333 \div .75 = \$145,777$$

31. (A) It is personal in nature. There is no dominant tenement.

32. (A)

33. (B) Through income or depreciation.

34. (D) Offer was not in accordance with the listing.

35. (C) An easement in gross transfers with the servient tenement, but not with a dominant tenement, because there is none.

36. (D) An agency agreement requires consent.

37. (C) Must inform the owners as to anything that could affect their interests.

38. (D) Adverse possession confers title.

39. (C) It is not an offer.

40. (D) The agency duty requires these to go to the principal.

41. (B) A quiet title action is a *legal process.*

42. (C) A mechanic's lien.

43. (D) Since the net would decrease and we capitalize the net to determine value.

44. (B) Owner must protect children, who are liable to trespass because of the attraction, from danger.

45. (D) And defeasible means it can be defeated or lost.

46. (D) VA loans don't cover rental property, and FHA only covers housing.

47. (D) Between the parties, recording is not necessary. While a legal description is usually required to obtain title insurance, it is not needed to convey title. Only the grantor signs.

48. (C) Fannie Mae buys and sells existing loans.

49. (A) An easement was never personal property and is not joined by accession. Fixtures are appurtenances but are not easements.

50. (A) Although an owner can borrow on the stock.

51. (C) Others could be fixtures.

52. (C)
$$40 \times 40 = 1,600 \text{ square feet.}$$
$$\text{Floor } 1,600 \times 1.13 = \$1808$$
$$\text{Roof } 1,600 \times 1.96 = \$3136$$
$$\text{Walls } 40' \times 10' = 400$$
$$400 \times 4 = 1600$$
$$1600 \times 2.38 = 3808$$
$$\text{Total Cost} = \$8752$$
$$\$8,752 \div 1600 = \$5.47/\text{sq. ft.}$$

53. (A) And a deed for real property.

54. (C) *B* and *D* would be unreasonable restraints on alienation, and *A* is a violation of the Fair Housing Act.

55. (B) Neither spouse can break the joint tenancy by a separate conveyance.

56. (C) The value of income property is arrived at by capitalizing the net. Higher interest rates would raise the capitalization rate.

57. (B)

1st payment $1800 \times .09 \times .5$ (½ year)	$81
2nd payment $1200 \times .09 \times .5$	$54
3rd payment $600 \times .09 \times .5$	$27
Total	$162

58. (C) Taxation is not under police power.

59. (A) Personal loans of more than $25,000, business loans, and loans of four or less installments where no interest is charged are exempt.

60. (C)

$$\text{net} \div .06 = \$300,000$$
$$\text{net} = .06 \times 300,000 = \$18,000$$
$$\text{at } 8\%, \$18,000 \div .08 = \$225,000$$

61. (B) Or reconciliation.

62. (B) A lease for one year or less need not be in writing.

63. (D) Sellers often finance at below-market rates in order to consummate a sale.

64. (A)

65. (C) Judgment lien is a general lien.

66. (C)

67. (C) A grantor has a reversionary interest. A third party has a remainder interest.

68. (C) Book value does not necessarily reflect market value.

69. (A) Property can be conveyed to a real person using a fictitious name, but not to a fictitious person. The grantee and the property granted must be definite.

70. (A) While in many states nonuse will end a prescriptive easement, the time period is much longer.

71. (C) The duplex that sold had a monthly gross multiplier of 140: 67,200 ÷ 480 = 140. Applying the same rent multiplier to the units renting at $275 each: $550 × 140 = $77,000.

72. (B) A promise for a promise.

73. (B) The North ½ has ½ mile on the sides. The S ½ of that has ¼ mile on the sides and the N ½ of that has ⅛ mile on 2 sides and 1 mile on the other 2 sides.

74. (D) Since the lots are improved the Interstate Land Sales Act does not apply.

75. (D) It comes off the sales price. Cash is given or received to balance out the closing statements.

76. (B) A thin market means few sales, so it is difficult to get comparables.

77. (B) Or it would be steering.

78. (C) Buyers determine the value, appraisers estimate.

79. (D) From the facts given, the broker had good fortune. If he knew that the value was in excess of $4,000, he would have had a duty to tell the owner.

80. (C) To tell the prospective buyer would be unfair to the other offeror, as it would give a competitive advantage. The broker must, however, tell the owner. One solution would be to go to both prospects for sealed bids.

TEST C

1. Which of the following would **NOT** be a cause of functional obsolescence?

   (A) Over-improvement
   (B) Eccentric design
   (C) Lack of central heating
   (D) Proximity of a nuisance

2. A township was bisected by a straight line from the NW corner of Section 6 to the SE corner of Section 36. Each of the two parcels thus formed contain how many acres?

   (A) 320
   (B) 23,040
   (C) 11,520
   (D) 1,320

3. What is the most likely response to violation of a deed covenant?

   (A) An action for money damages
   (B) An action for specific performance
   (C) Forfeiture
   (D) An action for an injunction

4. The fact that no two pieces of property are identical is the reason for:

   (A) punitive damages
   (B) specific performance
   (C) the Statute of Frauds
   (D) the Parol Evidence Rule

5. The responsibility for disclosure under RESPA rests with the:

   (A) seller
   (B) broker
   (C) lender
   (D) title company

6. Part of a legal description reads "T7NR4W." The South boundary of the township so described would be how far north of the base line?

   (A) 42 miles
   (B) 6 miles
   (C) 36 miles
   (D) 60 miles

7. Duress applied to one party to a contract makes the agreement:

   (A) unilateral
   (B) void
   (C) voidable
   (D) illegal

8. The shortest distance between Sections 5 and 31 of the same township would be:

   (A) 4 miles
   (B) 5 miles
   (C) 6 miles
   (D) 7 miles

9. An offer has been accepted on a 10-acre parcel, when the broker learns that the buyer has been buying up land in the area at a much higher price. The broker should:

   (A) notify the seller of the facts
   (B) recommend that the seller breach the contract
   (C) do nothing, as the seller is obligated to convey
   (D) do nothing, as agency has been completed with the procurement of the buyer

10. Real estate commissions are ordinarily a:

    (A) flat fee
    (B) percentage of the seller's equity
    (C) percentage of the sales price
    (D) percentage of the actual cash received

11. A real estate broker's duties to the principal do not include:

    (A) due care
    (B) financial trust
    (C) employee/employer relationship
    (D) loyalty

12. An owner would **NOT** use an unlawful detainer action against a tenant who:

    (A) refuses to pay rent
    (B) violates a lease provision
    (C) fails to make payments after exercising a purchase option
    (D) holds over after lease expires

13. The following would be required to have a real estate license:

(A) a developer selling more than 10 homes
(B) an attorney in fact selling property for a principal
(C) a trustee selling under court order
(D) an attorney at law taking a listing

14. Normally an investor would provide for the return of the investment in the:

(A) capitalization rate
(B) interest rate
(C) operational costs
(D) principal payments

15. Which of the following actions would NOT prevent a claim of adverse possession?

(A) Physically barring entry of adverse user
(B) Ousting the adverse user
(C) Ordering the adverse user to desist
(D) Giving the adverse user express permission to use the property

16. Which of the following is an advantage to buyers of FHA financing over most conventional loans?

(A) Shorter processing time
(B) Fully amortized
(C) Minimum property requirements
(D) FHA insurance

17. An investor's equity could be best described as:

(A) the original down payment
(B) what the investor has in the property
(C) the appraised value
(D) the difference between the market value and the indebtedness against the property

18. A broker who accepts a deposit on one of his or her listings is probably acting as:

(A) the agent of the seller
(B) the agent of the buyer and the seller
(C) an independent contractor
(D) the agent of the buyer

19. One tenant in common may NOT:

(A) use the property without paying co-tenants for the use
(B) place an easement over the property
(C) lease his or her interest without approval of other co-tenants
(D) sell his or her interest without approval of other co-tenants

20. A subdivider must comply with the Interstate Land Sales Act for subdivisions of:

(A) 5 or more parcels
(B) 25 or more parcels
(C) 50 or more parcels
(D) 100 or more parcels

21. When title is conveyed to two persons who are not married, and no mention is made of how they are to take title, ownership is presumed to be:

(A) in severalty
(B) as tenants in common
(C) as joint tenants
(D) as a tenancy in the entirety

22. The Torrens system is:

(A) a system of title registration
(B) a system of title insurance
(C) an appraisal method
(D) a system of land-use control

23. What would a landlocked property owner ask the court for?

(A) An easement by prescription
(B) An easement in gross
(C) An easement by necessity
(D) Adverse possession

24. One-quarter of a township equals:

(A) 160 acres
(B) 320 acres
(C) 5,760 acres
(D) 23,040 acres

25. Which of the following deeds would fail to transfer title?

   (A) A deed to John Jones using his stage name "Mr. Magic"
   (B) A deed made to Henry Schmidt Et Ux
   (C) A deed made to Henry or Henrietta Schmidt
   (D) A deed made to Henrietta Schmidt and husband

26. A financing statement would be removed from record by:

   (A) a receipt for payment
   (B) an abandonment
   (C) filing a termination statement
   (D) recording a quitclaim deed

27. The owner of a property with a condition subsequent has:

   (A) a remainder interest
   (B) a defeasible estate
   (C) less than a freehold interest
   (D) an estate for years

28. Truth in Lending is also known as:

   (A) Credit Act of 1968
   (B) Regulation Z
   (C) Federal Usury Law
   (D) Fair Housing Act

29. A planning commission customarily regulates all **BUT:**

   (A) parks and playgrounds
   (B) streets
   (C) construction methods and material
   (D) land use

30. With a capitalization rate of five percent, each additional dollar of expenses affects the value of income property by:

   (A) raising it $20
   (B) lowering it $20
   (C) lowering it $10
   (D) lowering it $5

31. Adjacent property owners are entitled to:

   (A) lateral support
   (B) structural support
   (C) emblements
   (D) easements of convenience

32. A tenant in common:

   (A) can sell his or her interest without approval of other owners
   (B) has interest equal with other owners
   (C) has exclusive right of possession
   (D) has survivorship rights

33. The purchaser's down payment is considered:

   (A) borrowed funds
   (B) leveraged funds
   (C) equity funds
   (D) capital funds

34. Use the following illustration to answer the question below.

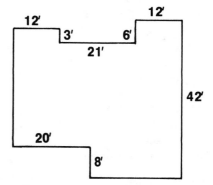

   The total square footage of the house is:

   (A) 1,382 sq. ft.
   (B) 1,440 sq. ft.
   (C) 1,568 sq. ft.
   (D) 1,670 sq. ft.

35. An offer is terminated by:

   (A) rejection by offeror
   (B) rejection by offeree
   (C) revocation by offeree
   (D) a request for an extension by offeree

36. Against a recorded deed from the owner of record, the party with the weakest position is:

    (A) a party with a prior unrecorded deed who is not in possession
    (B) a party in possession with a prior unrecorded deed
    (C) a tenant in possession with nine months left on the lease
    (D) a painter who is half finished painting the house at the time of sale and has not been paid

37. A $7,000 investment in a straight mortgage earns $210 in 90 days. What is the annual percentage return?

    (A) 9%
    (B) 11%
    (C) 12%
    (D) 14%

38. Which of the following best describes waiver of a contractual breach?

    (A) Ratification
    (B) Reformation
    (C) Rescission
    (D) Estoppel

39. What deductions does a homeowner have for tax purposes?

    (A) Interest expense
    (B) Insurance cost
    (C) Depreciation
    (D) Maintenance expense

40. Betty Smith took title to property in the name Elizabeth Smith. When she sold the property, she signed Betty Smith as grantor. The buyer has:

    (A) a cloud on the title
    (B) only color of title
    (C) an exception on the deed
    (D) clean title

41. A cooperative owner:

    (A) pays separate taxes for the unit
    (B) has a leasehold right of occupancy
    (C) has a separate mortgage on the unit
    (D) owns the structure as a tenant in common

42. The building residual method of appraisal would be used to determine the value of the:

    (A) land alone
    (B) building alone
    (C) building and the land
    (D) unearned increment

43. In computing capital gains, an owner would be interested in:

    (A) taxes paid
    (B) maintenance expense
    (C) condition of the property
    (D) improvements made

44. For a new FHA home-purchase loan, the insurance payment:

    (A) cannot be added to the loan amount
    (B) is paid by the lender
    (C) is a one-time payment by the borrower
    (D) is a charge with every monthly payment

45. A real estate salesperson, in selling the listing of another broker, would be directly responsible to:

    (A) her own broker
    (B) the owner
    (C) the buyer
    (D) the listing broker

46. An owner of an interest in land who has the right to impose conditions on its future use has:

    (A) a life estate
    (B) a fee simple
    (C) a nonfreehold interest
    (D) an estate for years

47. To find the gross multiplier of a property which has been sold:

    (A) divide the sale price by the gross income
    (B) divide the gross income by the sale price
    (C) multiply the sale price by the gross income
    (D) divide the sale price by the net income

48. A good example of functional obsolescence would be:

    (A) a building which, because of wear and tear, is no longer suitable for the purpose
    (B) an overimproved structure
    (C) an encroaching use
    (D) political change which has reduced value

49. Which is the correct order of events?

    (A) Judgment, attachment, execution
    (B) Judgment, execution, attachment
    (C) Execution, attachment, judgment
    (D) Attachment, judgment, execution

50. An appraiser would **NOT** define excess land as land:

    (A) not utilized by the improvements
    (B) in excess of that used for comparable properties
    (C) that does not add to the total property value
    (D) that produces excess income

51. A women's rights group established a non-profit housing project which gave preference to single women with children. Their action is:

    (A) proper if the organization is also non-profit
    (B) proper if there is no racial discrimination
    (C) improper under the Civil Rights Act of 1866.
    (D) improper under the 1974 amendment to the Civil Rights Act of 1968

52. K sold to M, but M inadvertently recorded the deed in the wrong county:

    (A) K still has good title
    (B) between K and M, M has good title
    (C) M's recording, though improper, still gives constructive notice of M's interests
    (D) a new deed will have to be issued and properly recorded

53. Assume a metes and bounds description starts in the center of a section and thence goes in a straight line to the Northeast corner of the section thence South 2,640′ along the East Section line and thence in a straight line to the point of beginning. The parcel so described would contain:

    (A) 320 acres
    (B) 160 acres
    (C) 80 acres
    (D) 40 acres

54. *Waiver* would best be described as a:

    (A) bilateral agreement which returns the parties to a previous position
    (B) bilateral agreement which leaves the parties as they are
    (C) unilateral act which affects the position of both parties to a contract
    (D) revocable act

55. On a buyer's closing statement, the following would **NOT** be shown:

    (A) cost of unused insurance
    (B) impound account of loan being assumed
    (C) points to be paid by seller
    (D) unpaid taxes

56. Market value is best defined as:

    (A) assessed value
    (B) the maximum price a willing informed buyer would pay to a willing informed seller
    (C) average sale price for similar properties
    (D) utility value

57. When a new mall opened, rental income for the old mall was reduced by $4,600 per month. Using a 12½ percent capitalization rate, what was the loss in value for the old mall?

    (A) $36,800
    (B) $441,600
    (C) $69,000
    (D) $538,976

58. Failure to meet the requirements set forth in a contract is a:

    (A) waiver
    (B) breach
    (C) novation
    (D) reformation

59. What can give a mortgage priority over a prior recorded mortgage?

(A) A subrogation clause
(B) A subordination clause
(C) A defeasance clause
(D) A blanket encumbrance

60. A verbally agreed to a six-month lease of a store, but prior to occupancy she changed her mind. Her verbal agreement is:

(A) enforceable
(B) illegal
(C) unenforceable because of the Statute of Frauds
(D) voidable by her

61. Which of the following would **NOT** terminate an offer?

(A) A request by offeree for more time for acceptance
(B) Revocation by offeror
(C) An acceptance contingent upon a change in price
(D) The death of the offeror

62. A broker soliciting listings in an area where Vietnamese families have been moving in decides not to solicit the Vietnamese, as they are all new owners. The solicitation:

(A) is proper, because the Vietnamese who have recently moved into the area are unlikely to be moving out
(B) is proper because it was not based on prejudice
(C) is illegal because of the Civil Rights Act of 1968
(D) is redlining

63. In appraising a building, the appraiser would consider all of the following **EXCEPT:**

(A) location
(B) tax appraisal
(C) vacancy factor
(D) reproduction cost

64. A life estate holder purchased the interest of the remainderman. The life tenant now holds:

(A) a fee simple
(B) a life estate for two lives
(C) a tenancy in common
(D) two separate estates

65. Market value is really determined by:

(A) buyers
(B) sellers
(C) listing brokers
(D) appraisers

66. J and A owned Greenacres with the right of survivorship. J died, willing his entire estate to a friend, making no provision for his wife and three minor children. The ownership of Greenacres would be with:

(A) the friend and A
(B) the wife and A
(C) the wife and children and A as tenants in common
(D) A alone

67. The term *tax shelter* is generally associated with:

(A) real property tax
(B) income tax
(C) sales tax
(D) personal property tax

68. A four-sided parcel of land has 2,640 feet on one side. At right angles to this side is a side 5,280 feet long. Parallel to the shorter side is a side of 5,280 feet. The ends of the two parallel sides of 2,640 feet and 5,280 feet are connected. The resulting acreage is:

(A) 640 acres
(B) 480 acres
(C) 320 acres
(D) 460 acres

69. Before closing, the seller and buyer agree to rescind their sale. The buyer asks the broker for the return of his deposit. The broker should:

    (A) return the deposit in full
    (B) deduct the commission due and return the balance
    (C) keep one half of the commission due and return everything else
    (D) hold all monies for a court determination as to the broker's rights

70. When the word *fee* is used in connection with ownership of real property it refers to:

    (A) commission
    (B) a conveyance charge
    (C) the price paid
    (D) an estate of inheritance

71. A writ of attachment levied on real property:

    (A) forces its sale
    (B) can be filed in anticipation of a contractual breach
    (C) is a lien on the real property
    (D) is filed after a judgment

72. Which of the following is incompatible with joint tenancy?

    (A) Right of possession
    (B) Survivorship
    (C) Probate
    (D) Equality of interest

73. The W ½ of the NW ¼ of the NW ¼ of the SE ¼ of the SW ¼ of a section was to be paved for parking at a cost of 38¢ per square foot. The total paving cost will be:

    (A) $41,382
    (B) $10,345
    (C) $20,691
    (D) $5,173

74. A suit by a principal against a broker who failed to follow instructions will probably result in:

    (A) loss of broker's license
    (B) fine and/or jail
    (C) money damages
    (D) exoneration, since a broker is not required to obey instructions. Broker only has to procure buyer.

75. The premium for title insurance is paid:

    (A) monthly with the mortgage payment
    (B) on an annual basis
    (C) upon issuance of the title policy
    (D) by the original subdivider for all subsequent holders

76. Which of the following **CANNOT** be owned in fee simple?

    (A) A condominium
    (B) Property owned as tenants in common
    (C) Property owned as a joint tenant
    (D) Leasehold rights

77. When improvements are accidentally made on the land of another:

    (A) the owner of the land will probably take title by accession
    (B) the improver has the right to buy the property at its tax-appraised value
    (C) the improver is allowed to remove the improvements, providing any damage is repaired
    (D) the improver is allowed to use the property of the other person by encroachment

78. A grantor sold a farm, retaining all mineral, oil, and gas rights. Eight years later the grantor wishes to enter and drill for oil. What are the rights of the grantor?

    (A) If the deed did not provide for an easement, the grantor must drill from outside the property.
    (B) The grantor can enter, so long as the grantor does not interfere with the land's agricultural use.
    (C) While the grantor can enter and drill, the owner must be compensated for any loss suffered because of the drilling operation.
    (D) The grantor has an implied easement for the purpose of extracting minerals, oil, or gas.

79. The purpose of the Federal Fair Housing Act is to:

    (A) eliminate all racial prejudice
    (B) provide livable housing for all citizens
    (C) provide equal housing for all citizens
    (D) provide equal housing opportunity

80. Restrictive covenants are customarily enforced by:

    (A) the district attorney of the county where the property is located
    (B) the lender
    (C) the planning commission
    (D) owners

GENERAL TEST

PLEASE TURN TO REVERSE SIDE FOR STATE TEST.

PLEASE PRINT THE FOLLOWING:
YOUR NAME

LAST | FIRST | MI

STREET ADDRESS

CITY | STATE | ZIP

TEST CENTER LOCATION (CITY, STATE)

TEST BOOKLET NO.

1ST THREE LETTERS OF LAST NAME

I.D. NUMBER FROM ADMISSION TICKET OR SCANNABLE APPLICATION

SOCIAL SECURITY NUMBER

TEST CENTER CODE

TEST DATE

| | YR. |

JAN, FEB, MAR, APR, MAY, JUN, JUL, AUG, SEP, OCT, NOV, DEC

HAVE YOU EVER TAKEN THIS EXAMINATION BEFORE? YES O NO O

FOR WHICH LICENSE ARE YOU TAKING THIS EXAM? BROKER O SALESPERSON O

WHICH PART OF THE EXAMINATION ARE YOU TAKING?
GENERAL O STATE O BOTH O

IN SIGNING BELOW I HEREBY AFFIRM THAT:
I AM THE UNDERSIGNED AND HAVE SIGNED MY CORRECT NAME ON THE SIGNATURE LINE BELOW. IN ADDITION TO PASSING THE EXAMINATION FOR LICENSURE, I MUST MEET ALL STATE REQUIREMENTS. I UNDERSTAND ALL EXAMINATION BOOKS ARE SECURE MATERIAL AND THAT NO BOOK OR PORTION THEREOF IS TO BE COPIED, TRANSMITTED TO ANY OTHER PERSON OR REMOVED FROM THE EXAMINATION ROOM. I WILL NEITHER ASSIST NOR RECEIVE ASSISTANCE FROM ANOTHER CANDIDATE OR USE ANY NOTES, MANUALS OR OTHER AIDS.

SIGNATURE | DATE

ANSWERS: TEST C

1. (D) Forces outside the property itself would be economic obsolescence.

2. (C) There are 36 sections in a township. 36 × 640 acres = 23,040 total acres. The township has been cut into 2 equal parts of 11,520 acres each.

3. (D) Restrictive covenants can be enforced by anyone subject to the covenants. Normal remedy is an order to cease (injunction).

4. (B) Because of the uniqueness of each piece of property, money damages are not adequate.

5. (C) It is a lender disclosure act. Disclosure compliance is not a broker obligation.

6. (C) Since there are 6 townships between the South boundary and the base line, with each township being 6 miles square.

7. (C) At the option of the injured party.

8. (A) Sections 8, 17, 20, and 29 are between them.

9. (A) You have a duty to inform the seller of all material facts. You could be liable for damages if you induce a breach of contract.

10. (C)

11. (C) A broker is not an employee. The broker is an agent.

12. (C) The action for this would be foreclosure.

13. (D) The attorney is acting as a broker, not in a legal advisory position. An owner "developer" can generally sell as a principal without a license.

14. (A) If a building had a 50-year economic life, the capitalization rate could be raised two percent to provide for the return of the investment (2% × 50 years = 100% return).

15. (C) Must actually stop adverse use. When permission is granted, the use is no longer adverse.

16. (C) Home must meet quality standards. FHA insurance protects the lender, not the buyer.

17. (D) The equity increases with inflation.

18. (A) The listing generally authorizes accepting the deposit.

19. (B) Cannot affect the future rights of the other co-tenants without all of them agreeing. All co-tenants must agree to an encumbrance.

20. (B)

21.   (B) Since there are two, it could not be in severalty.

22.   (A) Title is registered with a registrar who issues a certificate of title.

23.   (C) Not available in all states.

24.   (C) A township contains 36 sections of 640 acres each, or 23,040 acres.

25.   (C) Not a definite grantee.

26.   (C)

27.   (B) Because it can be lost by the happening of a condition.

28.   (B) Of the Federal Consumer Protection Act of 1968.

29.   (C) This would be regulated by building department.

30.   (B) The net is lowered, so it lowers value. By capitalizing one dollar, we find the value of one dollar of expenses: $1 \div .05 = \$20$.

31.   (A) From both structures and land. Statutes provide for notices and duties when you excavate below a neighbor's foundation.

32.   (A) An undivided interest without the right of survivorship. Equal right of possession, but interests do not have to be equal.

33.   (C)

34.   (C) (1) $3 \times 12 =$ 36 sq. ft.
         (2) $6 \times 12 =$ 72 sq. ft.
              (3) $8 \times 25 =$ 200 sq. ft.
         (4) $28 \times 45 = \underline{1260}$ sq. ft.
                      1568 sq. ft.

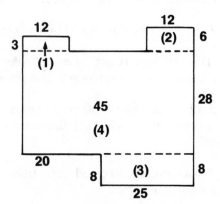

35.   (B) Offeror revokes and offeree rejects.

36.   (A) Since there was no possession and no recording, the owner had no constructive notice of the other person's interest. There is constructive notice of interests in *B* and *C*. The painter has lien rights.

37.   (C) $210 return for 90 days (¼ of year)
            $\times$ 4
            ————
            $840 annual return

$$840 \div 7000 = 12\%$$

38. (A) Agreeing to the performance as given.

39. (A) Property taxes are also a deduction.

40. (A) Needs a quitclaim from "Elizabeth" or recorded proof that Betty and Elizabeth are the same person.

41. (B) Under a proprietary lease.

42. (B) You find the income attributable to the land and deduct from the total income to find the income of the improvements. Capitalize this income to determine value attributable to the building.

43. (D) Capital gains is the difference between book value and sales price. Improvements increase the book value.

44. (C) And it can be added to the loan.

45. (A) Direct responsibility.

46. (B) Only a fee owner can place restrictions beyond his or her interests.

47. (A)

48. (A) Overimprovement is built-in obsolescence.

49. (D) Attachment is prior to a judgment, and execution is after the judgment has been rendered.

50. (D)

51. (D) A 1974 amendment bans sex discrimination.

52. (B) But the deed should be recorded in the proper county.

53. (C) This is ½ of a ¼ section:

54. (C) An act by one party which leaves both parties as they are.

55. (C) This would not affect the buyer.

56. (B)

57. (B) $4,600 per month × 12 = $55,200:
                 55,200 ÷ .125 = $441,600

58. (B)

59. (B) The prior mortgagee agreed to be subordinate to a later recorded mortgage.

60. (A) Leases for one year or less do not have to be in writing.

61. (A) This is not a rejection. *C* is a counteroffer that rejects the original offer.

62. (C) Soliciting listings on the basis of race is a violation of the Fair Housing Act.

63. (B) The value previously placed by another appraiser is not a factor in considering the present value.

64. (A) Ownership of all interests are merged together.

65. (A)

66. (D) Since they owned in joint tenancy (with the right of survivorship).

67. (D) Regular income is sheltered from taxation.

68. (B) 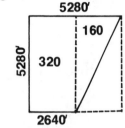 The half of a section contains 320 acres and the ½ of a half section contains 160 acres.

69. (A) Although the broker could have a claim against the owner for the commission.

70. (D)

71. (C) Filed prior to a judgment to prevent the property from being conveyed.

72. (C) Joint tenancy avoids probate.

73. (C)

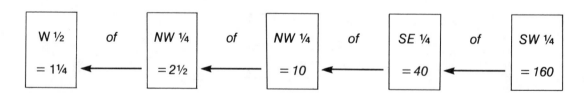

Realizing there are 640 acres in a section and computing backwards we find that the parcel contains 1¼ acres:

$$1.25 \times 43560 = 54,450 \text{ square feet}$$
$$.38 \times 54450 = \$20,691.$$

74. (C) This is a civil case. Action would have to be taken by Real Estate Department to lose a license.

75. (C) It is a one-time premium.

76. (D) A leasehold is occupancy only; a fee simple is ownership of the property.

77. (C) Court might allow you to buy the property at a fair value if removal was not practical.

78. (D)

79. (D) By eliminating discrimination in the sale and rental of housing.

80. (D) The remedy sought is usually an injunction.

GLOSSARY

WORDS AND PHRASES OF REAL ESTATE

This glossary has been designed as a quick reference to help students to understand the language of the real estate profession. A complete vocabulary review before your state examination will also serve to bring together into an understandable whole the many different facets of real estate which you have been studying.

As a quick aid, remember that words ending in "or" are givers: don*or*, grant*or*, option*or*.

Words ending in "ee" are receivers: don*ee*, grant*ee*, and option*ee*.

Words ending in "trix" refer to a woman: administra*trix*, execu*trix*, and testa*trix*.

abatement A legal action to stop a nuisance.

abstract A copy of every recorded document dealing with a property. It is examined to determine whether there is marketable title.

abstractive method A means of obtaining land value by deducting the value of improvements from the total property value.

abstract of judgment A condensation of a judgment of a court. When recorded, it becomes a general lien on the property of the debtor within the county where recorded.

accelerated depreciation Any method of depreciation for tax purposes which gives greater initial depreciation than the straight-line method.

acceleration clause A clause in a note making all payments due upon the happening of some event (such as missing a payment or selling the property).

accession Obtaining title because of attaching or joining property to other property.

accord and satisfaction Accepting a different consideration than agreed. Usually where there is a dispute as to performance and a party accepts less than originally bargained for.

accounts payable Money that must be paid out to others.

accounts receivable Money due a business.

accretion The gradual building up of soil by action of water or wind.

accrued depreciation Depreciation to date; measured by the difference between the replacement cost new and the present value.

acknowledgment A declaration certifying that the signing of an instrument is the signer's own free act. Customarily made before a notary.

acre A measure of land equal to 43,560 square feet.

action in personam Legal action taken against a person. A judgment from such an action, when recorded, would be a general lien against all of the property of the debtor in the county where recorded.

action in rem Legal action taken against property. A judgment from such an action, when recorded, is a specific lien against the particular property involved in the action.

administrator A man appointed by a probate court to administer the estate of a deceased (a woman is an administratrix).

ad valorem A tax according to value. Real property taxes are considered to be ad valorem taxes.

adverse possession A means of obtaining title from another by open, adverse, hostile, and continuous use for a statutory period of time. In some states it also requires payment of taxes.

affidavit A statement sworn to under oath or by affirmation before a notary.

affirmation A formal declaration as to the truthfulness of a statement. Made by a person whose religious beliefs prohibit swearing under oath.

after-acquired interest An interest acquired by a grantor after he or she has conveyed the property. Under some deeds, this after-acquired interest is said to pass to the grantee.

age-life tables Appraisal tables which indicate the economic life for various types of structures.

agency A contractual relationship where one person (an agent) represents another (a principal).

agent A person representing another, acting in his or her behalf.

air rights The right of a property owner to the reasonable use of the airspace over his or her property. Air rights are considered to be real property, and can be separately leased or conveyed.

alienation clause *see due on sale clause*

alluvion Soil added gradually to land by action of water. The soil belongs to the land it is added to by this accretion process.

ALTA American Land Title Association; also, a type of title insurance policy providing extended coverage to the lender. The same extended coverage may also be available for the buyer.

amend escrow instructions A change in the escrow instructions after they have been signed. The signatures of both buyer and seller are required to amend the instructions.

amenities Features of a property which enhance the satisfaction and use of the property. (Extra bath, flower garden, mature shade trees, etc.)

anchor bolt A bolt that ties the mudsill (the lowest board in a house) to the foundation.

anchor tenant A major tenant, usually located at one end of a shopping center. Lesser shops benefit by being between anchor tenants.

annexation Adding to something, as when a city annexes outlying land.

anticipatory breach An action or statement of a party prior to performance due date that indicates the party will breach the contract. The other party can bring suit upon anticipatory breach without waiting for an actual breach.

appraisal An estimate of value.

appurtenance Rights, benefits, and attachments which transfer with real property. Examples: buildings, easement rights, water rights, etc.

arbitrage Taking advantage of interest rate differential by buying at one interest rate and selling at a higher interest rate by either land contract or the use of a wraparound loan.

ARM (adjustable rate mortgage) A mortgage where the interest rate is tied to an index, such as the T-bill rate. They generally have a maximum interest swing.

artificial monument A surveyor point for metes and bounds descriptions, which is man-made; such as an iron stake, a fence, a canal, etc.

ASI (Assessment Systems, Inc.) An independent testing organization that prepares the *Real Estate Assessment for Licensure* examination.

as is A statement intended to mean that the seller is not warranting the condition of the property. It does not protect the seller in cases of concealment or fraud. Some courts hold that it only applies to readily observable defects, and not to known but undisclosed latent defects.

assemblage The act of bringing adjacent parcels of land under one ownership; the opposite of subdividing. It usually results in an increase in value. *See plottage.*

assessed value Value placed by tax assessor.

assessment The amount of taxes levied against a property.

assets Property owned by or owed to a business or person.

assignee One who receives an assignment.

assignment The complete transfer of a person's rights to another. The assignee takes over the rights and duties of the assignor.

assignor One who makes an assignment.

assumption Assuming the responsibilities for an obligation and agreeing to be personally liable for the obligation. A deficiency judgment might be possible against an assignee.

attachment The legal seizure of property of another prior to a judgment when there is belief that it will not be available after judgment.

attestation The act of witnessing. Attest is to bear witness. Formal wills require witnesses.

attorney in fact A person operating as an agent under a power of attorney (not an attorney at law).

attornment An agreement between owner and sublessee that the owner will recognize the sublease and the sublessee will pay the owner should the sublessor's interests be foreclosed.

avulsion The sudden tearing away or loss of real property by action of water, such as a river changing course.

bailment Giving possession of personal property to another but retaining title. Examples: storing goods in a warehouse, renting a trailer, giving existing mortgages to a lender as security for a loan, etc.

balance sheet Financial statement showing assets and liabilities. The balance sheet shows net worth.

balloon payment A final installment of an unamortized loan which exceeds the previous payments.

band of investment method A procedure to determine the capitalization rate to be used for a particular property under the income approach.

bankers' interest Interest based on a 30-day month and a 360-day year.

bankruptcy A legal procedure to eliminate unsecured debts. To eliminate secured debts, the security must be surrendered.

bargain-and-sale deed A deed for consideration which uses the term *Bargain and Sale*. It contains no warranties other than implied ownership by the grantor.

baseboard A molding placed against the wall on the floor around a room.

batten Wood strips used to cover joints. Used in board and batten siding.

beam A horizontal structural member giving support to a structure.

bearing walls A wall with a footing under it that bears the load of the structure.

bench marks A marker placed by a government surveyor and used by surveyors as a reference point.

beneficiary The person receiving payments under a deed of trust. Similar to a mortgagee.

beneficiary statement A statement of a lender of the balance due on a loan.

bequeath To give personal property by will.

bequest Personal property which is given by will.

betterments Actual improvements to real estate (not repairs).

bilateral contract A mutual exchange of promises where each promise is consideration for the promise of the other.

bill of sale Written agreement transferring title to personal property.

binder Insurance coverage given by an agent prior to the issuance of a policy or payment of premium.

blanket mortgage   A mortgage covering more than one property.

blended mortgage rate   A refinance rate which is less than the current market rate but more than the old rate.

blind advertising   An advertisement which fails to indicate that the advertiser is a real estate agent.

blockbusting   Inducing panic selling for gain by the fear of loss in value because of a neighborhood change. Illegal under Civil Rights Act of 1968.

board foot   A unit of measurement of lumber equal to 144 cubic inches (a board 1 foot × 1 foot × 1 inch).

book value   Cost plus improvements less depreciation taken. The value an asset has for bookkeeping purposes.

boot   Money, personal property, or debt relief given to even off a trade. Boot is taxable to the person receiving it.

bracketing   Process of selecting a value which lies between selling prices of comparable properties having greater and lesser amenities. Used in the market comparison method of appraisal.

broker   An agent employed by a principal for real estate transactions. Only a broker can employ a salesperson.

broker's net income   An income figure which does not consider a vacancy factor, collection costs, or management expenses.

BTU (British Thermal Unit)   The unit of heat needed to raise one pound of water one degree Fahrenheit. It is used to rate the capacity of heating and air conditioning units.

budget mortgage   A loan where borrower pays one-twelfth of estimated property tax and insurance payment with each monthly payment.

building line   The setback from the lot line.

build-up method   A process for arriving at a capitalization rate by rating a risk-free, management-free investment and then adding for risk and management problems.

bulk sales act   A part of the Uniform Commercial Code; requires recording and publication of sales not in the course of normal business. Applies to the sale of stock in trade when a business is sold. If it is not complied with, the sale is void as to the vendor's creditors, who can then treat the stock as if the vendor still owned it.

bulk zoning   Zoning for density with height, setback, and open space requirements.

bundle of rights   All rights incidental to ownership such as rights to lease, use, encumber, sell, etc.

business opportunity   A business including stock, fixtures, and goodwill.

buydown   A financing technique in which a seller makes a property more attractive by paying a lender points to lower the effective interest rate on a mortgage.

bylaws   The rules as to how a corporation shall be governed; sets forth the authority of its officers.

capital assets   Physical assets such as land, buildings, and equipment, usually for a business or trade. Capital assets other than land may be depreciated.

capital gain   Profit from the sale of business or investment property. Long-term capital gain applies to assets held over six months.

capitalization method   An appraisal method whereby the net income of an investment property is capitalized to determine its value. The net income is divided by a capitalization rate.

capitalization rate   A desired rate of return for an investment which is divided into the net income to determine a property's value.

capital loss Loss from a sale of a capital asset or other real property.

cash flow The net spendable cash left over after all cash outlays are subtracted from the gross income.

CC&R's *see restrictive covenants*

certificate of eligibility Obtained by the veteran to be eligible for a VA loan. Veteran must submit discharge information.

certificate of occupancy Frequently required before a new structure can be occupied. Usually provided by the building inspector.

certificate of title Evidence of title issued by registrar under the Torrens Title System.

chain A surveyor measurement of 66 feet.

chain of title The actual history of a property showing all conveyances from the original government conveyance (patent). An abstract includes only the recorded history, so may differ from the chain of title.

chattel An item of personal property.

chattel mortgage A mortgage of personal property. Has been generally replaced by financing statements under the Uniform Commercial Code.

chattel real A personal property interest in real property such as a lease, mortgage, trust deed, land contract, or shares in a real estate syndicate.

check 24 × 24-mile area formed by guide meridians and parallels under government survey that correct for the curvature of the earth.

closing statement The final accounting showing all debits and credits in the sale of real property or a business. Also known as a Settlement Statement.

cloud on title A claim or document which casts doubt on the marketability of title.

codicil An amendment to a will. It requires the same formalities as the will itself.

coinsurance A requirement that a property carry a minimum coverage (usually 80% of replacement cost) in order to collect 100% of the loss. If a person carries only a percentage of the amount required then that person only gets that percentage of the loss suffered.

collateral That property which secures a loan.

color of title Appearing to have title, but because of some defect, not having title at all, as when a person has a deed from a party who had previously been declared insane.

commercial acre The amount left from an acre after deducting land for streets, walks, etc.; less than 43,560 square feet.

commingling Mixing personal and principal's funds. Considered grounds for disciplinary action.

commission An agent's fee or percentage for successfully completing a sale or lease.

common law The unwritten law of England established by precedent. The English Common Law is the basis for our statutory real estate law.

community property Property acquired during marriage which is considered equally owned by both spouses. Community property states presently are Arizona, California, Idaho, Louisiana, Nevada, New Mexico, Texas, Washington, and Wisconsin.

compensating balance Requirement of lender that borrower keep a specified balance on deposit with the lender.

compensatory damages Money damages awarded to indemnify the injured party for a loss because of the wrongful act of another.

complete escrow An escrow where everything necessary to be done has been accomplished.

compound interest Interest which compounds upon interest as well as principal. Since interest is paid monthly on normal real estate loans, the interest is simple interest, not compound interest.

condemnation Legal action to take property for public use by eminent domain. It also is the process of declaring property unfit for use.

conditional loan commitment A promise to make a loan on a property to a buyer yet unknown, as long as

condition precedent A condition which must happen prior to the vesting of title in another. Until the condition, title remains with the grantor.

condition subsequent A present transfer of title with the condition that title shall revert to the grantor upon the happening of some event. the buyer otherwise qualifies for the loan.

condominium A vertical subdivision with common ownership of land and common areas and individual ownership of the units.

conservator A person appointed by the probate court to manage and protect the assets of one who is unable to handle his or her own affairs.

consideration Something of value given or promised in exchange for a promise, act, or property of another. A promise made without consideration is considered void and unenforceable.

constructive eviction An act of a property owner which interferes with the quiet possession of the tenant. It allows the tenant to consider the lease at an end and discharges the tenant from further obligations.

contingent remainder A remainder interest in property which will only vest if some contingency is met, such as the holder outliving a life tenant.

contour lines Lines on a topographic map which follow elevations. Lines close together indicate a steep slope, and lines far apart indicate a level area.

contract An agreement between two or more parties which is enforceable by law.

conventional loan A loan made by a conventional lender; usually by savings and loan institutions, without government guarantee or insurance.

conversion Taking property entrusted to you and converting it to your own use; a form of larceny.

corner influence An increase in value of commercial property because of the additional traffic and exposure of being on two streets.

corporation A separate legal entity. Shareholders are not personally liable for debts of the corporation.

cost approach A method of appraisal whereby the cost to replace the structure is calculated. The accrued depreciation is determined and deducted from the replacement cost, and the land value is then added to determine the value of a property.

covenant A promise that runs with the land.

CPM (Certified Property Manager) A member of the Institute of Real Property Management of the National Association of Realtors®.

crawl space The space between the ground and the floor on houses not built on a slab or with a basement.

cripple Vertical piece of 2″ × 4″ board above or below an opening (window or door).

CRV (Certificate of Reasonable Value) Appraisal required for VA loans.

cubage The number of cubic feet contained in a structure.

cul-de-sac A dead end street ending with a rounded end. It is desirable for housing, as there is no through traffic.

curable depreciation   Depreciation which can be economically corrected.

curtesy   A common-law right of a husband in the estate of his deceased wife. Some states have made this a statutory right to a life estate in the wife's property.

datum plane   A surveyor's plane from which elevations and depths are measured.

dealer   A person who makes a regular part of his or her income by buying and selling property. Dealers are not eligible for capital gains even though they may hold an asset over six months, because it is considered to be their regular income.

declaration of homestead   A formal procedure of recording a homestead declaration. It protects the homestead from unsecured creditors up to a statutory amount.

declaration of restrictions   A declaration recorded by the subdivider of the restrictive covenants. In each deed the subdivider usually incorporates the restrictions by referencing the recording of the document.

declining balance depreciation   An accelerated method of depreciation used for tax purposes, whereby a percentage of the straight-line depreciation is taken from a constantly declining balance.

dedication   The gift of real property to a governmental unit, usually by a subdivider in order to gain approval. If the dedication is given for a particular purpose and that purpose is later abandoned, then the land dedicated may revert to the grantor.

deed   Document which conveys title in real property from a grantor to a grantee.

deed in lieu of foreclosure   Deed from owner to lienholder. Unlike foreclosure, does not wipe out junior encumbrances.

deed of reconveyance   A deed given by the trustee to the trustor when the trustor has fully paid the beneficiary. Used for trust deeds to remove the lien in the same manner as a satisfaction is used to remove a mortgage.

default   The breach of a promise or agreement.

defeasance clause   A clause in a mortgage which defeats or cancels the mortgage upon the full payment as agreed, or provides for forfeiture should the conditions not be fulfilled.

defeasible estate   An estate that is subject to forfeiture should some event take place (fee on a condition subsequent).

deferred maintenance   Maintenance that has been neglected.

deficiency judgment   A judgment obtained when foreclosure sale does not satisfy a debt. Difficult to obtain in many states because of restrictions on them. In some states they are not allowed.

degree   A measurement for angles used in metes and bounds descriptions. A degree is 1/360 of a circle.

demise   The transfer of a leasehold interest.

deposit receipt   Also known as a purchase contract or offer to purchase. An offer by a buyer, which becomes a binding contract when accepted by the seller.

depreciation   A loss in value of property from any cause.

depth table   An appraiser's table which determines additional value attributable to additional depth.

dereliction (or reliction)   Land which is created by the recession of water. It belongs to the adjacent landowners.

descent   Property passing to heirs.

devise   The passing of real property by will.

devisee   The person receiving real property by will.

devisor   The testator or testatrix who is transferring real property by will upon his or her death.

discounting a loan   Selling of a loan for less than its face value (common with second mortgages or loans bearing low interest rates).

discount loan   A loan where the interest is deducted in advance. It results in a higher effective rate of interest, since the total sum borrowed is not actually received.

disintermediation   The sudden withdrawal by savings from lending institutions. It results in a tight money market.

documentary stamps   Also known as revenue stamps. Formerly a federal tax on real property conveyances which, when abandoned, were picked up by many states.

dominant tenement   An estate using the land of another under an easement. The easement is an appurtenance to the dominant tenement.

double escrow   The use of one escrow to both purchase and resell a property.

dower   A wife's common-law right in the estate of her husband should she survive him. In some states it is a statutory right, such as one-third interest.

downzoning   A change in zoning resulting in a lower density use or lower use.

dragnet clause   A clause extending a mortgage to cover future obligations which may arise between the parties. Used in an open-end mortgage.

due on sale clause (alienation clause)   A type of acceleration clause in a note that makes all future payments due when a property is sold. Prevents an assumption of the loan.

duress   Use of force or threats to make a person act. Makes a contract voidable.

earnest money   A deposit made by an offeror with an offer to show that the offeror is serious.

easement   The right of a person to use land of another.

easement in gross   A personal easement to use land of another where there is no dominant tenement being benefited.

economic life   That period for which improvements give a return attributable to the improvements alone.

economic obsolescence   A decline in value caused by forces extraneous to the property itself.

effective age   An age placed on property for appraisal purposes based upon the condition of the property. It may be more or less than the chronological age.

effective gross income   The gross income less the vacancy factor and an allowance for collection loss.

ejectment   An action to eject (oust) an encroacher or a trespasser.

emblements   *See fructus industriales*

eminent domain   Government right to take private property (title or easement) for public use. It is not under the police power, since the owner is paid for the property taken.

enabling act   A legislative act which confers power on local governments that they would not otherwise have had. Zoning powers were given under enabling acts.

encroachment   A trespass by placing an improvement on or over the land of another.

encumbrance   Anything that affects title or limits use such as liens, easements, restrictions, etc.

environmental impact report   A report required for projects which may have a significant effect on the environment.

Environmental Protection Agency   Agency which enforces federal environmental standards.

Equal Credit Opportunity Act   Federal act which prohibits credit discrimination based upon age, sex, race, or marital status.

Equal Dignities Rule   If an act must be in writing, then the agency appointing someone to perform the act must also be in writing.

equity   The difference between the value of a property and the liens against it. It also means what is right or just.

equity of redemption   The right of a mortgagor to redeem after foreclosure; governed by state statute.

erosion   The wearing away of soil by acts of wind and/or water.

escalator clause   A clause in a contract or lease which provides for payments to rise or fall.

escape clause   A clause which lets a party out of contract responsibilities in the event of stated situations.

escheat   The reversion of property to the state when a person dies both intestate and without known heirs.

escrow   A neutral depository to handle real estate closings as the agent for both the buyer and the seller.

escrow account   *See impound account*

estate   An interest in property.

estate at will   An estate for an undetermined time period. Lessee has possession at the will of lessor.

estate for life   A freehold interest whereby a person has property for his or her life or the life of some other-named person. The life tenant cannot encumber the property beyond his or her interest. At the end of the estate, the interest either reverts back to the grantor or passes as a remainder interest to a third party.

estate for years   A lease for a definite period of time. It is the result of an express agreement.

estate of inheritance   An estate which can be inherited, such as a fee simple.

estoppel   A doctrine whereby a party is barred from raising a defense when that person's acts or words induced another party to act to his or her detriment.

exception in a deed   An exclusion in the deed. Deeding only part of the property.

exchange value   The value a property has as to other goods.

exclusionary clause   *See exception in a deed*

exclusive agency listing   A listing whereby the broker is the exclusive agent of the owner and is entitled to a commission if the broker or any other agent sells the property. If the owner sells the property without an agent, then the broker is not entitled to a commission.

exclusive right to sell listing   A listing whereby the agent is entitled to a commission if the property is sold during its term by anyone, including the owner.

exculpatory clause   A clause in a contract excusing a party for injuries to another. It is frequently used by lessors in leases. It does not affect the rights of third parties who may be injured on the premises.

execute   To sign a document.

executed contract   A contract where all performance has been completed.

execution of judgment   The action of the sheriff in seizing property of the debtor to satisfy a judgment.

executor   A man appointed by a will to administer the estate of a deceased. A woman is an executrix.

executory contract   A contract which has yet to be performed.

exemplary damages   Punitive damages which are awarded in excess of compensatory damages when an action was performed with willful intent.

express contract   A contract which is stated verbally or in writing, as opposed to an implied contract where it is understood but not stated.

extended coverage policy   Extends basic fire policy (fire, lightning, and smoke) to cover additional perils such as windstorm, hail, riot, etc.

extension of a lease   Continued occupancy under the terms of an existing lease. (A lease renewal is actually a new lease.)

fair credit reporting act   Allows a person to know what is in his or her credit file and to have explanations inserted and information investigated and removed if wrong.

Fannie Mae (FNMA)   A private corporation which sets the market in FHA and VA and conventional loans by buying and selling loans.

Farm Home Administration   Insures, subsidizes, and makes loans in rural areas. Preference is given to veterans.

FDIC (Federal Deposit Insurance Corporation)   Insures bank deposits. Federal banks must belong. State banks may be insured. (For savings and loan associations, see FSLIC.)

Federal Home Loan Bank   Provides a credit system for savings and loan associations to borrow from.

Federal Home Loan Mortgage Corporation (FHLMC or Freddie Mac)   A subsidiary of the Federal Home Loan Bank which serves as a secondary mortgage market for savings and loan associations.

Federal Land Bank   A farm credit administration agency which provides financing for farm purchases.

Federal Reserve System   A federal agency which regulates the money supply, interest rates, and reserve requirements of member banks.

fee simple   Highest ownership possible. No time limit, and it can be transferred or inherited. Also known as fee simple absolute. (The word Fee means an inheritable estate.)

fee tail   An estate where conveyance is limited to the descendants of the grantee.

fictitious name   A name which does not include the surname of every principal in a business. In order to sue as the fictitious name, the fictitious-name statutes must be complied with (publication and recording).

fiduciary   The financial trust relationship of an agent to the principal.

financing statement   A notice filed by a lender on a personal property loan to give the public notice that the goods are security for the loan. (Under Uniform Commercial Code.)

fire block   A horizontal block between studs to prevent a fire from rising through a wall.

fire wall   A wall built of fireproof material to limit or contain a fire.

firm commitment   A loan commitment made for a particular borrower and property.

fixture   A former item of personal property which has become so connected to the realty that it has become part of the real property.

flat lease   A level-payment lease with no escalation clause. Also known as a gross lease.

floor space   Interior square footage measured from the inside walls.

footing   Concrete poured in the ground upon which the foundation rests. Spreads the building load directly to the soil.

foreclosure   Legal procedure whereby the lender forces the sale of property to pay indebtedness in the event of default.

foundation   The masonry substructure upon which the building rests. The foundation rests on the footing.

fraud An intentional act or omission to deceive another to the detriment of the other party.

freehold A higher interest-category of estates (fee simple and life estates) as opposed to non-freehold estates, which are leasehold interests.

front foot Some commercial and waterfront property is sold based on a price per linear front foot.

fructus industriales Emblements. Annual crops and plants resulting from human cultivation. They are generally considered to be personal property, and the tenant has the right to remove them after a lease expires.

fructus naturales Trees and perennial crops and uncultivated natural growth. Generally considered real property.

FSLIC (Federal Savings and Loan Insurance Corporation) A federal agency which insures savings and loan accounts in federal savings and loan associations. State savings and loan associations can also be insured.

functional obsolescence Built-in obsolescence by design or construction.

gable roof A roof in which the two opposite planes slope down from a ridge line.

gambrel roof A roof with a steep lower slope and a flatter upper slope. It is found on some barns and on Dutch Colonials.

gap loan A standby loan, usually at a higher interest rate, where the borrower intends to obtain better financing. It is also known as a swing loan.

general power of attorney A broad power given by a principal to an agent which enables the agent to act for the principal. (A specific power of attorney only allows the agent to act in the manner and area specified.)

gift deed A deed given for love and affection. Creditors of the donor can reach the property if it can be shown that the gift was made while the donor was insolvent in order to evade creditors. A recorded gift deed does not take precedence over a prior unrecorded deed by the grantor for value.

GNMA (Government National Mortgage Association or Ginnie Mae) A federal corporation which provides assistance for federally aided housing projects by purchasing mortgages that are at below-market interest rates. Funds are raised through the sale of government-backed securities.

government survey The survey system used for most of the nation whereby land is measured from principal base lines and meridians and laid out in townships and sections.

graduated payment mortgage (GPM) A loan where early payments are lower and increase during the term of the loan. Makes it easier for young people to purchase property.

grandfather clause A regulation which permits existing things or uses to continue despite new laws against them. Applies to uses in existence prior to zoning.

grant A transfer of title.

grant deed A deed used in some states in conjunction with title insurance whereby the seller warrants that title has not been previously conveyed and that there is nothing against the property that the seller knows of which has not been disclosed to the buyer.

grantee The person who receives the grant from the grantor.

granting clause Clause in a deed indicating that title is passing.

grantor The person who makes the grant to the grantee.

grantor/grantee index A recorder's index system by grantor/grantee names. It makes it easy to research a title.

GRI (Graduate Realtors® Institute) Professional designation which requires seminar attendance and courses of study.

gross income   The total income before any expenses or deductions.

gross multiplier   An appraisal method to get an approximate idea of vaue, where gross income is multiplied by a gross multiplier. Does not take into account unusual expenses.

gross lease   *See flat lease*

gross profit   Gross sales less the cost of the merchandise. To obtain net profit, all other expenses must also be deducted.

ground lease   A lease of land only. Tenant puts in the improvements.

ground rent   The portion of the rent which would be attributed to the land rather than improvements.

guardian   A person lawfully charged with managing the property of another who is legally incapable.

habendum   The *have and to hold* clause in a deed indicating the extent of ownership being transferred, such as fee simple or life estate.

hard money loan   A cash loan, rather than seller financing.

header   A beam over a window or door.

head lease   A master lease where the lessee subleases portions of the premises.

hereditaments   Any item capable of inheritance.

highest and best use   That use which results in the greatest net attributable to the land and/or building.

hip roof   A roof where all four sides slope to a ridge line.

hold-harmless clause   A clause where one party agrees to indemnify the other for any loss suffered because of the contract or lease.

holdover clause   A clause in a lease which provides for a very high rent should the tenant fail to vacate at the end of a lease. It makes a holdover situation unlikely.

holdover tenant   Tenant retaining possession after expiration of lease. *See tenancy at sufferance*

holographic will   A handwritten signed and dated will; no witnesses are needed.

homeowners' policy   A comprehensive insurance policy covering fire, vandalism, theft, liability, and other hazards.

homestead   A home on which a declaration of homestead has been filed which protects the home from unsecured creditors up to a statutory amount.

HUD   Federal Department of Housing and Urban Development.

hypothecate   To give something as security without giving up possession.

illegal   In violation of an existing law.

illiquidity   An asset which is not readily convertible to cash. Real estate is considered to be illiquid.

illusory contract   An agreement which appears to be binding, but where one party is actually not bound; not enforceable.

implied contract   An agreement which is not expressly stated but is implied by the actions of the parties.

implied easement   An easement implied when the grantor conveys property which is landlocked by other property of the grantor or where the grantor created the use, then sold the parcels separately.

impound account (escrow account)   A reserve for taxes and insurance kept by the lender to which the borrower pays along with regular principal and interest payments.

incentive zoning   Zoning that allows commercial use of the first floor of office structures.

incompetent A person who, because of age or mental capacity, lacks the legal ability to contract.

increment Any increase in value.

incurable depreciation Depreciation where the cost of correction is prohibitive.

index lease A lease tied to an index such as the consumer price index.

index method A method of determining cost of replacement by taking the actual costs when built and applying the increases in the construction cost index since that date.

informal description A description of property which is not a legal description, such as by street address or name of owner.

ingress A means of entering.

injunction A court action to cease and desist from a course of action.

interest rate The percentage of a loan balance charged by the lender for use of the money.

internal rate of return A method of measuring returns on investment that considers tax consequences.

interpleader action An action requested by a party to determine rights when two or more people claim to have an interest in property, such as an action brought by a broker where both buyer and seller demand the broker turn over trust funds to them.

Interstate Land Sales Act Federal disclosure act for projects of 25 or more unimproved lots to be sold in interstate commerce.

intestate Dying without a will. Property passes according to state statute as to intestate succession to the heirs.

inverse condemnation An action by an owner to force a government unit to take property when by its action it has wrongfully restricted use.

involuntary lien A lien imposed without the consent of the landowner, such as a tax lien. A mortgage is a voluntary lien.

joint and several Agreement to be liable together as well as separately.

joint liability Each party agrees to be liable together equally for an obligation.

joint tenancy An undivided interest with the right of survivorship. Owners must take title at the same time, by the same instrument, with equal interests, and equal rights of possession.

joint venture A partnership for a particular undertaking only. It differs from a normal partnership in that one partner alone in a joint venture cannot obligate the other joint venture partners.

joist Horizontal boards which support a floor or ceiling.

judgment Final order of a court as to money owed. When recorded, the judgment becomes a general lien on the property of the debtor.

junior lien A subordinate lien as determined by time of recording or nature of the lien.

laches The loss of the right to enforce an agreement because the delay in bringing action worked to the detriment of the other party.

land contract Also known as a *Contract for Sale*. The seller keeps title while the buyer gets possession. Title passes when the property has been fully paid for.

lateral support The support a landowner has a duty to provide to adjacent property owners.

lease A tenancy agreement between the landlord (lessor) and tenant (lessee).

legacy A bequest of money by will.

legal description A description of real property either by government survey, metes and bounds, or reference to recorded lot, block, and tract.

lessee   A tenant under a lease.

lessor   Landlord who has given a lease.

leverage   Use of other peoples' money to make money. Purchasing real property with a minimum down payment is a use of leverage.

license   A revocable privilege to use the land of another.

lien   An encumbrance which is secured by real estate.

lien theory   The theory that a mortgage is a lien and not a transfer of title (majority of states). *See title theory*

life estate   An estate in property for the life of a person. It may not be inherited.

like for like   An exchange of similar property which qualified for a tax-free exchange; for example, real property for real property.

limited partnership   A partnership where one or more of the partners have liability limited to the extent of their investment only.

link   A surveyor's measure equal to 7.92 inches.

liquidated damages   Agreeing in advance as to the amount of damages for nonperformance when exact damages may be difficult to ascertain. If they are so unreasonable that the court considers them a penalty, they will not be enforced.

lis pendens   A recorded notice of a pending lawsuit concerning a property. Though not a lien, it provides constructive notice in a property.

listing   An agency agreement between owner and broker where the owner authorizes the broker to attempt to find a buyer, and to pay an agreed commission should the broker succeed.

littoral property   Property located on shore of lake or ocean.

littoral rights   Right of a property owner to reasonable use of lake, pond, or ocean water bordering the property (rights to flowing water are riparian rights).

livable floor space   Space measured by the interior of each room. It excludes interior walls and closets.

loan-to-value ratio   The percentage of value which will be loaned on a property.

lock-in clause   A clause which allows prepayment providing full interest is paid as if the loan had gone to maturity. The borrower is locked in as to interest.

longitude and latitude   Longitude is measured in terms of north-south meridians; latitude is referenced by lines parallel to the equator. Both are measured in degrees (°), minutes (') and seconds (").

MAI (Member, Appraiser's Institute)   A professional designation of the American Institute of Appraisers of the National Association of Realtors®.

mansard roof   A French-style roof with a steep lower slope and a very gentle upper slope.

margin of security   Lenders security which is the difference between the mortgage amount and the value of the property.

market comparison approach   An appraisal method where value is based on sales of comparable properties.

marketable title   A title that is clear of objectionable liens and encumbrances. A merchantable title.

market price   Price actually paid.

market value   Price a willing, informed buyer would pay to a willing, informed seller.

mechanic's lien   A specific lien by contractor, subcontractor, materialman, or laborer for work performed for a property but not paid for.

menace Threat of force that makes a contract voidable.

merger The joining of a lesser right into a superior right so as to extinguish the lesser one. For example, a tenant having an estate for years buys the property in fee simple; the lease is extinguished, since the owner and tenant are one and the same.

meridians Government surveyors' north-south lines which intersect base lines. Land is measured from the intersection of these lines.

metes and bounds Land description by measurements and boundaries.

MGIC (Mortgage Guaranty Insurance Corporation) A private mortgage insurance (PMI) carrier.

mile A linear measure of 5,280 feet.

mill One-tenth of a cent or 1/1000 of a dollar; written as .001. Property taxes are often expressed in mills.

minor Any person under contractual age.

monument A fixed surveyor's marker for a metes and bounds description; can be natural, such as a rock or tree, or artificial, such as an iron stake.

mortgage A security device for real estate. In lien-theory states, the seller retains title and gives the mortgagee a lien. In title-theory states, the mortgagor retains possession but gives the mortgagee title as security.

mortgagee One who receives the mortgage. A lender or a seller (under a purchase-money mortgage).

mortgage loan correspondent A firm that arranges the sale of existing loans in the secondary mortgage market.

mortgage note The note which reflects the promise to pay the mortgage debt. The mortgage is security for the note.

mortgagor The owner or buyer of property who gives the mortgage.

mortgage warehousing Interim financing where a lender or correspondent borrows on the stock of mortgages until they can be sold.

mudsill or sill The lowest board on a house which rests on the foundation. It is often of redwood to resist rot.

multiple listing A listing, usually an exclusive right to sell listing, which is given out to a group of cooperating brokers who are members of a multiple listing service.

mutual savings banks Banks owned by depositors and paying dividends, not interest, to their depositors. Located in several Northeastern states, they can make real estate loans anywhere in the nation.

naked title Legal title only without other rights of ownership. For example: a trustee under a deed of trust.

NAR National Association of Realtors®.

NARELLO (National Association of Real Estate License Law Officers) Made up of real estate commissioners from each state.

narrative report An appraisal written in a narrative form. The most comprehensive form of appraisal report.

National Flood Insurance Act Legislation which makes flood insurance available in communities which have developed a flood-protection plan.

natural monument A surveying point for metes and bounds descriptions which is natural, as opposed to man-made. Examples: tree, rock, river bank, etc.

negative cash flow An investment or business which requires regular infusion of cash, since the cash outlay exceeds the cash receipts.

negative fraud Fraud which results from failure to disclose rather than from an affirmative act.

neighborhood   An area of social conformity.

net-net lease   Tenant pays all expenses except taxes and insurance.

net-net-net lease   A lease where tenant pays all expenses including taxes and insurance and gives lessor a net amount as rent.

net listing   A listing where the broker receives as commission that portion of the sales price which exceeds the listing price. Illegal in some states.

net profit   Profit after all expenses (excludes payment on principal of loans or taxes on the profit).

net spendable   *see cash flow*

net worth   The difference between total assets and total liabilities.

nominal   The rate stated in the instrument. Can also mean minimum.

nominal damages   A token amount awarded by the court when there are no actual damages resulting from a wrongful act.

nominee   A new person who is designated to perform under a contract in the place of another. Unlike an assignment, when there is a nominee, the original person is totally relieved of his or her obligations.

non-freehold estate   A leasehold interest.

non-institutional lender   Lender other than banks, savings and loan associations, and insurance companies. Examples: pension funds and private individuals.

note   A signed instrument which acknowledges a debt and agrees to pay it either on demand or at a set date in the future. The mortgage or trust deed secures the note in real estate transactions.

notice of completion   A notice filed by an owner which starts a statutory period in which mechanics' liens must be filed.

notice of default   A notice given under a trust deed which sets statutory period for trustor to pay up his or her obligations.

notice of nonresponsibility   A notice filed by owner to protect the property from liens for work authorized by another person, i.e., tenant.

notice to quit   A statutory notice given by a landlord to the tenant to vacate the premises.

novation   The substitution of one agreement for another, or the substitution of parties to the agreement.

nuisance   A use of property which interferes with the quiet enjoyment by others of their properties. An abatement action can be taken to stop (abate) the nuisance.

nuncupative will   An oral deathbed will for personal property of low value. It must be reduced to writing by the witnesses. Not valid in all states.

objective value   The market value as opposed to subjective value, which is use value.

obligatory advances   Loan advances required to be made by a lender under an agreement as construction progresses.

observed condition method   The method of determining effective age of a property by its condition.

obsolescence   Loss in value due to reduced desirability because of built-in design (functional obsolescence) or forces outside the property itself (economic obsolescence).

offset statement   Statement by lender as to the current status of a loan (balance due). *See beneficiary statement*

open-end mortgage   A mortgage which can be increased in the future up to an agreed-upon maximum amount. *See dragnet clause*

open listing   A nonexclusive agency whereby the owner agrees to a fee only if the broker is the one to first procure a buyer under the exact terms of the listing or any other terms that the owner agrees to.

open mortgage   A loan that can be prepaid without penalty.

option   A noncancelable right given by an owner to another to buy a property at an agreed-upon price within a stated period of time. To be valid, consideration must have been given to keep the offer open.

optionee   Party who purchased the option and has the right to exercise it.

optionor   Owner who gives the option.

orientation   The way a structure is placed on a site.

origination fee   Points paid to obtain a loan.

or more **clause**   A clause which allows prepayment without penalty.

packaged mortgage   A mortgage that includes personal property as well as real property.

parol evidence rule   The rule that bars verbal (parol) evidence from being used to show that a contract means other than what it says. Parol evidence can be used to clarify ambiguities or to show fraud.

participation loan   Loan agreement where the lender receives a share of the revenue or profits in addition to the interest. The lender takes on equity share as a limited partner or stockholder as partial consideration for the loan.

partition action   A legal action to break a joint ownership.

party wall   A common wall on the property line maintained by both owners.

patent   The original conveyance of land from the government.

payback period   Period of time it will take for the income generated by a property to return the investment (down payment).

penny   A measure for nails shown as the letter "d." The larger the penny, the larger the nail.

percentage lease   A lease where the rent is a percentage of the gross income.

percolation   The ability of soil to absorb water. Percolation tests are required in many areas before a permit will be issued for a structure requiring septic system.

perfect escrow   An escrow in which all signed documents and funds have been deposited with the escrow and it is ready for closing.

periodic tenancy   A rental from period to period which renews itself automatically unless a notice is given by lessor or lessee.

personal property   Property which is not classified as real property.

per stirpes   Inheritance by right of representation. Children share equally in the share their deceased parent would have received. This is different from per-capita distribution, where all heirs obtain the same amount.

physical deterioration   Depreciation caused by age and use.

pitch   The slope of a roof. Usually expressed in inches per foot; a five-twelfths pitch would drop 5 inches in each horizontal foot. Generally, roofs with steeper pitch have longer lives than more gently sloped roofs.

PITI   Used to denote that a payment includes principal, interest, taxes, and insurance.

planned development project   A development containing areas owned in common such as recreational area.

planning commission   A group of appointed officials responsible for planning and zoning.

plat   A map or plan of a subdivision showing individual lots.

plate   A horizontal board (2" × 4") to which studs are nailed. There is both a top and bottom plate (sole plate).

plot plan   Layout of a lot showing the placement of the structure in relationship to lot lines.

plottage   The increase in value from the process of assemblage (joining several adjacent parcels to form a larger parcel).

POB   Point of beginning (metes and bounds description).

points   A fee charged by the lender which amounts to advance interest. It makes up for an interest rate the lender considers too low. Each point is one percent of the loan amount.

police power   Power of the state to enforce order, safety, health, morals, and general welfare. No compensation is given for financial losses resulting from the exercise of police power. It cannot be delegated to a nongovernmental body. Examples: zoning, health code, and building code enforcement.

power of attorney   A written agency agreement given by a principal to an attorney in fact to act in his or her behalf.

prepayment penalty   A penalty for prepaying a loan prior to the payment schedule of the note.

prescription   Obtaining an easement by open, hostile, and continuous use for a statutory period of time.

primary financing   First mortgages and trust deeds.

primary mortgage market   The actual granting of loans from the lender to the borrower.

principal   One who engages an agent to act in his or her behalf.

principle of anticipation   Value will change based on anticipated future use and income.

principle of change   Real estate values do not remain constant.

principle of competition   When extraordinary profits are being made, competition will enter the area and profits will drop.

principle of conformity   A property will have its maximum value when it is in an area of similar properties.

principle of dependency   The value of a parcel changes based on changes in the use of surrounding parcels.

principle of diminishing returns   As demand is met, new units will result in a lower return.

principle of integration and disintegration   Property goes through three phases of development: integration, equilibrium, and disintegration (growth, stability, and decline).

principle of substitution   A person will not pay more for a property than it would cost for a property of equal utility and desirability.

principle of supply and demand   The greater the supply, the lower the value; the less the supply, the higher the value. The greater the demand, the greater the value. The less the demand, the less the value.

pro-forma financial statement   An estimated operating statement based upon anticipated returns and expenses. It is used where there is no real experience.

progression   The increased value of a less expensive home resulting from more expensive homes being around it.

proprietary lease   Lease by a cooperative to a shareholder providing a right to occupy a unit.

proration   To apportion based on actual time to the date of closing, as with taxes, insurance, rents, etc.

puffing   A statement of opinion given in a sale. Not a warranty.

punitive damages   Exemplary damages beyond actual damages awarded for a wrongful, willful act, for the purpose of punishing the wrongdoer.

purchase-money mortgage A mortgage given by the buyer to the seller to finance the purchase. The seller is financing the buyer. Actual cash does not change hands.

purchase saleback or purchase leaseback Investor buys property and sells or leases it to original owner. Normally used by an owner to free capital for operational purposes.

quantity survey A detailed method to determine replacement cost by pricing out all the elements of a structure in the same manner as a builder would estimate costs.

quiet enjoyment Right of an owner or tenant to use the property without interference.

quiet title A court action to determine ownership rights.

quitclaim deed A deed conveying whatever interest the grantor may have without making any claims as to ownership.

rafter The diagonal roof beams running from the eaves to the ridge of the roof.

range A vertical row of townships, measured east and west from the meridian.

ratification The approval of an act of the agent by the principal when the agent exceeded his or her authority. By taking the benefits of the act, the principal also accepts its obligations.

real estate board An organization of brokers and associates (salespeople).

real estate investment trust (REIT) Unincorporated group of 100 or more investors who have limited liability. Taxed on retained earnings only under federal law.

Real Estate Settlement Procedures Act (RESPA) A federal disclosure act requiring borrower be given an estimate of settlement costs and an information booklet. Administered by HUD.

real property Land and that which goes with the land (appurtenances).

realtist A real estate broker who is a member of the National Association of Real Estate Brokers.

Realtor® A broker-member of the National Association of Realtors® (NAR).

receiver clause A mortgage clause which allows mortgagee to appoint a receiver to collect rents between the period of commencement of foreclosure and final foreclosure.

reconveyance deed The deed from the trustee to the trustor when the trustor has satisified the debt to the beneficiary.

recordation The act of recording with the county recorder which serves to give constructive notice to all of the instruments recorded.

recorded lot block and tract system Legal description based on approved subdivision description.

recovery fund A fund maintained by many state real estate departments to repay persons who suffer losses because of wrongful acts of licensees. Recovery is up to a statutory limit and usually requires an uncollected judgment against the licensee.

redlining Refusing to make loans within designated areas. Considered to be a violation of the Civil Rights Act of 1968.

reformation A court action to rectify a mistake in a deed or contract so it reads as it was intended to read.

regression A loss in value because a home was placed in an area of less expensive homes.

release clause A clause in a blanket encumbrance allowing separate releases from the encumbrance by paying stated sums of money.

reliction *See dereliction*

remainder depreciation   The depreciation which an owner has left to take.

remainder interest   An interest that a third person has in property after the death of a life tenant.

renewal of lease   A new lease. An *extension* of a lease continues the old lease.

replacement cost   Cost of replacing a structure of the same desirability and utility value.

rescission of contract   Setting aside the contract and placing the parties back in the condition they were in prior to the contract (as opposed to waiver, which leaves them as they are).

reservation   The retention of a right such as an easement when property is conveyed. (An exception retains part of the property.)

reserve for replacement   A reserve fund established to replace an asset.

restricted license   A probationary license granted by some states after a license has been revoked, suspended, or denied.

restrictive covenants   Private beneficial restrictions whereby owners are restricted in the use of their property. Examples are minimum size, setbacks, height limitations, etc. They are also known as CC&R's (covenants, conditions, and restrictions).

revenue stamps   *See documentary stamps*

reverse mortgage   The mortgagee pays the loan amount in monthly payments to the mortgagor (like an annuity). When the mortgagor dies or sells, the loan is paid back.

reversionary interest   An interest whereby a property reverts to the original grantor upon occurrence of some event, such as the death of a life tenant.

rezoning   Changing the zoning, as opposed to a variance, which is an exception to the zoning.

ridge board   The highest board in a house. It is between the tops of the opposing rafters.

right of first refusal   A right sometimes given to a tenant to be able to meet the price and terms at which the owner is willing to sell the property to another party. The owner must first offer it to the right holder before a sale can be made to another. Unlike in an option, the owner is under no requirement to sell.

right of prior appropriation   A right of water use based on who was first user. Primarily in Western states.

right of way   The right to pass over land of another, such as in an easement.

right of correlative user   Right of a landowner to the reasonable use of underground percolating water (water table).

riparian right   Right of landowner to reasonable use of the flowing water located on, under, or adjacent to his or her property.

rollover mortgage (Canadian Rollover)   Short-term mortgage at fixed rate, with payments based on a long-term amortized loan. Lender refinances when due at the prevailing rate.

R value   A measure of insulation effectiveness.

safety clause   A clause in a listing which grants the broker a commission for a sale made within a specified period of time after a listing expires, if the broker submits the name of the buyer to the owner within a stated period of time as a party with whom he had negotiated prior to the expiration of the listing.

sandwich lease   A lease where the lessor is not the owner.

sans   Without.

satisfaction of mortgage   Given by the mortgagee to the mortgagor when the mortgage has been satisfied. By recording, it removes the lien.

seal   An impression or stamp to authenticate the signature on a document. Required in some states on formal documents. Generally "(seal)" or the letters "L.S." are sufficient.

seasoned loan   A loan with a payment history. Such a loan is desirable on the secondary mortgage market.

secondary financing   Second mortgages or trust deeds.

secondary mortgage market   The buying and selling of existing mortgages.

secret profit   An undisclosed profit of the agent.

section   A parcel of land one mile square containing 640 acres, formed by government survey.

security agreement   A security interest which a creditor retains in personal property of a debtor (under Uniform Commercial Code).

separate property   Property owned individually by a spouse in which the other spouse has no interest.

servient tenement   An estate which is used by another under an easement.

setback   Building-line distance from the lot line.

severalty ownership   Ownership by one person alone.

sheathing   A covering over studs and rafters. May be plywood, boards, or composition board over which the siding or roofing is placed.

sheriff's deed   A deed given by the sheriff when property is sold for execution of a judgment or sheriff's foreclosure sale.

short rate   A less-than prorated refund when insured cancels a policy.

soil pipe   The sewage pipe carrying waste from a building to the sewer or septic system.

Soldiers and Sailors Civil Relief Act   A law which restricts foreclosure of a person in service.

special assessment   A charge against a property for a specific improvement such as street or sewer. It is usually assessed on a front-foot basis.

specific performance   A legal remedy of requiring a party to perform as agreed. It will ordinarily be granted where money damages are not adequate.

split rate   Use of separate capitalization rates for land and improvements.

spot zoning   Small areas of zoning use which do not fit with the general use of the area (frequently resulting from political influence).

square footage   Measurement by taking exterior dimensions, excluding the garage.

Statute of Frauds   Requires certain contracts including those dealing in real estate to be in writing.

Statute of Limitations   Sets forth the time limit in which legal action must be taken or rights will lapse.

step lease   Lease with graduated increases.

stock cooperative project   A cooperative where each owner owns stock in the project and has the right to occupy a unit.

straight-line depreciation   A method of depreciation whereby an equal amount is deducted each year over the life of the asset.

straight note   A note where interest only is paid, with the entire principal payable on due date.

straw man   A substitute used to conceal the identity of an actual purchaser.

studs   Vertical 2″ × 4″ boards in a wall. Usually 16 inches on center (from center of one to the center of the next stud).

subdivision   A land division in accordance with state subdivision laws.

subjective value   The use value to the owner.

subject-to mortgage   An agreement that allows the buying of real estate without agreeing to pay an encumbrance. Buyer is not personally liable on the loan, so a deficiency judgment is not possible. Buyer must make payments, however, or lienholder will foreclose.

sublease   A lease given by the original lessee, who becomes a sublessor. The sublessee is the tenant of the sublessor and not of the original lessor.

subordinate   An agreement that a loan will be secondary to another encumbrance.

subrogation   The substitution of one party for another as to his or her interests.

surrender   Mutual agreement of the parties to end a lease. All further obligations of the parties are terminated.

survey   A location or verification of property lines by a surveyor.

survivorship   Upon the death of a joint tenant, the tenant's interests cease to exist, and all interests remain undivided with the survivors.

sweat equity   Equity earned through owner's construction or improvements.

syndicate   A limited partnership for investment purposes.

take-out loan   Permanent financing which replaces (takes out) the construction loan.

tax collector   Collects property tax and conducts tax sales.

tax deed   The deed given at a tax sale.

tax roll   Total assessed valuation of all taxable property.

$$\text{tax rate} = \text{needed revenue} \div \text{tax roll}$$

tax sale   Sale of property to satisfy real property tax lien.

tax shelter   Way of excluding income from taxes by such means as depreciation, which is a paper expense and can offset other income.

tenancy at sufferance   A tenant holding over at the expiration of a lease. No notice is required to eject the former tenant.

tenancy at will   A tenancy for an indeterminate period.

tenancy by the entirety   A form of joint tenancy for husbands and wives. Neither spouse can separately convey to break the tenancy.

tenancy in common   Ownership by two or more persons, each of whom has an undivided interest without the right of survivorship.

tender   An unconditional offer to perform (legal tender is money).

termination statement   Statement filed to remove a personal property lien of a financing statement.

testate   To die with a will.

testator   A man who has a will.

testatrix   A woman who has a will.

tier   A horizontal row of townships, measured north and south from the base line.

time is of the essence   A statement which makes prompt performance mandatory.

title   Ownership. Title is passed by deed.

title theory   The theory that a mortgage is a transfer of title to secure a loan, and not just a lien (minority of states).

topography   The surface elevations of a property.

Torrens title   A system of registering ownership where the government keeps the registers.

township   An area established by U.S. Government Survey which is six miles square and contains 36 sections.

trade fixture Personal property installed by a tenant to carry on a trade or business; remains personal property, and can be removed by the tenant any time prior to the lease expiration.

trading on equity Borrowing money on equity in property in order to invest it at a higher rate of return.

trespass A wrongful intrusion on the land of another.

trust deed Transfer of title from the trustor (borrower) to a trustee (third party) as security for a note to a beneficiary (lender).

trustee The third party who holds the trust deed.

trustor The debtor who gives title to the trustee as security for the loan.

Truth in Lending Part of Consumer Credit Protection Act, also known as Regulation Z. It is a disclosure act requiring lender to show the interest as an Annual Percentage Rate (APR).

ultra vires An act outside the authority of the person acting. That person is personally responsible for his or her actions.

unconscionable contract A contract which is so unfair or harsh that the court will refuse to enforce it.

undue influence Taking advantage of another because of a unique position of trust, such as doctor-patient or attorney-client.

unearned increment An increase in value that is not due to any effort of the owner.

Uniform Commercial Code Standardized commercial laws adopted throughout the nation.

unilateral contract A promise in exchange for an act; accepted by the offeree's performance.

unit in place method An appraising method whereby cost is priced per unit, such as price per square foot.

unlawful detainer Legal eviction procedure.

usury An unlawful rate of interest.

valid Enforceable by either party.

valid escrow Escrow in which an agreement has been reached and there has been conditional delivery of transfer agreements (deeds) to escrow. Delivery is conditioned upon escrow receiving all required funds and/or liens.

valley An internal angle in a roof. Metalwork is often used in a valley to prevent leaks.

variable rate mortgage (VRM) *See ARM*

variance An exception to zoning.

vendee The buyer.

vendor The seller.

verification A sworn statement before an officer of the court as to the correctness of the contents of an instrument.

vested A present or sure interest which cannot be revoked.

vested remainder A remainder interest that cannot be defeated, such as a remainder interest to a life estate. The remainder holder or heirs are bound to get the property.

void Having no legal effect.

voidable Capable of being voided by one party only. Valid until voided.

voluntary lien A lien placed by an owner, such as a mortgage.

wainscoting The treatment of the lower portion of a wall in a different manner than the rest of the wall; half paneling.

waive To give up or relinquish a right.

waiver Accepting something less than contracted for. A waiver leaves the parties as they are. Rescission places them back as they were.

Code of Ethics[1]
of the
National Association of Realtors®

Revised and Approved by the
Delegate Body of the Association
at its 75th Annual Convention
November 15, 1982

Preamble . . .

Under all is the land. Upon its wise utilization and widely allocated ownership depend the survival and growth of free institutions and of our civilization. The REALTOR® should recognize that the interests of the nation and its citizens require the highest and best use of the land and the widest distribution of land ownership. They require the creation of adequate housing, the building of functioning cities, the development of productive industries and farms, and the preservation of a healthful environment.

Such interests impose obligations beyond those of ordinary commerce. They impose grave social responsibility and a patriotic duty to which the REALTOR® should dedicate himself, and for which he should be diligent in preparing himself. The REALTOR®, therefore, is zealous to maintain and improve the standards of his calling and shares with his fellow REALTORS® a common responsibility for its integrity and honor. The term REALTOR® has come to connote competency, fairness, and high integrity resulting from adherence to a lofty ideal of moral conduct in business relations. No inducement of profit and no instruction from clients ever can justify departure from this ideal.

In the interpretation of this obligation, a REALTOR® can take no safer guide than that which has been handed down through the centuries, embodied in the Golden Rule, "Whatsoever ye would that men should do to you, do ye even so to them."

Accepting this standard as his own, every REALTOR® pledges himself to observe its spirit in all of his activities and to conduct his business in accordance with the tenets set forth below.

Article 1

The REALTOR® should keep himself informed on matters affecting real estate in his community, the state, and nation so that he may be able to contribute responsibly to public thinking on such matters.

Article 2

In justice to those who place their interests in his care, the REALTOR® should endeavor always to be informed regarding laws, proposed legislation, governmental regulations, public policies, and current market conditions in order to be in a position to advise his clients properly.

Article 3

It is the duty of the REALTOR® to protect the public against fraud, misrepresentation, and unethical practices in real estate transactions. He should endeavor to eliminate in his community any practices which could be damaging to the public or bring discredit to the real estate profession. The REALTOR® should assist the governmental agency charged with regulating the practices of brokers and salesmen in his state.

Article 4

The REALTOR® should seek no unfair advantage over other REALTORS® and should conduct his business so as to avoid controversies with other REALTORS®.

Article 5

In the best interests of society, of his associates, and his own business, the REALTOR® should willingly share with other REALTORS® the lessons of his experience and study for the benefit of the public, and should be loyal to the Board of REALTORS® of his community and active in its work.

1. Published with the consent of the NATIONAL ASSOCIATION OF REALTORS®, author of and owner of all rights in the Code of Ethics of the NATIONAL ASSOCIATION OF REALTORS®, © NATIONAL ASSOCIATION OF REALTORS® 1982— All Rights Reserved. The NATIONAL ASSOCIATION OF REALTORS® reserves exclusively unto itself the right to comment on and interpret the CODE and particular provisions thereof. For the NATIONAL ASSOCIATION's official interpretations of the CODE, see INTERPRETATIONS OF THE CODE OF ETHICS; NATIONAL ASSOCIATION OF REALTORS®.

Article 6

To prevent dissension and misunderstanding and to assure better service to the owner, the REALTOR® should urge the exclusive listing of property unless contrary to the best interest of the owner.

Article 7

In accepting employment as an agent, the REALTOR® pledges himself to protect and promote the interests of the client. This obligation of absolute fidelity to the client's interests is primary, but it does not relieve the REALTOR® of the obligation to treat fairly all parties to the transaction.

Article 8

The REALTOR® shall not accept compensation from more than one party, even if permitted by law, without the full knowledge of all parties to the transaction.

Article 9

The REALTOR® shall avoid exaggeration, misrepresentation, or concealment of pertinent facts. He has an affirmative obligation to discover adverse factors that a reasonably competent and diligent investigation would disclose.

Article 10

The REALTOR® shall not deny equal professional services to any person for reasons of race, creed, sex, or country of national origin. The REALTOR® shall not be party to any plan or agreement to discriminate against a person or persons on the basis of race, creed, sex, or country of national origin.

Article 11

A REALTOR® is expected to provide a level of competent service in keeping with the standards of practice in those fields in which the REALTOR® customarily engages.

The REALTOR® shall not undertake to provide specialized professional services concerning a type of property or service that is outside his field of competence unless he engages the assistance of one who is competent on such types of property or service, or unless the facts are fully disclosed to the client. Any person engaged to provide such assistance shall be so identified to the client and his contribution to the assignment should be set forth.

The REALTOR® shall refer to the Standards of Practice of the National Association as to the degree of competence that a client has a right to expect the REALTOR® to possess, taking into consideration the complexity of the problem, the availability of expert assistance, and the opportunities for experience available to the REALTOR®.

Article 12

The REALTOR® shall not undertake to provide professional services concerning a property or its value where he has a present or contemplated interest unless such interest is specifically disclosed to all affected parties.

Article 13

The REALTOR® shall not acquire an interest in or buy for himself, any member of his immediate family, his firm or any member thereof, or any entity in which he has a substantial ownership interest, property listed with him, without making the true position known to the listing owner. In selling property owned by himself, or in which he has any interest, the REALTOR® shall reveal the facts of his ownership or interest to the purchaser.

Article 14

In the event of a controversy between REALTORS® associated with different firms, arising out of their relationship as REALTORS®, the REALTORS® shall submit the dispute to arbitration in accordance with the regulations of their board or boards rather than litigate the matter.

Article 15

If a REALTOR® is charged with unethical practice or is asked to present evidence in any disciplinary proceeding or investigation, he shall place all pertinent facts before the proper tribunal of the member board or affiliated institute, society, or council of which he is a member.

Article 16

When acting as agent, the REALTOR® shall not accept any commission, rebate, or profit on expenditures made for his principal-owner, without the principal's knowledge and consent.

Article 17

The REALTOR® shall not engage in activities that constitute the unauthorized practice of law and shall recommend that legal counsel be obtained when the interest of any party to the transaction requires it.

Article 18

The REALTOR® shall keep in a special account in an appropriate financial institution, separated from his own funds, monies coming into his possession in trust for other persons, such as escrows, trust funds, clients' monies, and other like items.

Article 19

The REALTOR® shall be careful at all times to present a true picture in his advertising and representations to the public. He shall neither advertise without disclosing his name nor permit any person associated with him to use individual names or telephone numbers, unless such person's connection with the REALTOR® is obvious in the advertisement.

Article 20

The REALTOR®, for the protection of all parties, shall see that financial obligations and commitments regarding real estate transactions are in writing, expressing the exact agreement of the parties. A copy of each agreement shall be furnished to each party upon his signing such agreement.

Article 21

The REALTOR® shall not engage in any practice or take any action inconsistent with the agency of another REALTOR®.

Article 22

In the sale of property which is exclusively listed with a REALTOR®, the REALTOR® shall utilize the services of other brokers upon mutually agreed upon terms when it is in the best interests of the client.

Negotiations concerning property which is listed exclusively shall be carried on with the listing broker, not with the owner, except with the consent of the listing broker.

Article 23

The REALTOR® shall not publicly disparage the business practice of a competitor nor volunteer an opinion of a competitor's transaction. If his opinion is sought and if the REALTOR® deems it appropriate to respond, such opinion shall be rendered with strict professional integrity and courtesy.

Note: Where the word REALTOR® is used in this Code and Preamble, it shall be deemed to include REALTOR-ASSOCIATE®. Pronouns shall be considered to include REALTORS® and REALTOR-ASSOCIATES® of both genders.

The Code of Ethics was adopted in 1913. Amended at the Annual Convention in 1924, 1928, 1950, 1951, 1952, 1955, 1956, 1961, 1962, 1974, and 1982.